Guillermo Cabrera Infante

TEXAS PAN AMERICAN SERIES

Guillermo Cabrera Infante

Two Islands, Many Worlds

By Raymond D. Souza

UNIVERSITY OF TEXAS PRESS   AUSTIN

Designed by Liz Menon

Requests for permission to reproduce material from this work should be sent to
Permissions, University of Texas Press, Box 7819, Austin, TX 78713-7819.

∞ The paper used in this publication meets the minimum requirements of
American National Standard for Information Sciences—Permanence of Paper
for Printed Library Materials, ANSI Z39.48-1984.

Souza, Raymond D., 1936–
    Guillermo Cabrera Infante : two islands, many worlds / Raymond D. Souza.
      p.   cm. — (Texas Pan American series)
    Includes bibliographical references (p.   ) and index.
    ISBN 0-292-77695-0 (cloth : alk. paper). — ISBN 0-292-77708-6 (paper : alk.
    paper)
    1. Cabrera Infante, G. (Guillermo), 1929–   .   I. Title. II. Series.
PQ7389.C233Z86 1996
863—dc20   95-43620

Acknowledgements on page 196

For Richard David Souza,

who embodies our father's courage

and our mother's will to endure.

Contents

Preface

THIS BOOK COMBINES BIOGRAPHICAL MATERIAL WITH LITERARY criticism and endeavors to portray the complexity of the character and works of Guillermo Cabrera Infante in their many facets. It is the account of how a man faced many trials and overcame them through the creative act of writing. During his lifetime, Cabrera Infante has moved in a variety of artistic and geographic contexts, enduring the vicissitudes of exile from Cuba. He became a British citizen in 1979 and writes with equal ease in both English and Spanish. He has distinguished himself with daring and innovative novels, essays, short stories, and film scripts written in both languages, and he has won major literary awards in France and Spain as well as a Guggenheim Fellowship in the United States. Cabrera Infante is, in every sense of the word, a multilingual and multicultural author. He is now widely regarded as the most accomplished living Cuban writer and as one of the finest novelists from the Spanish-speaking world.

After directing the most important cultural supplement of the first years of the Cuban revolution, Cabrera Infante, with the journal, fell from grace in 1962. A stint in the Cuban Embassy in Brussels came to an end in June 1965, when he returned to the island to attend his mother's funeral. He then spent four harrowing months dealing with a bureaucratic maze of suspicion before obtaining a nondiplomatic exit visa. When Cabrera Infante abandoned his native land in 1965, he also left behind a family tradition of social activism; both his parents were longtime members of the Communist Party. After being hounded out of Franco's Spain, he took up residence in London in 1966. Moving to England was one of the few options open to him and he was attracted by the opportunity to work in British films. His first years in England were economically difficult and complicated by persistent visa problems. Disaster struck in 1972 when he was overwhelmed by a lifetime of real and imagined ills and was hospitalized. The road back to health and a productive life was challenging and arduous. These circumstances have tempered his personality and writings and have marked important milestones in his creative odyssey.

The preparation of a literary biography always involves a figurative invasion of privacy and at times a literal one as well. I am indebted to Cabrera Infante and his wife Miriam Gómez for making their home and papers available to me and for providing a constant critical discourse in which to frame my ideas. I also wish to thank their daughters, Ana and Carola, and their grandchildren (particularly the two who showed up one day dressed as Batman and Superman) for allowing me access to their private lives and for providing glimpses of a writer in a number of personal contexts. I recall an evening dinner at the Cabrera Infantes with Ana and Carola and their English husbands, Trevor and Edward. A Cuban meal prepared by Miriam was followed by pastries my wife Martha had purchased at Harrod's. The only threat to the harmony of the evening was the scramble for dessert. After dinner, we were drinking coffee in the living room when Cabrera Infante abandoned his favorite black chair to carry his empty cup and saucer to the kitchen. In a flamboyant gesture of mock surprise, Miriam Gómez, the former actress, placed her right hand on her chest and gasped for air. As he returned to the living room, he was greeted by an unexpected and vigorous round of applause from all the members of the family. Back in his leather chair, he turned to me and confessed: "They said I only did that to look good for you." And after a slight pause, he added with a touch of English detachment: "Evidently, I overplayed my hand." Cubans have always struck me as remarkably candid and forthright, particularly as compared to the polite reserve of someone from a New England town steeped in English tradition. For me, doing research in London was a cultural as well as an academic homecoming.

I am also appreciative of other individuals and groups for direct and indirect help in the preparation of this study. These include, among others, John Brushwood, Peter T. Johnson, Herminia Novás Calvo, and Martha Souza as well as the research staffs at the Library of Congress, the firestone Library at Princeton, New Jersey, and the

Library of the University of Miami. I wish to thank the Center for Humanistic Studies at the University of Kansas for travel funds, the Kansas General Research Fund for summer grants, and the University of Kansas for a sabbatical leave. When available, English translations of works originally published in Spanish have been used—unidentified translations are my own.

R.D.S.
Lawrence, Kansas
December 30, 1994

Guillermo
Cabrera Infante

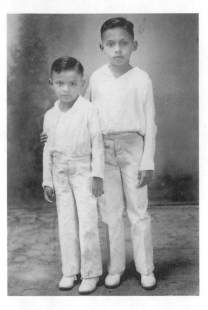

Sabá and Guillermo, Gibara, 1937.
(Family archive. All photos in this section
are courtesy of Cabrera Infante.)

Gibara, 1956. (Photo by Cabrera Infante.)

Guillermo with his maternal uncle
"Infante the Kid," Havana, 1941.
(Family archive.)

Zoila and Guillermo Sr., Havana 1948.
(Photo by Germán Puig.)

The unforgettable Pepe Castro.
(Photo by Jesse Fernández.)

Reading Kerouac in a bar in Santiago de Cuba, 1959.
(Photo by Jesse Fernández.)

Guillermo, c. 1951.
(Photo by Nestor Almendros.)

Guillermo, 1958. (Photo by Martínez Paula.)

Cain and Leal on television in Havana, c. 1958.
(Photographer unknown.)

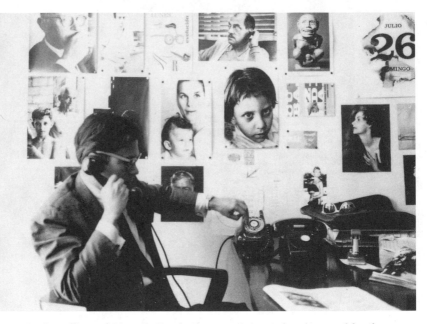

In the offices of *Lunes de Revolución*, 1961. Among the photos of family
members on the wall are pictures of Sartre, Hemingway, and Garbo.
(Photo by Mario García Hoyo.)

After the closure of
Lunes de Revolución, 1962.
(Photo by Anders Ehnmark.)

With Miriam Gómez, New York 1982. (Photo by Nestor Almendros.)

The family in London, 1970.
Guillermo and Miriam Gómez;
upper left, Ana, with Carola beside
her. In the foreground, the regal
"Offenbach."
(Photo by Michael Thompson.)

At the Barcelona Film Festival with José Luis Guarnerten, 1989.
(Photo by Sam Shaw.)

A
Distant
Place

THERE ARE AS MANY STORIES AS MILES BETWEEN THE TOWN OF Gibara on the northeast Atlantic coast of Cuba and 53 Gloucester Road in the South Kensington section of London. These two areas mark important intervals in a creative odyssey that includes Gibara, Havana, Brussels, and London, with Gibara and Brussels representing formative and transitional stages in Guillermo Cabrera Infante's career, and Havana and London the full expression of his literary talents. There have been other significant sojourns along the way, notably in Hollywood, Madrid, and New York, but the most compelling object of his creative energies has been Havana, where he lived from 1941 to 1962 and for four months in 1965. His last trip to the Cuban capital, which was triggered by the sudden illness and untimely demise of his mother during the first days of June, became a Kafkaesque experience, the substance of nightmares. In addition to coping with an unnecessary death, Cabrera Infante barely succeeded in leaving the country with his two daughters. He spent months dealing with a bureaucratic maze of suspicion before the right contacts made it possible for him to acquire an exit visa.

Prior to his family's move to Havana in 1941 when he was twelve years old, Gibara in Oriente Province formed the geographic center of his existence. According to the *Atlas de Cuba,* the average temperature in Gibara during July exceeds 82 degrees Fahrenheit (32). Because of its torrid climate, Heberto Padilla has referred to that location as "the entrance hall to hell. People from there never sweat. Neither Cabrera Infante, Pablo Armando Fernández, César López, nor my wife, Belkis Cuza, all of them from there, has been seen to sweat one drop. They tremble with chills amid the flames; in the Cuban winter, they would wrap themselves up as if on the North Pole."[1]

In Cabrera Infante's case, this singular characteristic is most likely due to a biological adaptation that occurred over an extensive period of time. The native inhabitants of the Amazon basin, for example, do not perspire—in a hot, humid climate, it is a waste of energy and does not cool the body. Interestingly, because he has lived in England since 1966, Cabrera Infante now has difficulty tolerating the heat or at least, in good English fashion, begins to complain when the temperature exceeds 70 degrees Fahrenheit. Other notables from Oriente Province include Reinaldo Arenas, Fulgencio Batista, and Fidel Castro, an indication that the area operates as a sort of jack-in-the-box in Cuban cultural and political history, springing a variety of surprises on an unsuspecting populace.

A racially homogeneous town of some ten thousand inhabitants when Cabrera Infante lived there, Gibara was the site of Columbus's initial landfall on the island during the first voyage and the area where members of his crew discovered tobacco. Cabrera Infante grew up in a family divided between smokers and nonsmokers, and he is happy to count himself among those who partake of this, for him, pleasant vice. A third of the cramped refrigerator in his London apartment still is devoted to the storage of cigars, much to the dismay of his wife, Miriam Gómez, an excellent gourmet cook, who would prefer to use the space for food. Although he has a keen appreciation for tasty culinary fare, there are few things he is less forgiving of than a bad cigar. Cabrera

Infante's long and happy association with tobacco is chronicled in *Holy Smoke* (1985), which is, among other things, a recasting of Sir James Matthew Barrie's *My Lady Nicotine* (1890), Sir Compton Mackenzie's *Sublime Tobacco* (1957), and Fernando de Ortiz's *Contrapunteo cubano del tabaco y el azúcar*, 1940 (*Cuban Counterpoint, Tobacco and Sugar*, 1947).

Cabrera Infante includes among the pro-tobacco faction of his family his maternal great-grandparents, Sebastián Castro and Caridad Espinoza. Caridad was born in Cuba but her husband was from Almería, Spain. Sebastián fought on the Spanish side during the first Cuban struggle for independence, but he did not participate in the final conflict that resulted in Cuban independence and the U.S. occupation of the island. When victorious Cuban troops entered Gibara, Sebastián greeted them dressed in his old Spanish uniform, not knowing what to expect. As the columns passed, he saluted a Cuban general on horseback who responded to Sebastián's gesture in a respectful manner. The general's magnanimous reply "made a Cuban for life" of Cabrera Infante's great-grandfather.[2] Despite Sebastián's and Caridad's persistent use of tobacco (he smoked, she chewed), they lived long lives. It is through Caridad Espinoza that Cabrera Infante can claim a bloodline that extends back to the island's original native inhabitants, a source, among other things, alluded to in a self-mocking passage from the fictional portrayal of his life, *La Habana para un Infante difunto*, 1979 (*Infante's Inferno*, 1984): "I waited for her in bed, in darkness, still under the sheets, still naked, an Indian in his tepee . . ."[3]

The same branch of the family tree also produced a great-uncle (the son of Caridad and Sebastián) who hated tobacco and God. A materialistic eccentric who often shaved his head, José Castro Espinosa (better known as Pepe Castro among his friends and as Crazy Pepe to his detractors) was an amateur inventor, a vegetarian, and a man of strong and often contradictory convictions. An admirer of Friedrich Wilhelm Nietzsche, Pepe embraced Nazism when he discovered that Hitler was a vegetarian and a nonsmoker. The names he gave his children, Noelia, Gildo, and Nereyda, are manifestations of his whimsical nature as well as his interest in sound. He had a stormy relationship with his wife, Luisa Ortega, whom he eventually left. Cabrera Infante remembers her as the neighborhood ogre who was an avid collector of sports memorabilia; she confiscated any ball that strayed onto her property. Despite Pepe Castro's bizarre beliefs and strange causes, Cabrera Infante referred to him in an interview with Danubio Torres Fierro as "the kindest man I have known, incapable of even witnessing the killing of a chicken."[4]

Cabrera Infante published an affectionate and revealing portrait of Pepe in 1979, "Mi personaje inolvidable" ("My Unforgettable Character"), and a large photograph of his favorite relative still graces a wall of his London apartment. In the photograph a shirtless Pepe is leaning against a wall and his slim body and thin left arm seem to form a part of the barrier. But a large and oversized head arches forward as if it were defying gravity and declaring independence from its torso and surroundings. Pepe has a wry grin on his face, and mischievous eyes offer a mocking challenge, providing the viewer an image of a spirit prone to conflict with its environment, an incorrigible, endearing hero. Pepe Castro is one of the few people whom Cabrera Infante refers to as a mentor in his writings, and he was an important figure during the writer's formative years in Gibara. Cabrera Infante points out in his portrait that Pepe hated to write and that his world and existence revolved around the spoken word. These attitudes became important components in *Tres tristes tigres,* 1967 (*Three Trapped Tigers,* 1971), particularly in the characterization of Bustrófedon.

The tobacco dichotomy extended into Cabrera Infante's immediate family since his mother smoked and his father refrained and disapproved. This difference was one of many incongruities in a relationship that still puzzles their eldest son. Cabrera Infante does not understand why his mother married his father and feels she could have selected someone more devoted to her than a man completely dedicated to the Communist Party. He believes that she never received adequate recognition or compensation for all her years of sacrifice for her husband's causes, a not uncommon fate for women who take up with true believers, and one that their children frequently share. They were married in 1927 and with a few other individuals organized the local Communist Party in Gibara in 1933. Cabrera Infante was born on 22 April 1929, just two months after Leon Trotsky's expulsion from the Soviet Union.

Zoila Infante Castro (1909–1965) was educated in a convent and was admired in Gibara for her beauty. A vivacious and outgoing woman, Zoila enjoyed the movies, theater, and baseball, and she frequently took her children with her to such functions since her husband eschewed most entertainment. Emotionally spontaneous and a skilled conversationalist, she relished social contacts and was adept at making visitors to her home feel welcome and comfortable. She was adroit at focusing her feelings on the people around her and she appreciated harmonious human contacts. She must have found her husband's capacity for indifference difficult to handle. Despite her congeniality, she was not given to formalities and was known to ridicule the social pretensions of some of her husband's relatives. At times Zoila suffered from severe migraines and was known to spend as many as three days in bed and to take up to twenty-nine aspirins to seek relief. Cabrera Infante apparently inherited this tendency from his mother and used to suffer from this malady, especially on the left side, but he has not experienced such a headache in many years. Unlike her spouse, who was reluctant to entertain callers who had fallen out of the good graces of the Party, Zoila established her own norms and was capable of defying both her husband and the Party. Zoila's formidable character probably came from her mother, Angela Castro, a serious and devout agnostic, though her mother Caridad maintained an altar in her home.

Despite her Catholic background, Zoila shared two characteristics with the atheistic Pepe Castro, an unusual tolerance for contradiction and a tendency to resist established norms. She hung on a wall of her home portraits of the Sacred Heart of Jesus and Joseph Stalin, an unlikely combination of icons of blood, one the embodiment of self-denial and the other of the sacrifice of others. Zoila tended to disregard facts that were disagreeable, and both she and her husband found it hard to see things they wished were not true. She also had some peculiar ideas about the raising of children and believed that traditional roles could be modified by changing the words that referred to them. As a result, her children always called their parents by their first names and never used any reference to mother or father, a practice that Cabrera Infante feels only created confusion.

This custom, their political activism, and Zoila's everlasting sociability undermined their children's emotional security. Guillermo and his brother Sabá often played second fiddle to their parents' political concerns. It was most likely her anarchistic tendencies and romantic nature that attracted Zoila to her husband. He was a handsome man and she was prone to confuse her emotions with reality. With his persuasive skills, he convinced her to join the Communist Party at a time when it was a risky and dangerous venture. However, his rebelliousness was selective, for although he resisted the established political and economic order, he was slavishly devoted to the Party. A confirmed Stalinist whose thoughts and actions were directed by his political affiliation, he, with his wife, considered Trotsky a demon of evil. Zoila unwittingly replaced the religious extremism of her grandmother with the political fanaticism of her husband. The tyranny of religion was replaced by that of history.

Guillermo Cabrera López (1900?–1990) was in many respects the opposite of his wife. Shorter and stockier than the slender and fair Zoila and considerably darker in complexion, Guillermo senior was of a gentle and serious disposition. Unlike Zoila, he was more likely to identify with ideals rather than individuals—he seemed more interested in saving humanity than his own family. He hated arguments and scenes and avoided them at all costs but was persistent and even stubborn at hanging on to things he cherished. As a result, he was prone to inaction and momentary paralysis of the will, reactions that frequently frustrated those around him. Guillermo senior was extremely frugal and extended the life of razor blades by sharpening them on the rim of a glass, a practice he had learned from Pepe Castro. For him, a tube of toothpaste was good to the last drop; he would repeatedly fold it until it had surrendered its last trickle. Quiet, serious, and reflective, he was a model of sobriety and correct behavior when at home, sometimes to the point of prudishness. He did not encourage or approve of his son's interest in literature and was indifferent to aesthetic matters, but he did enroll him in an English Institute after the move to Havana. He had, however, a dark side to his personality that Cabrera Infante has discussed in a little-noted but revealing essay published in the Canary Islands.

Originally given as a speech in Santa Cruz de Tenerife, the site of his paternal grandfather's birth, "Del gofio al golfo" ("From Gruel to the Gulf") is a sort of physical and psychological homecoming, a frank and candid reappraisal of origins. In it he discloses that women "of all races, colors, and creeds" were his father's only passion and that his was a "clandestine" obsession.[5] He also referred to his father as a "secret womanizer" in *Infante's Inferno*.[6] This explains many aspects of the relationship between Zoila and her husband, particularly a barely detectable and vague estrangement that came to characterize their marriage. As individuals frequently do when they wish to express a hidden frustration, Zoila displaced her anger onto some of the things most dear to her spouse, in this case the Party and its publications. If one assumes that the son was sensitive to his mother's unacknowledged feelings, it may explain Cabrera Infante's own recognition of an emotional distancing from his father during his teenage years.

Over the years, Guillermo senior and Zoila became estranged, and she was not above heaping verbal abuse on her unfaithful spouse. In the same article, Cabrera Infante also mentions with some reluctance a number of legacies from his father: "But I have always carried my father within me without recognizing it: in my spirit, in my social conduct, in my physical appearance—even in my clinical eye for women."[7] Cabrera Infante has exorcised some of these influences through his writings, but another legacy by way of his paternal grandfather has cast a longer shadow.

Francisco Cabrera was a skilled ironworker who forged balconies, railings, and windows that can still be seen in Gibara. Shortly after the birth of Guillermo senior, Francisco Cabrera returned to his native country with his Cuban wife and new son for a visit. He had been depressed and his physician, assuming that his patient was suffering from a form of melancholia caused by homesickness, suggested that he return for an extended stay. After the sojourn in the Canary Islands, they returned to Gibara. When Guillermo senior was approximately two years old, a violent family tragedy occurred in Gibara. Francisco Cabrera returned one day from a walk along the banks of the Cacoyugüín River carrying his wife Cecilia López in his arms. They had quarreled and she was bleeding profusely from a bullet wound in her forehead. Francisco ordered that someone send for a doctor and then locked himself in his room. When family screams confirmed that his wife had died, he shot himself in the temple.

The repercussions of this murder-suicide in the life of their young son are hard to gauge, but the tragedy could explain Guillermo senior's uncompromising commitment to the Cuban Communist Party. It must have filled an emotional void in his life and offered a degree of permanence. The tragedy also may have contributed to his determination to survive, his will to endure whatever the cost. He was raised by different relatives including an older sister, uncles, and his maternal grandmother, Cecilia González, a tyrannical woman who resented her grandson's presence. She was not above reminding him that his father had killed her daughter. Whether the treatment he received at the hands of his bitter grandmother was a factor in his later attitude toward women cannot be known, but it is not unusual for a persistent philanderer to resent and dislike women. Cecilia's taunting was replaced later in his life by the ridicule he received for his affiliation with the Communist Party, and finally by Zoila's resentment over his unfaithfulness. Guillermo senior was adept at making himself the object of the derision of others.

In his Canary Islands talk, Cabrera Infante frankly discussed his personal connection to Francisco Cabrera: "I must confess that I have ended up being the father of my father. I am a reasonable person, but hidden within me there is a flow of irrationality that threatens to rise violently as in my murderous and suicidal grandfather."[8] In his particular case, violence is more apt to find verbal expression, as anyone who has been the object of his feared barbs can attest, but his comments allude to his well-known hospitalization in 1972 and to there being biological and genetic factors in his illness. It is likely that he has contended with angels of joy and demons of despair a good deal of his life, and that cumulative circumstances overwhelmed him in that year.

Although he never knew his paternal grandparents, several members of that branch of the family form a part of his colorful memories of Gibara, especially two of his father's uncles, Matías and Bartolomé López. Cabrera Infante remembers Matías, a tall, thin bachelor from southern Spain, for his Gongoristic appearance, epigrams, and library. Zoila must have acquired some of her unusual ideas about raising children from him. Guillermo recalls Matías admonishing his parents: "you must keep in mind that children should not be educated with the heart but with the brain."[9] Years later in *Infante's Inferno,* this advice was reported as being scrupulously followed by his father but disregarded by his emotional mother: "I ended up educated by my mother's heart, not my father's brain."[10] Matías had intellectual pretensions and used the pseudonym "Socrates" in columns he wrote for the local press. After his death, Cabrera Infante's father acquired his modest library, and it was in that collection that the young and curious writer discovered in 1942 the erotic delights of the *Satyricon.*

Bartolomé López is recalled in family lore as a strict autocrat whose authoritarian ways produced rebellious offspring; one son even ran off with a circus. He relished presiding over formal and elaborate meals for his extended family because they provided opportunities for him to exert his authority and for proper homage to be paid to the acknowledged leader of the family dynasty. During one of those regal occasions, a careless or malicious participant indiscreetly broke wind in a startling and loud fashion. Bartolomé, his dignity offended by an act he considered a deliberate affront, immediately shot to his feet, his face flushed with anger. He started to deliver a declaration of reproach, but he was so enraged that he fell over dead instead. He has the distinction of being the only person that Cabrera Infante has ever known "who was killed by a fart."[11]

The intimacies and eccentricities of life in a town in a rural area of the island combined with a close relationship with nature. Cabrera Infante's home was only a few blocks from the sea, so morning swims were a common practice. During his years in Gibara he had many pets, including dogs, birds, and a goat. He remembers hunting birds (one orgy of destruction produced serious remorse), a plague of dragonflies, and an invasion of crabs that was so persistent that it was not unusual to find one in the drawer of a dresser. However, unlike many Spanish American novelists who have extolled and exploited the prodigious wonders of the Americas, such memories have not formed the basis of his texts. Indeed, stories that do feature nature, such as "La voz de la tortuga" ("The Voice of the Turtle"), leave the reader with an aversion to aspects of the natural environment. Although Gibara left him with an appreciation and interest in nature that has lasted a lifetime, he finds its cruelty difficult to accept. While working at his desk one day in his London apartment, he had the misfortune to witness a jay killing and devouring a sparrow, a spectacle that caused him to faint. He is equally unforgiving of human abuse of the environment—the careless treatment of trees still shocks him. During his association with the Cuban journal *Carteles* in the 1950s, he spearheaded a campaign to reduce the destruction of trees in Havana.

In the chronologies of his life that he has published, Cabrera Infante points out that he was taken to the movies for the first time by his mother when he was twenty-nine days old to see *The Four Horsemen of the Apocalypse*. This anecdote suggests that cultural creations intrigue him more than nature, and that the creative and destructive forces of civilization concern him more than those of the natural order. The images on the screen and the printed page would eventually prevail over the natural environment as culture displaced nature. Third-rate productions were more likely to be found outside of a movie house than in it. In 1929 the Teatro Unión Club was the only movie house in Gibara, but by 1939 two others had opened, the Roxy and the Ideal.

Other aspects of popular culture also attracted his interest, and none more powerfully than comic strips. When he was approximately four years old, a devotee of his mother started bringing the Sunday paper to his home on a regular basis. He still vividly recalls the intense excitement he felt as he awaited the arrival of the cherished cartoons, particularly *Dick Tracy* and *Tarzan*. Every weekend was Christmas. He also discovered that daily newspapers had comics. His only problem was that he did not know how to read. When family members, undoubtedly fatigued by numerous requests, finally refused to read them to him, he decided to learn on his own. The first word he succeeded in deciphering was "which," and once that feat was accomplished, his confidence soared.

He remained an avid consumer of comic strips into the 1940s and was especially intrigued that motion could be conveyed in an essentially static medium. The attraction of this art form on his imagination has been so powerful that he has referred to it as "a contaminating influence," one that began before he could read and that was more intense than the movies.[12] When one reads a comic strip, the eye moves from one frame to another and the mind establishes connections between the independent units. But each frame exists as a singular entity, as a fragment that is at the same time dependent on and independent of the images around it. This technique of assembling fragments later became one of the hallmarks of works that incorporated vignettes such as the Spanish version of *Así en la paz como en la guerra,* 1960 (*Writes of Passage,* 1993), *Three Trapped Tigers,* 1971, and *Vista del amanecer en el trópico,* 1974 (*View of Dawn in the Tropics,* 1978).

Although most of his memories of Gibara are pleasant, there were events related to his parents' political activities that were markedly traumatic. Cabrera Infante remembers being awakened by the commotion in his home at eight o'clock on the morning of 30 April 1936. The postman, a good friend of his father named Joseíto, arrived that day with a package of propaganda materials from party headquarters in Havana, followed by two members of the rural military police. Warned by the silent gestures and facial expressions of the sympathetic letter carrier, his mother dashed into the house with the package and headed for a back door. When the turmoil awoke Guillermo, he saw a succession of figures running down the hall, first his mother, then his three-year-old brother (Sabá), and finally men in uniform with drawn revolvers. He was so terrified that he dashed to a neighbor's home barefoot and in his underwear, but he could not relate what was happening. Disregarding orders to halt, Zoila ran out of the house and into the patio, intent on destroying the incriminating evidence. A few weeks after the event, one of the men who had pursued her informed a relative that he had not fired at Zoila because of his fear of hitting the nearly naked child. Sabá had unwittingly upstaged his older brother; the invader of the realm was now its savior.

Zoila was arrested at the house and her children sought refuge in the homes of neighbors. At about ten that evening, Guillermo senior turned himself in to the authorities. His action provoked disbelief among many family members and criticism from the Party, but it does indicate that he had a strong sense of responsibility. Zoila and Guillermo senior were sent to prison in Santiago de Cuba for several months. Zoila's father, who at that time was a lieutenant in the local police force, intervened and saw to it that they were transported to Santiago by train rather than by car. He wanted to ensure that there would be no opportunity for a spontaneous application of the "ley de fuga," which allowed authorities to kill any prisoner who attempted to escape. The country evidently was experiencing one of its periodic epidemics of restless captives. The family had had some experience with this practice during a rebellion of black military personnel in the Cuban army in 1912. Pepe Castro, who then held the rank of sergeant, was ordered to apply the subterfuge to two black civilians. Rather than pass the responsibility down to a subordinate as others had done, he cheerfully accepted it. He then took the prisoners into the countryside, turned them loose, and shot some vultures instead.

The drastic and unexpected separation from his parents, particularly his mother, was a stressful experience for Cabrera Infante, serious enough to provoke disturbing dreams, concern among his relatives, and medical consultations. Reality became a nightmare and terrifying dreams tore at the fabric of everyday life. His fertile imagination, stimulated in part by the many movies he had seen, began to run wild. An adjective from a phrase in a song his mother used to sing was converted into a noun denoting a diabolical figure that pursued him. A voice whispered into his ear commanding him to perform mathematical calculations beyond his ability. When these nightmares subsided, they were replaced by other hallucinations that occurred on Fridays.[13] As far as he is concerned, many of the insecurities of his childhood can be directly attributed "to the brutal way I realized that I was losing my mother."[14] The separation from his parents lasted six months, an inordinate amount of time for a seven-year-old child, considering the circumstances. The event had all the makings of an imperative toward uncertainty and shame. Zoila's death in 1965 from the incompetent medical treatment of a minor problem occurred with equal and unexpected rapidity. In that year, Guillermo would lose both his mother and his country.

There are indications that Guillermo was an anxious child before the incarceration of his parents in 1936. He was enrolled in kindergarten at the age of four, but he found the experience so unsettling that he was taken out of school. He did not return for two years, at which time he started first grade at a private Quaker school, Los Amigos. His first educational experience occurred a few months after the birth of his brother Alberto (Sabá) in April 1933. His parents had prepared him for the arrival of a sister, and he was so disappointed with the unexpected result that he claims to have attempted to remedy the situation by modifying his brother's anatomy with a pair of scissors. Whether the event took place or not is immaterial; the anecdote effectively conveys an emotional state as well as his novelistic approach to his own history. The anecdote communicates a fear of being displaced by a younger sibling, one who Cabrera Infante asserts was favored by his mother and whom he refers to in *Infante's Inferno* as "my inseparable appendix."[15] Why go to school when there was more serious business at hand, like the important tasks of maintaining Zoila and Guillermo senior's attention and defending his turf from an interloper? He started developing mysterious physical symptoms and remembers awakening his parents one night in a panic after having experienced the strange sensation of a finger sinking into his navel. Interestingly, a sister born in 1928 had been strangled by her umbilical cord, and another died shortly after birth of an infected navel in 1940. Separation was fraught with many dangers.

During his parents' imprisonment in 1936, Guillermo spent time with his maternal grandparents, Cándido Infante and Angela Castro Espinoza. The stern and humorless Angela interrupted her grandson's first amorous encounter with a beautiful, green-eyed cousin when she discovered them naked together, an episode described in *Infante's Inferno*. For his part, Cándido, tipping his hand more than he realized, criticized his wife for disciplining their adventurous grandson for following his natural inclinations. Shortly after that disruptive episode, Angela learned that Cándido was involved in an affair and, deeply wounded by the betrayal, she threw him out of their home and out of her life forever. It does not sit well with Cabrera Infante that his grandmother used him as a witness in the corroboration of his grandfather's infidelity, employing his then keen eyesight to confirm that Cándido was spending time with a paramour. Since he was fond of both grandparents, the calamity was a source of considerable guilt, an indication, perhaps, that he was acquiring his father's excessive sense of responsibility. It was not Guillermo's fault that the handsome Cándido, who had spent his youth toiling in sugarcane fields, was a womanizer, but emotions seldom follow the dictates of logic. The breakup of their marriage was a tragedy in the lives of both Angela and Cándido. Among Cabrera Infante's fondest memories of his maternal grandfather was Cándido's sense of humor, his ability to laugh and enjoy life in the face of adversity, a quality Cabrera Infante has carefully cultivated.

When Zoila and Guillermo senior were released from prison, they had economic problems because of their identification with subversive activities. Before his arrest, Guillermo senior had worked as a reporter and typesetter for a local newspaper, *El Triunfo,* but after his return, he was practically unemployable. The only work he found was as a bookkeeper. The family's financial situation became precarious, and they were compelled to live with relatives. The income generated by Zoila's work as a seamstress became crucial to their survival. Their eldest son was transferred from a private to a public school. In addition, Zoila's father was forced to resign his police commission. Their difficulties were complicated by the fact that the town was in a period of marked economic decline as the nearby city of Holguín took on many of the commercial activities previously centered in Gibara. The construction of a new highway to Holguín relegated Gibara to economic obscurity. But they continued their political activities and, undaunted by the twists and turns in the Party's policies, began to actively support Fulgencio Batista in 1938. Zoila, demonstrating consistency in her capacity to foster the cause of tyrants, became more enthusiastic about Batista than Stalin. However, in her favor, it should be pointed out that compared to the bloody Stalin, Batista was a small-time gangster. The collaboration with Batista had its benefits; the Cuban Communist Party was soon legalized and its newspaper, *Hoy,* came into existence.

In 1940 Zoila ran for a seat on the city council of Gibara as a representative of the Communist Party. After her defeat, she provoked a minor family squabble when she attributed her failure to some unfortunate posters that the enthusiastic Pepe Castro had placed around town. Although she lost the election, she discovered the charms and excitement of Havana during preparations for the campaign. Moving to the city became her new cause, and she began to wage an unrelenting campaign at home. Her new slogan became: "Havana, who sees you, loves you."[16] Her husband proved to be more pliable than the voters. Spurred on by his wife's entreaties and their dismal financial outlook, Guillermo senior went to Havana in 1940 in search of a job and his family followed in 1941.

Cabrera Infante believes that his life would have turned out quite differently if his mother had won the election. They would have remained in Gibara and she would have held office until 1944, a year in which economic conditions in Cuba might have made a transfer to the capital impossible. The move to Havana in 1941 was a pivotal event in Cabrera Infante's life. He left behind a poor but pleasant childhood in the country and encountered the grinding poverty of a major urban center. In Gibara he often was called "Gallego" and "Galleguito" by family members. The nicknames were bestowed on him by his maternal grandfather because his skin had been so crimson after his birth (there is some irony in his being born so vividly red), but in Havana the innocent child those names referred to began to disappear.

CHAPTER TWO

A Room Without a View

IN A PHOTOGRAPH TAKEN SHORTLY AFTER HIS ARRIVAL IN HAVANA, Cabrera Infante appears with an uncle, his mother's youngest brother. Affectionately known as "Infante the Kid," since he had been raised by his sister, the uncle is one of many relatives who later appeared in the pages of *Infante's Inferno*. The Kid looks confident and relaxed in the photo as he glances at the camera with a warm and gracious smile, but twelve-year-old Cabrera Infante peers at the world in a different manner. He glares at the camera in tough-guy fashion, with the smoldering meanness of a George Raft. But his thin and rigid body betrays him. The stance of the barely hunched figure conveys hesitation and insecurity—the nasty face does not match the frightened body. Forced to traverse the mean streets of the poor districts of Havana, where his singsong Oriente accent marked him as a rube and an outsider, he was on his way to cultivating a demeanor that would offer some protection from the local bullies.

The transition from Gibara to Havana was a painful experience for Cabrera Infante. The family moved from ample quarters in Gibara to a "room without a view of the street, like a cell."[1] Their lodging contained fewer than four hundred square feet and was shared by six people: the immediate family, the Kid, and Zoila's favorite niece, the green-eyed temptress who had initiated one of Guillermo's early erotic adventures, in the home of his maternal grandparents. To make matters worse, relatives would visit and stay for extended periods, as a grandmother, an uncle, or a cousin would appear from the provinces, but nothing seems to have discouraged Zoila from playing the woman who lived in a shoe. Although Havana is a port city, they no longer had easy access to the sea or the woods, and family pets were left behind. A tranquil town was replaced by a busy city, and their cramped quarters and proximity to a variety of noisy neighbors, with whom they shared a single bathroom, destroyed any sense of privacy.

They resided for a short time at 822 Monte but then moved to 408 Zulueta, into the tenement that is described in great detail in the opening pages of *Infante's Inferno*. They lived on the second floor and were one of fifteen families crammed into fifteen rooms. Located near the Payret Theater and a block from the Capitol building and the tree-lined Prado Boulevard, 408 Zulueta was in the old social and commercial center of the city, not far from some of Havana's most notorious red-light districts. Narrow side streets were often cramped with traffic and pedestrians, and the senses were overwhelmed with the sights and sounds of a bustling city. Local color was enhanced by the frequent presence of sensual and provocative women who somehow could transform the most mundane activities into erotic statements. Guillermo's emerging sexuality found ample stimulation in his new neighborhood, which was frightening and overpowering, but not dull. A boring excursion or errand could become an adventure at any moment.

Although he later wrote in *Infante's Inferno* that "the streetlamps were so poor back home that they couldn't even afford moths,"[2] living in poverty was not a troublesome issue for Cabrera Infante while he lived in Gibara. However, the situation was quite different in Havana. In Gibara, he was unaware that his family was poor, but it was so apparent in Havana that he avoided telling his acquaintances where he lived. "I was genuinely ashamed of living in that place," he once explained.[3] His most inquisitive friends found the way to his home on their own, and, if

Zoila was present when they arrived, they discovered a gracious hostess. In spite of his secretive ways, Cabrera Infante returned one day and found Nestor Almendros, the well-known cinematographer who won an Oscar in 1978 for the filming of *Days of Heaven,* engaged in an animated discussion with his mother.

If someone who had been a frequent visitor stopped appearing on a regular basis, Zoila would encourage him or her to come back. Her lively personality transformed their tiny quarters into a social center for friends and a refuge for political activists, although she was not above throwing out anyone who attacked one of her cherished political heroes. Even Carlos Franqui was welcome after his expulsion from the Communist Party, despite her husband's misgivings, but Guillermo senior knew from experience that once his wife had made a decision, nothing could deter her from her course. Franqui has indicated that many dreams and hopes were nourished in that warm environment where "there was always room for one more."[4] Franqui includes among the projects that began in that cramped but friendly environment the cultural magazine *Nueva Generación,* the society Nuestro Tiempo, and the generation that created and directed *Lunes de Revolución.*

Despite his political beliefs, Guillermo senior felt his son should know English, and he was enrolled in night school to learn that language, although the term had already begun. Cabrera Infante studied English five nights a week from 1942 to 1946 at an institute located on Havana Street between Muralla and Sol in a predominantly Jewish neighborhood. The only cost was a library fee of twenty cents per month. His instructor, a young man in his late twenties, also served as the principal. Emilio González possessed a good sense of humor and enjoyed playing with words in Spanish and English, much to the delight of his new pupil. Cabrera Infante was hooked. He acquired Emilio González's zest for language and he has been experimenting with words ever since. He also discovered that he had exceptional linguistic aptitudes. He later learned two other languages, French and Italian, and became especially fluent in the former. A more immediate application of these abilities occurred when his classmates in his regular school made fun of his Oriente accent. He made a conscious and successful effort to modify his speech, an indication of his linguistic versatility as well as his adaptability. The adolescent who tried to mask his fears with a mean face was developing effective survival skills.

He also cultivated other tactics to avoid physical harassment, taking on the role of the funny wise guy. He broached the subject in a passage from the fictional rendering of his life, *Infante's Inferno:* "What's more, since my high-school days, after passing my first inexperienced year in a Havana primary school, miraculously surviving the abuses of the local bullies, I entered the Institute with my right foot forward. Since then I had avoided being among the victims of violence by dint of wit, with a joke here, a wisecrack there, a grotesque gag yonder: playing the clown though at first I was one of those who were considered the weaklings, the four-eyed eggheads, the bookworms hated by the bullyboys, the tough guys."[5] He also learned to deal with adversity by turning it into a joke and by masking pain or fear with humor. On occasion, wit was used to mollify or deflect parental displeasure.

Although Guillermo senior knew he was increasing his son's opportunities by enrolling him in night school to study English, he scarcely could have imagined that his son would one day write movie scripts for British films and the Hollywood industry and live in the city where Karl Marx wrote his major work. When he visited his son in London in the summer of 1986, the first things he wanted to see were Karl Marx's tomb in Highgate Cemetery and Sherlock Holmes's residence in Baker Street. As Cabrera Infante has pointed out, "Sherlock Holmes is possibly the only fictional character that has been converted into a person with a residence."[6] Since he is not a great admirer of Marxism and has declared on several occasions that he prefers Groucho to Karl, Cabrera Infante took more than passing satisfaction in his conviction that his father's interests were the offspring of fantasy. But his father's insistence that he study English in Havana in the 1940s did result in the incorporation of a second major code into his literary discourse—the language and culture of the English-speaking world.

During the early years in Havana, Cabrera Infante's interest in popular culture in general and American culture in particular continued to grow. He was already an enthusiast of Cuban music, especially the bolero, and through films and radio he acquired a taste for American music, particularly swing and jazz. Listening to radio retransmissions by the Columbia Broadcasting Network each Sunday at four o'clock in the afternoon became a weekly ritual. During this period he became a fan of a performer with a sensuous, silky voice and cheerful personality— Dinah Shore. He even wrote the vivacious, blonde singer to request a photograph, and she replied with an autographed print. Films such as *Sun Valley Serenade* (1941) and *Orchestra Wives* (1942), which featured Glenn Miller and his Orchestra and the music of the era, heightened his enthusiasm. The first-mentioned movie highlighted the Miller arrangement of "Chattanooga Choo-Choo," accompanied by the dynamic dance routine of the Nicholas Brothers, spats and all, "possibly the greatest big band production number ever filmed."[7] Although the plot is hardly convincing, the precise and harmonious musical renditions are as impressive as when Cabrera Infante first saw the film in Havana in the early 1940s. Of the two movies, *Orchestra Wives* has the more engaging and believable story line. It also boasts snappy dialogue and an actor of Cuban background, Cesar Romero, as well as the future star Jackie Gleason. Cabrera Infante's enthusiasm for popular music and singers found ample expression in later creations, specifically in characters such as Estrella Rodríguez and Cuba Venegas in *Three Trapped Tigers,* and in his conceptualization of some of his works as musical compositions. Glenn Miller's modification of the lead instruments in a big-band production also demonstrated how innovation could be achieved by shifting the stressed components in an artistic creation.

In 1946 another teacher had an important impact on his life. Cabrera Infante remembers Juan Fonseca as a snob who refused to acknowledge the existence of students outside of class. He looked American in his crew cut, bragged of his son's exploits in the great war against Japan, and liked to dramatize literature. Cabrera Infante was not especially impressed with his class, but when Fonseca began to read passages from the *Odyssey* that dealt with Argus, his own love for dogs perked his interest. He went to the library of the Havana Institute where an aged, one-eyed librarian, who had been cruelly nicknamed Polyphemus by previous generations of students, helped him locate the works of Homer. He read the entire *Odyssey* and the *Iliad* as well and became seriously interested in literature. Up to that point in his life, his great ambition was to be a shortstop on a professional baseball team, although he had little or nonexistent talent for the sport. The world has Juan Fonseca to thank for saving it from Cabrera Infante the baseball player and for unknowingly nudging him toward his true profession. Many of his classmates shared his interest in baseball, but none were concerned with literature. Some, however, had an exceptional knowledge of music, particularly Sergio Rigol.

As Cabrera Infante's mastery of English increased, so did his father's ambitions for him. After he was awarded a Certificate in the Teaching of English in 1946 by the English Center, at his father's instigation Cabrera Infante made an unsuccessful attempt to become an instructor of that language. Shortly after that disappointment, he began to work occasionally as a translator for his father's employer, the Communist Party newspaper *Hoy*. He translated articles from the socialist press in the United States, and among the essays he recalls working on were commentaries on the radio show "Amos and Andy" and the Gore Vidal novel *The City and the Pillar*. During the same period he worked as a proofreader for the newspaper *Luz*. There also was an attempt by his father to enroll him in the Naval Academy, but his short stature put an end to that possibility.

A significant aspect of his association with *Hoy* was his contact with writers such as Nicolás Guillén, Carlos Montenegro, and Lino Novás Calvo; the future political mobster Rolando Masferrer; and his close friend Carlos Franqui. Like Cabrera Infante, Franqui was not a native of Havana. "Poor from birth, a peasant who didn't even have the benefit of a nearby city or town, Franqui was what is called in Cuba a *guajiro macho:* a hick from the sticks . . . he was discovered when he was a mere boy by an extraordinary teacher, Melania Cobo, a well-educated black woman . . . who loved painting and music."[8]

Franqui moved to Havana after completing his high school studies in the town of Santa Clara in the Province of Las Villas. According to Heberto Padilla, Franqui "attained a secondary education against enormous odds. From childhood he knew the coarseness of life that accompanies the children of misfortune."[9] A confirmed activist, he was intelligent and honest enough to resist a blind obedience to authority and he had a decidedly independent streak. "His most notable character trait was the extravagant combination of, on the one hand, an impassioned advocacy of literature, music, and painting and, on the other, a militancy amply demonstrated by his daring and courage under Batista's repression."[10] Franqui would eventually leave the Communist Party and become involved in Fidel Castro's 26th of July Movement. If there ever was a leader after the revolutionary triumph of 1959 whose appearance could be associated with traditional images of Christ, it was Franqui with his slim, angular face and full beard. Although he was politically active when Cabrera Infante met him, his consuming passion at that time was the arts.

One day members of the staff at *Hoy* were discussing an article translated by Cabrera Infante from *The Daily Worker* that asserted that Theodore Dreiser was the best North American novelist. Franqui expressed his disagreement with that claim and countered it with his own candidate—William Faulkner. It was the first time that Cabrera Infante had heard that name, made even less recognizable by Franqui's inaccurate pronunciation. Shortly after that discussion, Franqui gave Cabrera Infante an Argentinian edition of Faulkner's *The Wild Palms* translated by Jorge Luis Borges, a rendering that Cabrera Infante now considers superior to the original. The translation traveled well. Mario Vargas Llosa also has indicated that it was the first Faulkner book he read, and both became avid readers of Faulkner after that initial discovery.[11]

Cabrera Infante perused any translation he could obtain, including *As I Lay Dying,* which he located in the National Library. The first work by Faulkner that he read in English was *Intruder in the Dust,* which he acquired years later in an affordable Signet Book edition. But *The Wild Palms* proved to be the most lingering influence, and a copy of the 1939 edition of the work can still be found in his London library. That novel changed the way he read and forced him to consider carefully all the nuances of language. He was also attracted to a classic American topic, the theme of escape, the search for individual freedom by movement through space.[12] Parallels also exist between Faulkner's use of alternating chapters with two story lines and the organization of the Spanish editions of *Writes of Passage* into vignettes and short stories that are intertwined.

Cabrera Infante has contradictory attitudes toward Faulkner's work, admiring some of its qualities and despairing of others. He is drawn to the powerful characterizations and themes and is intrigued by the skillful use of shocking elements, but he no longer finds the tortured and convoluted style attractive. Although some of the stories in *Writes of Passage* evidence a careful reading of Faulkner, he is not one of the many Spanish American writers who have fallen under that writer's hypnotic spell. After he became familiar with Faulkner, he went on to read Erskine Caldwell, Ernest Hemingway, and John Steinbeck, pursuing his interest in all cultural manifestations of the English-speaking world. Cabrera Infante admires Hemingway's clean style, a mode he cultivated in *Writes of Passage* and *View of Dawn in the Tropics.* In 1947 or 1948, he also read *Ulysses,* by James Joyce, a writer whose works have been one of the most enduring influences on his writings, especially Joyce's "precociously acute awareness of eye-ear polarities."[13]

Carlos Franqui prompted Cabrera Infante's first literary venture in 1947. It all began with an article on Miguel Ángel Asturias that appeared in an issue of *Bohemia,* the most popular magazine in Cuba. *Bohemia* was an eclectic journal that appealed to a broad spectrum of readers, a hybrid that contained a wide range of articles. It was like *Newsweek,* the *New Yorker,* and the *National Enquirer* all rolled into one. The article on Asturias was accompanied by selections from his *El Señor Presidente.* In an interview with Anne Marie Mergier, Cabrera Infante recounted the events that lead to his first published story: "Several important magazines devoted long articles to that book. I remember perfectly the one in *Bohemia,* signed by Ramón Vasconcelos, a well-known journalist at that time. Vasconcelos praised Asturias to the skies. He cited examples of onomatopoeias, of verbalizations, of all the vanguardist elements in *El Señor Presidente.* Franqui and I were discussing not so much the novel as Vasconcelos's criticism. With all the insolence of my eighteen years I said to Franqui: 'If being a writer means playing with words like that, then I'm a writer . . .' Then Franqui dared me to write a story. I wrote it. Franqui read it, liked it, and sent me to *Bohemia* to see if they would publish it. What happened then definitively changed my life."[14]

Cabrera Infante went to the offices of *Bohemia* on Trocadero, the same street where Lezama Lima lived, and met for the first time the literary editor of the journal, Antonio Ortega. A well-educated man of extraordinary literary sensibility, Ortega was a Spanish exile from Asturias, one of the few "really aristocratic" individuals Cabrera Infante ever knew.[15] With his elegant taste in clothing, arching eyebrows, thin mustache, and long and moderately angular face, he looked like someone who had stepped out of a painting by Velázquez or El Greco. Despite his aristocratic appearance and demeanor, he had great sympathy for the unfortunate. He was the kind of individual who could write a novel about a stray dog and who once published an article about the death of Franklin Delano Roosevelt's Scottish terrier, Fala. Trained in the natural sciences, he had taught in Spain before he came to Cuba. Despite his scientific background, he refused to use a typewriter and wrote by hand. If he were alive today, he undoubtedly would be resisting the computer, a device that Cabrera Infante has avoided with great success. Ortega was approximately forty-four years old when the brash teenager who had been spurred on by a dare appeared at his door struggling to control his emotions. Ortega agreed to look at his manuscript and asked Cabrera Infante to come back a week later. When he returned, Ortega informed him that *Bohemia* was going to publish his story, "Aguas de recuerdo" ("Waters of Memory"), a work that is described in *Infante's Inferno* as "a heavy-handed and pretentious parody."[16]

Cabrera Infante attributes his interest in parody to the banter he learned from classmates in high school. Julio Matas recalls that he was a skillful mimic of the speech of friends, relatives, and public figures at that age: "I particularly remember the imitations he did of Herminio Almendros, the Spanish pedagogue, father of the now famous cinematographer Nestor Almendros, of Nestor speaking in Catalan with his father, of Nicolás Guillén, and of the Communist writer Mirta Aguirre."[17] This skill would find its ultimate expression in *Three Trapped Tigers* in his parodies of the style and personal mannerisms of several Cuban writers. Time has not diminished this talent, an ability that can make a conversation with him an instructive as well as entertaining experience.

Cabrera Infante was paid the equivalent of fifty dollars for his first publication in *Bohemia,* an amount that represented a small fortune to an impoverished youth in Cuba at that time. Intrigued by the success he had inspired, Franqui suggested his young charge write another story, and he eventually produced "Las puertas se abren a las tres" ("The Doors Open at Three"). That story also was published in *Bohemia,* earned an equal amount of money, and was included in the collection *Writes of Passage* when it first appeared in Spanish in 1960. Cabrera Infante was as delighted as a prospector who had discovered gold. He was amazed that one could be paid so handsomely for something that seemed so easy, but then, he had not yet tackled his first novel. Ortega must have seen something in the young man that he liked, or perhaps he recognized a raw talent needing cultivation and direction. When the inexperienced writer returned for their second meeting, Ortega suggested that he needed to expand his literary background, and he invited Cabrera Infante to his home to see his personal library.

Ortega and his wife lived on the corner of Amistad and Trocadero, very close to the offices and pressroom of *Bohemia*. Their home was in the Columbus section of the city, an area where decency and prostitution coexisted, and it was located only ten blocks from 408 Zulueta. It was an easy and pleasant stroll, most of it down the tree-lined Prado

Boulevard, where there was always something interesting to see, especially during the evening. Once he left the Prado for the side streets of Ortega's neighborhood, the sights became more compelling. Furtive glances into bordellos revealed seminude sirens. On one occasion he saw a stark naked woman running across Trocadero from one establishment to another, transforming the road into "an olympic street: nymphs running in the nude."[18] During visits to the Ortega residence, Guillermo could indulge himself with temptations of the mind and flesh. Carlos Franqui, having decided that his protégé should cross the thresholds of desire, took him to a brothel, "thinking there wasn't much difference in initiating me in Faulkner or fucking."[19] Overwhelmed by anxiety, fear, and guilt, he found the experience a disheartening failure.

In due time, Ortega surprised Cabrera Infante by offering him a position as his personal secretary, an appointment he was delighted to accept. He started spending evenings from eight to ten working on the organization and cataloging of the library, but he soon discovered that Ortega frequently preferred to talk about literary matters. Cabrera Infante was the beneficiary of Ortega's knowledge of Spanish and world literature, and his new guide introduced him to writers such as T. S. Eliot, George Orwell, Ramón del Valle-Inclán, and Azorín. Other writers visited Ortega in his home, including María Zambrano and Lino Novás Calvo with his wife Herminia del Portal; on one occasion Cabrera Infante met Luis Cernuda there. He sometimes found it difficult to concentrate on the task at hand when Ortega's conversations with guests appeared more interesting. In addition to receiving an introduction into literary circles, he was learning that it was possible to survive in exile, a skill that Cabrera Infante could scarcely have appreciated at that juncture in his life. Antonio Ortega suffered the fate of being a political fugitive twice in his life, first from his native Spain after the fall of the Republic in 1939, and then from Cuba after Fidel Castro and his revolution came to power in 1959. Ortega left Havana in 1960 and would die in exile eight years later in Caracas.

Since he was a writer of fiction of some accomplishment who had won a literary award in Spain and the Hernández Catá Prize in Cuba in 1945 and had published the novel *Ready* in Havana in 1946, Ortega could advise Cabrera Infante on creative matters as well. He even shared some of his own manuscripts with his new pupil. When Guillermo returned to 408 Zulueta one evening the proud possessor of a copy of the manuscript of a collection of stories, Zoila was immensely impressed with the confidence that Ortega had bestowed on her son. A believer in the sacred power of the word, she encouraged her son's flirtations with literature, much to the dismay of her husband, who preferred that his son seek a more practical livelihood. Cabrera Infante had to deal early in his career with this paternal imperative toward inadequacy. His father, the worrier, must have felt that his impulsive wife was leading their son down the primrose path to poverty. Whatever deep-seated compulsions had caused him to lead a life that had deprived his family of material comforts, he was not anxious to see his son repeat the pattern. He had reason for concern, because after his contact with Ortega, Cabrera Infante's interest in his studies declined markedly. A proclivity to spend the day in libraries rather than class became a persistent habit.

In addition to working in Ortega's library, Cabrera Infante started evaluating manuscripts and writing literary notices for *Bohemia*. One of his first covered the 1949 recipient of the Nobel Prize in Literature— William Faulkner. He even did research on the Nobel laureate in the library of the U.S. Embassy, an indication that he took the assignment seriously and that he did not want to squander the opportunity. He went on to work as a critic-at-large for *Bohemia* from 1951 to 1953.

Franqui and Ortega facilitated his entrance into a number of positions in the journalistic world of Havana. He worked as a proofreader for several newspapers in addition to his occasional assignments for *Bohemia* and the *Mensuario Nacional de Cultura*. His other activities during this period included involvement in the founding and editing of two periodicals, *Nueva Generación* and *Nuestro Tiempo*. He participated along with Carlos Franqui, Rine Leal, Matías Montes Huidobro, and others in the initiation of the first-mentioned journal. Although *Nueva Generación* had a brief and undistinguished existence, Cabrera Infante did publish his first movie reviews in it. Cabrera Infante's association with the second journal ended when Carlos Franqui discovered that *Nuestro Tiempo*, which was the name of both the journal and a cultural society, had been infiltrated by the Communist Party. During this general period, Cabrera Infante also completed a summer program in cinematography at the University of Havana in 1949. Two years later he and four friends (Germán Puig, Ricardo Vigón, Nestor Almendros, and Tomás Gutiérrez Alea) founded the Cuban Cinemateca. At about that same time he met Marta Calvo, whom he married in 1953. Marta had showed up at 408 Zulueta acting as a chaperon for her sister, who was pursuing the object of her affections, Juan Blanco.

Guillermo also gained a degree of notoriety in October 1952, when he was arrested and fined for having published in the 19 October issue of *Bohemia* the short story "Balada de plomo y yerro" ("A Ballad of Bullets and Bull's-Eyes"). In that work, a secondary character becomes a minor nuisance when he wanders through a group of assassins awaiting the appearance of their victim. The drunken American, sporting all the accoutrements of an obnoxious tourist including yellow pants, mouths obscenities in his own language as he staggers down the street: "'Ah wanna a chiquita banana/ to suck mah bohs at Havana/ To suucckk mah baalls at Havaaannaa.'"[20] The imaginary Chiquita Banana, the Juan Valdez of another generation of North American advertisers, extolled the virtues of the tropical fruit in colorful radio jingles. She ended her heavily accented pitch with the admonition to avoid placing bananas in the refrigerator. In Cabrera Infante's text the caricature resonates on several levels, combining repulsion and humor as it undermines the stereotypes of two cultures. The government's antics might have been judged less severely by posterity had it taken the position that the story's use of obscenity was an affront to national dignity.

The year before his arrest, Cabrera Infante's family had moved from the unpleasant room at 408 Zulueta to an apartment in Vedado near the corner of Twenty-seventh Street and the Avenue of the Presidents, a change prompted, in part, by his brother's relapse of tuberculosis. Antonio Ortega had located the apartment and Cabrera Infante had insisted on the move because their quarters at 408 Zulueta were simply unhealthy. He contributed two-thirds of his monthly salary to the rent. This significant and pleasant improvement in their living quarters was countered by a reversal in the nation's political fortunes. On 10 March 1952, the government was overthrown in a military uprising orchestrated by former president Fulgencio Batista. A shadowy figure in Cuban politics who kept turning up like a bad penny, Batista had decided to occupy center stage again. This coup suffocated democracy in Cuba and eventually paved the way for the growth of revolutionary fervor.

"A Ballad of Bullets and Bull's Eyes" is the story of political gangsters who assassinate the wrong man. Little did Cabrera Infante know that his work would occasion the appearance of official gangsters at his Vedado apartment who would provide him with a personal tour of some of the government's more unsavory institutions. He was booked, inter-rogated, and incarcerated with a number of criminals who were kinder to him than his keepers. He had the good fortune to fall under the protective wing of a notorious bank robber of Lebanese background, Jorge Nayol Nasser. After a few days, friends and family secured his release, but there was a hearing later during which he was fined an amount larger than he could pay, prevented from pursuing a degree at the School of Journalism for two years, and prohibited from publishing under his own name.[21] The loss of his studies at the School of Journalism was apparently not a great tragedy since he has declared that "to be admitted you had to prove that you could read the headlines without moving your lips."[22] If we can believe Cabrera Infante's published and oral accounts of his ordeal, he suffered the ultimate indignity when one of his fellow prisoners criticized "A Ballad of Bullets and Bull's Eyes" for its inauthenticity (it should be pointed out that nearly everyone in Cuba read *Bohemia*). The prison's resident literary critic implied that the story rendered the simple act of murder as too complicated an enterprise.

According to Cabrera Infante, his arrest was really directed at *Bohemia,* and his role was that of a "scapegoat." The whole affair "was a kind of settlement of accounts between the director of *Bohemia* and the Minister of the Interior."[23] Irritated with the journal's critical stance toward the government, some officials regarded the appearance of obscenity in its pages as a good pretext for political mischief under the guise of defend-ing the morality of the realm. No matter that there was little morality to protect. Antonio Ortega had edited out Spanish obscenities before the publication of the story, but since he did not know English, the others were left intact. The publisher of *Bohemia,* Miguel Angel Quevedo, cleverly defended the journal by claiming innocence of the meanings of the words, so the logical and legal choice was the author.

Cabrera Infante's unexpected arrest provoked a flurry of activity among his family and friends. His father even consulted the Communist Party's legal representative. It fell on Juan Blanco to represent him, and he and Antonio Ortega resolved the issue of the fine. Cabrera Infante's five-day imprisonment was a traumatic event that must have recalled at some level of his consciousness the emotional turmoil of his parents' incarceration in 1936. On his release, the craving for emotional security must have been intense. According to him, the ordeal "accelerated the catastrophic process of my getting married to my first wife."[24] Marta had been experiencing difficulties with her family and during Guillermo's imprisonment she moved in with his parents. Zoila was particularly taken with the young woman—Marta must have filled the void caused by the two infant daughters Zoila had lost. On his release from prison, Guillermo found himself outflanked at home and facing the implied obligation of marriage. Marta Calvo had provided timely assistance during the crisis and her concern and commitment were genuine. A brunette whose dark and ardent eyes revealed intense and persistent emotions, Marta was a single-minded young woman who had been trained in a convent school like Zoila. She had the ability to see and deal with the need of the moment, a characteristic that made her adept at coping with emergencies, but that did not provide analytic insight. She was also tenacious and reluctant to relinquish anything she fancied. Impressed and moved by her response to his plight, Cabrera Infante did not realize that there could be similarities between being under lock and key and the state of holy deadlock.

In 1954 Antonio Ortega became the director of *Carteles,* a weekly magazine similar to *Bohemia,* and he appointed Cabrera Infante as the feature writer for films during that same year. Initially, his assignment consisted of two columns a month, but when they were successful, it became a weekly responsibility. At first Ortega reviewed his work carefully, but after a period of time Cabrera Infante was given complete autonomy for all practical purposes. Because of the conditions of his sentence the previous year, he could not use his name and resorted to pseudonyms in all his publications. The most widely known is Caín (Cain), the one he employed for his film reviews, but several others were utilized for other pieces. He recalls employing as many as four or five different pen names, but he only remembers two, which are reminiscent of the eccentricity of Pepe Castro: Jonás Castro, the one most used, and S. del Pastora Niño. In addition, many items were published without any indication of the author's identity.

A photographic essay published under the pseudonym Jonás Castro in the 5 August 1956 issue of *Carteles* attracted considerable attention, not all of it desirable. "La belleza de la bomba" ("The Beauty of the Bomb") consisted of twelve spectacular pictures of atomic explosions, vivid images of beauty and destruction whose symmetrical or twisted forms have haunted the human imagination since they first appeared. The introduction and the comments that accompanied the photographs focused on the infernal aspects of human creativity and combined aesthetic appreciation with moral revulsion. Many were disturbed by his approach to the specter of global nuclear death, which replaced a singular horror with a variety of reactions, converting a universally acknowledged symbol with one meaning into an image of multiple significance. For those content to locate evil in an external other rather than an inner self, the synthesis was unacceptable, but in fairness to the offended it must be admitted that Jonás Castro was as mischievous as any of Cabrera Infante's other personae. Other articles published under that pen name included "Los espectadores las prefieren rubias" ("Spectators Prefer Them Blonde") and "El bikini tiene más de 2,000 años" ("The Bikini Is More Than Two Thousand Years Old").[25] The reaction to "The Beauty of the Bomb" was not lost on Cabrera Infante. It convinced him that combining the word and image could be a powerful technique, an approach he would use in other works such as *Un oficio del siglo veinte,* 1963 (*A Twentieth Century Job,* 1991).

Among his other achievements at *Carteles,* Cabrera Infante was appointed managing editor in 1957, a post once held by Alejo Carpentier. These positions provided him with important outlets for his literary and film interests and consolidated the beginnings of a fruitful career. His editorial work involved the selection of national and foreign literary texts for publication, and during this period he translated two stories by Frank O'Connor and James Joyce. In 1957 he also traveled to New York and Mexico City. Cabrera Infante worked for *Carteles* until the journal was suspended by the revolutionary government in 1960 and its facilities taken over by a new state publication, *Verde Olivo.*

Ortega responded to the young and inexperienced writer by offering him a friendship and professional relationship that were decisive in his literary career. Cabrera Infante's esteem for Ortega is underscored by his references to him in his writings as a mentor, a status accorded another important figure, Pepe Castro. Cabrera Infante has published literary portraits of both of these men. A loyalty to individuals is one of his laudable characteristics. He was instrumental in arranging the republication a few years ago in Spain of *Yemas de coco y otros cuentos,* the manuscript that Antonio Ortega had allowed him to read in 1947. The collection of stories originally had been published in a small edition by the Universidad Central de las Villas in 1959.

Although these two mentors were quite different in temperament and background, they shared certain qualities, including a propensity to teach and what can be termed an acute critical sensibility. The latter characteristic was manifested in Pepe Castro in a skeptical attitude and in the recognition of cause-and-effect relationships, and in Antonio Ortega in a fine aesthetic sensibility and an appreciation for quality. The fact that Pepe Castro did not always practice what he preached and had a dismaying tendency to embrace strange causes prematurely did not go unnoticed, but it only increased his appeal. Pepe Castro imbued Cabrera Infante with an awareness of oral language and Ortega with an understanding of the written word. Pepe shared with Zoila a zest for living, although he did not challenge life as directly and as passionately as she did. She also was quite different from her husband, who faced adversity not by confronting it, but by avoiding it or simply persevering. Cabrera Infante has always admired his father's ability to survive, and he has acquired that facility in the face of many misfortunes.

In addition to the guidance of his immediate family, Cabrera Infante had been fortunate to acquire mentors in Gibara and Havana who contributed significantly to his development. After the move to Havana in 1941, the family made several trips to Gibara to visit relatives and to keep in touch with roots. In 1943 Cabrera Infante's maternal great-grandfather, Sebastián Castro, died at approximately one hundred three years of age. Two years later Zoila's father Cándido passed away in Holguín, calling for the wife who had banished him from her life several years earlier. There also was the lingering possibility of a permanent return to Gibara if circumstances in the capital became unbearable or economic conditions forced them back. But after 1947 the trips became infrequent and slowly Havana became home, although there were no dramatic improvements in their financial situation. By the 1950s Gibara was a golden memory and Havana a painful reality, but one with challenging possibilities.

CHAPTER THREE

A Momentary Splendor

IN A PICTURE TAKEN BY THE ACCOMPLISHED PHOTOGRAPHER
Jesse A. Fernández in June 1959, Cabrera Infante is sitting at a table in a
bar in Santiago de Cuba, a city he had discovered less than four years
earlier. He is seated alone at a round table, wearing sunglasses that wrap
around his face, intently bent over a book by Jack Kerouac. In the
foreground there is a bottle of Hatuey beer and a half-filled glass. The
profile of an Indian chief graces the bottle's label, a reminder of the
historical personage whose name the product bears and whose destiny
Cabrera Infante would chronicle in *View of Dawn in the Tropics*. An icon of
resistance in Cuban legend, Hatuey (the chief) is remembered for refusing
to be converted to Catholicism at the stake because he did not want to
share a promised afterlife with his Spanish executioners. Cabrera Infante's

hunched figure and the table he is sitting at occupy the lower left portion of the photograph. In the background, there is a long bar and behind it rows of glistening bottles. Above all the glass and the bar, a large billboard slants forward, displaying in opulent splendor four languid, Rubenesque nudes. The mural extols the quality of another beer: "CRISTAL. ¡Está como nunca!" ("CRISTAL. Better than ever!"). A neon sign to the right of the billboard touts the same beverage. Two bartenders or waiters are seated behind the bar, engaged in idle conversation, and to the right a patron's relaxed arm dangles behind a chair. The informal ease of the setting contrasts subtly with the intense concentration of Kerouac's reader.

This remarkable photograph captures three important elements in Cabrera Infante's work: literature, sensuality, and popular culture. It also reveals his capacity to focus his attention on a particular task irrespective of the setting, an ability acquired after years of living in cramped and noisy quarters and working in tumultuous newsrooms. The sunglasses indicate that he was cultivating a movie persona. Other photographs taken during this period show a Cabrera Infante quite different from the twelve-year-old captured with his uncle the Kid in the 1941 picture. Now attuned to the image, he no longer regarded the camera as an adversary, and the pictures reveal a more confident person and one more at ease with his surroundings. By 1959 he had acquired considerable editorial experience and had established himself as the most important film critic in Havana. His cinematic activities had even included an interview with Marlon Brando. He also received a degree in professional journalism in 1956, and by 1959 he was the father of two daughters, Ana and Carola.

It was a euphoric period in Cuban history. Batista and his bruised ego abandoned the country in the early morning hours of January 1 and the revolutionary government began to assume power that same day. Cabrera Infante was soon involved in several cultural activities. As reforms moved through society, new publishing houses and journals were established and he was engaged in many of the changes. He also traveled abroad with governmental delegations and accompanied Fidel Castro on several trips. He returned from one tour with new insights into the popular leader's personality—Castro became enraged in Brazil when Nat King Cole attracted larger audiences than he did. The trip to Brazil left Cabrera Infante traumatized by what he had learned about the revolutionary leader. Despite his misgivings, he had not concluded that the revolution and the man were one and the same. During this time, Cabrera Infante was urging Cubans living abroad to return to their homeland and inviting foreigners to see his rejuvenated country—Cuba was better than ever.

Although Jesse Fernández (1929–1987) had been born in Cuba, his parents were from Asturias and returned to Spain during the Machado dictatorship "just in time for the Spanish Civil War."[1] After a long and difficult period in Spain, they eventually returned to Cuba. Cabrera Infante first met Jesse Fernández in October 1957 in New York City, where Jesse was working as a photographer for *Life* magazine. In February of 1958 Fernández was on special assignment in Havana when the world champion auto racer, Juan Manuel Fangio, was kidnapped in a downtown Havana hotel by revolutionaries. Since the object of his captors was to attract world attention to their cause, Fangio was soon released unharmed. This use of a hostage to further a political agenda was a prelude to the later extensive use of this tactic on the international political scene.[2] Cabrera Infante attempted to arrange an interview between Fernández and the kidnappers without success.

After the defeat of Batista in 1959, Cabrera Infante persuaded Jesse to return to the island of his birth for an extended period. Cabrera Infante had traveled with the group that accompanied Fidel Castro on his April 1959 trip to the United States, and while in New York City he took the opportunity to go off on his own to visit friends such as Edmundo Desnoes, Pablo Armando Fernández, and Heberto Padilla and to urge them to return to Cuba. Jesse Fernández and Cabrera Infante worked for the same publications in Havana and toured the country together, compiling a photographic record of their travels to places as remote as Gibara. Cabrera Infante was on the road, roaming the island with a remarkable photographer. Evidently more astute than most, Fernández elected to return to New York at the end of the year. Despite the general optimism of the first months of the revolution, there were many disturbing signs. Power was being concentrated in the hands of one man, there was a complete lack of any system of checks and balances, and governmental decisions appeared arbitrary to anyone not privy to hidden agendas. As far as the general populace was concerned, Fidel Castro was above the restraints of mere mortals.

Cabrera Infante was introduced to Jesse Fernández in October 1957 by Humberto Arenal at a Madison Square Garden celebration thrown by

Mike Todd to commemorate the first year of his film, *Around the World in Eighty Days*. The celebration received detailed coverage and publicity and was broadcast for ninety minutes by CBS Television with George Jessel serving as the emcee. Eighteen thousand guests somehow mingled with twenty-four bands, two orchestras, elephants, and "some 14,000 free gifts, including an airplane, motorboat and eight automobiles."[3] Above it all was the famous balloon from the movie. The party was a follow-up to a more modest gathering of two thousand guests in the Battlesea Festival Garden in London. Cabrera Infante met many notables during the activities surrounding Mike Todd's extravaganza, at a reception held at the Museum of Modern Art, and during interviews and photographic sessions with Jesse Fernández. He wrote: "Jesse was a bounty hunter with a hit list: He tracked down Elizabeth Taylor, beautiful and vulgar, her husband Mike Todd, just vulgar, Victor McLaglen, enormous and affable, Tony Curtis and his still carnally desirable Janet Leigh, Sir Cedric Hardwicke, haughtily mounted on a humpback, nocturnal camel, David Niven, laughing, remote, simulating a smile: It was a moveable and fast-moving feast."[4]

He also encountered Marlene Dietrich and the legendary Josef von Sternberg, who directed several of Dietrich's films, including *The Blue Angel*. The years of apprenticeship, which began in obscure movie houses in Gibara, were yielding results. During his first visit to New York City in 1955, he had viewed a hundred movies in twenty-nine days, many at the Film Library of the Museum of Modern Art. One of the results of those activities was the establishment of a loan program of films from New York to the Cuban Cinemateca in Havana. He also viewed on stage Tennessee Williams's *Cat on a Hot Tin Roof*, William Inge's *Bus Stop*, and Adler and Ross's musical comedy *Damn Yankees*. Cabrera Infante spent many days and nights during his 1957 stay dashing around the city with Jesse Fernández in his red Austin Healey. They visited several nightclubs and listened to jazz played by the likes of Thelonious Monk, one of the founding figures of bebop. During a return visit in 1959, he heard Miles Davis and John Coltrane at the Blue Note Club. Although exciting, such excursions were not new to him since he wandered Havana in similar fashion before and after his trips to New York City. His nocturnal meanderings would provide an imaginative vehicle for the portrayal of similar adventures in the restless movement of several of the characters in *Three Trapped Tigers*.

On a brisk autumn morning in October 1957, Cabrera Infante and Fernández stumbled upon the scene of a gangland slaying moments after it had taken place in the Grasso Barbershop in the luxurious Park Sheraton Hotel. They had stopped to use a rest room and instead found chaos and confusion. The notorious Alberto "The Executioner" Anastasia, whose infamous Murder Inc. had decimated the ranks of rival mobs in the 1930s and who had overcome several charges of homicide, had been shot to death by two masked gunmen. Fernández, frustrated because he had missed the opportunity to photograph Alberto Anastasia's sudden death in a barbershop, began to lament what might have been. He even speculated that he could have taken a photo of the crime in progress. The more pragmatic Cabrera Infante, showing a flash of his father's caution, quickly pointed out that such an action could have been a one-way ticket to oblivion.

They arrived soon enough to acquire information and pictures for an article that was published in the 10 November 1957 issue of *Carteles*. Cabrera Infante began "Muerte en la barbería" ("Death in the Barbershop") with a personal but third-person account of his accidental appearance at the hotel. This is followed by a narrative rendering of the event that even describes the victim's last sensations. The focus then shifts to a historical summary of Anastasia's life. The gangster's story forms the central section of the text and the article closes by reversing the procedure used at the beginning by returning to the narration of the assassination and ending with Cabrera Infante's eyewitness account. The segmentation is astutely handled and is reminiscent of the crime stories of Lino Novás Calvo, particularly his "Angusola y los cuchillos" ("Angusola and the Knives"), which first appeared in *Bohemia* in December 1947. Cabrera Infante's blending of fact and fiction or history and narration in this journalistic endeavor is a strategy that he would use extensively in later works. He also attempted to convey the unreality of the entire event with several references to film but closed with the observation that "he had not just seen a movie but a slice of life he did not know."[5] Since he and Jesse Fernández were returning from an interview with the German film director Helmut Kautner when they came upon the brutal scene, the references to the movies in the article reflect the extension of an actual experience.

The murder must have reminded Cabrera Infante of the carnage that had taken place in Havana on 13 March of the same year, when approximately forty-one individuals were killed during an unsuccessful attack on the Presidential Palace.[6] Several friends perished in the frustrated attempt to assassinate Batista, and the tragedy has haunted him ever since. During the assault on the Presidential Palace, another attack was directed at the broadcasting studios of CMQ Radio, with the objective of announcing the death of Batista. It also failed and two survivors, Carlos Figueredo and Joe Westbrook, sought refuge in the apartment of Zoila and Guillermo senior, but they only stayed a short time. It was decided that the apartment was not a secure hiding place because the family's maid was dating a soldier and the director of the motorcycle police of Havana, Oscar González, lived next door. After the two men separated, Joe Westbrook was killed during a police raid. Figueredo survived and, after the revolutionary government came to power, was eventually assigned the task of interrogating political prisoners.

Many of the politically slanted vignettes of the Spanish version of *Writes of Passage* and some of the narrative segments in *View of Dawn in the Tropics* were inspired by those events. In the latter-mentioned text, the fates of Westbrook and Figueredo are chronicled in the vignette "When he was a waiter." The events of March would receive more elaborate artistic treatment in the 1991 screenplay, "The Lost City," written for Paramount Pictures. Although the assaults had been suicidal, their near success destroyed the myth of governmental invincibility, and they eventually helped galvanize public opinion against Batista. The mood in Cuba became more grim in 1957 as the desire for change gained momentum.

In that same year, Cabrera Infante began writing for the underground press and offered what assistance he could to revolutionary associates as a messenger or transporter of arms. His close friend Carlos Franqui founded *Revolución* clandestinely in 1956. Padilla wrote: "Officially, Franqui was a journalist who worked for Channel 2 in Havana: behind the scenes, he was organizing the urban opposition to Batista. He took charge of propaganda and information and created the clandestine *Revolución,* which became the official organ of the 26th of July Movement after the fall of Batista."[7] Franqui was arrested and tortured in 1957 and went into exile after his release. He later joined Fidel Castro in the Sierra Maestra and "built Radio Rebelde from scratch. . . . [I]t broadcast not only the partisan truth but instructions for direct political action, such as sabotage and terrorism."[8]

Cabrera Infante's professional endeavors during the 1950s revolved around his journalistic activities, his development as a film critic, and his writing of short stories. Each of these enterprises evolved into a major achievement between 1959 and 1963: the appointment as editor of the newly created cultural journal *Lunes de Revolución* in 1959, the appearance of the volume of short stories *Así en la paz como en la guerra* (*Writes of Passage*) in 1960, and the publication of the collection of film reviews *Un oficio del siglo veinte* (*A Twentieth Century Job*) in 1963. His work for the press began with the journeyman tasks of proofreading and translation, moved on to occasional writing assignments, and culminated in important journalistic and editorial positions. The highlight of his journalistic career was his appointment in 1959 as the editor of *Lunes de Revolución,* the weekly cultural supplement of the daily newspaper *Revolución,* directed by Carlos Franqui. Zoila and her husband must have been satisfied with this achievement, since their son was now involved with a revolutionary journal dedicated to the fostering of change in society. With Franqui as his sponsor and collaborator, Cabrera Infante was ready to make his mark on Cuban cultural expression.

Lunes de Revolución was the most innovative, broadly based, and integrative journal in Cuba. There wasn't another intellectual supplement like it and there never was another after its demise. Reflecting the eclectic aesthetic concerns of both its founder and its editor, it was interested in all the arts as well as political and theoretical writings. Carlos Franqui has explained:

> From its inception *Lunes* had been very polemical. Our thesis was that we had to break down the barriers that separated elite culture from mass culture. We wanted to bring the highest quality of culture to hundreds of thousands of readers. We were motivated by a motto we got directly from José Martí: "Culture brings freedom." . . . We called into question all the commonplaces of Cuban history and literature. Even *Lunes*'s typography was a scandal for left- and right-wing prudes. We played with letters in the same way that Apollinaire, the futurists, the Dadaists, and the surrealists had done. And we included black and Cuban folk traditions as well. We tried to translate Cuban culture into visual symbols.[9]

Lunes published the works of writers and intellectuals from all over the world. Its eclectic orientation resulted in articles on topics as diverse as avant-garde art, eroticism, surrealism, Camus, Picasso, Sartre, and the radical left. A listing of the authors who appeared on its pages would read like a who's who of Cuban, Spanish American, and worldwide artistic and intellectual expression. There were also many authors who were relatively unknown at the time, such as Alvaro Cepeda Samudio, or who were in the early stages of their careers, like Carlos Fuentes. One of Antonio Ortega's stories appeared as well.

Political articles included extensive coverage of the Bay of Pigs (known as Playa Girón in Cuba) and Algeria. Cabrera Infante published an article in the 2 November 1959 issue that attacked the coverage the revolution was receiving in *Time* and *Life* magazines. There were special issues on China, José Martí, Anton Pavlovich Chekhov, and Rubén Martínez Villena. The magazine even published some of the writings of Trotsky, which must have perturbed more than one doctrinaire commissar and Stalinists like Zoila and her husband. In a retrospective essay, Cabrera Infante has explained: "We had the Surrealist credo as our catechism and Trotskyite politics as our aesthetics, mixed like bad metaphors—or heady drinks."[10] The journal also attacked the established aesthetic order in Cuba, which in those years meant the great poet and novelist José Lezama Lima. Heberto Padilla recalls: "I remember saying to Cabrera Infante that I wanted to blow up the baroque bastion that was the Trocadero home where Lezama lay wheezing."[11] Cabrera Infante and his colleagues were spreading their wings on a grand scale.

The activities at *Revolución* and *Lunes* were frenetic. Invitations to visit Cuba were issued to writers like Jean-Paul Sartre, Simone de Beauvoir, Françoise Sagan, Wright Mills, and LeRoi Jones. Sartre visited the offices of *Lunes* on Tuesday 8 April 1960 and an edition was dedicated to his work. Pablo Neruda arrived by boat in early December 1960 and stayed three weeks, much to the dismay of his rival, Nicolás Guillén. One hundred twenty-nine issues of *Lunes* were published before it was closed down by the government because of its independent stance and its insistence on artistic freedom. (One number that appeared after the explosion of the French ship *La Coubre* in Havana harbor in 1960 was unnumbered and undated.) Immediately following the controversy, three issues of *Lunes de Revolución,* numbers 115 through 117, dated 24 July, 31 July, and 14 August of 1961, were edited by Ithiel León and featured Laos, Vietnam, and Korea. The incident or pretext that brought it all to an end was the short film *PM,* an approximately twenty-three-minute documentary about nightlife around Prado and Neptuno streets in the old section of the city and on the waterfront across the bay from old Havana in the predominantly black Regla. The short was made by Cabrera Infante's younger brother, Alberto (Sabá), and Orlando Jiménez Leal, "at the time the youngest photographer in Cuba, capable of handling a Cinemascope camera when he was 14, quite a film feat."[12]

Cabrera Infante had helped with the completion of the documentary and had provided partial financing through the auspices of *Lunes.* He was interested in the project because of its subject matter and the producers' plans to apply the techniques and approaches of Free Cinema. Launched in England in 1956 in the same political and intellectual atmosphere that nurtured the New Left, Free Cinema advocated showing themes and plots relevant to the lives of the general public. According to Ephraim Katz, "it helped steer British commercial cinema in the direction of socially controversial subjects, dealing with contemporary problems against working-class settings." He also points out, "In a published manifesto, the aims of the movement were summed up thus: 'Implicit in our attitude is a belief in freedom, in the importance of people and in the significance of the everyday.'"[13] *PM* inadvertently lived up to many of these tenets, even to the extent of becoming controversial.

PM was shown without incident on *Lunes*'s television program on a Monday evening. However, when plans were made to exhibit it in a movie theater, permission was needed from the Cuban Film Institute, headed by the cunning and dangerous Alfredo Guevara. It was at this point that the film became a bone of contention between different governmental factions and the focus of political intrigues. When Orlando Jiménez and Sabá Cabrera innocently took the film to gain the necessary approval, it was seized and banned. In response to this action and others, some two hundred intellectuals and writers signed a letter of protest. The government responded with a plan to hold a series of public hearings, but few suspected what would happen. Three meetings were held during three consecutive weeks in the National Library. The protestors soon discovered that the scheduled meetings were really a public trial.

In retrospect, the timing of the protest was not auspicious, since the Cuban government had won a resounding victory with the defeat of the invasion at the Bay of Pigs in April and the first international convention of writers and intellectuals was about to take place in Havana. To avoid embar-

government postponed the meeting from June to August. To
Cabrera Infante and his closest collaborators on *Lunes* were
livious to the approaching disaster is hard to ascertain, but
frenzied energy may have had its roots in an unarticulated
vaguely sensed foreboding that it was all too good to last.

The denunciation of *Lunes* was presided over by a number of high-
ranking government officials including Prime Minister Fidel Castro, a
sign that serious trouble was brewing. Among those accompanying
Castro to the first meeting were the rotund and clownish president,
Osvaldo Dorticós, and the minister of education, Armando Hart, an
expert spewer of hate. An affair that apparently started out as a minor
matter was soon recognized as an attack against anyone associated with
Lunes. The meetings turned into an ordeal with a foregone conclusion.
The closure of the journal involved discussions at the highest levels of
the government and culminated in Fidel Castro's often cited speech,
"Words to the Intellectuals," in June 1961, in which he declared that all
was possible within the revolution, but nothing outside of it.

The demise of his cherished journal was a severe blow to Cabrera
Infante. Once again, as in October 1952, he had run afoul of the
authorities, only this time on a grander and more public scale. Many
individuals were involved and their lives were changed dramatically by
the events of that summer. In a photograph taken by Anders Ehnmark of
Stockholm during the difficult days after the closure of *Lunes,* Cabrera
Infante appears grim and taut. His left hand holds a cigarette to his
mouth, and he peers at the camera with troubled and bewildered eyes—
the quiet confidence of 1959 is gone. His parents were puzzled by his
stubborn insistence on defending abstract concepts of little consequence.
His father, forever the evader of confrontation, must have felt that his
original misgivings about his son involving himself with anything as
troublesome as words, and creative ones at that, had been justified. He
had taken up again with the unreliable and undisciplined Carlos Franqui,
the same man who once had been expelled from the Communist Party.

For her part, Zoila could not understand why such a fuss was being
made over a trivial matter. Any good Party member knew that the
acceptance of authority in the battle against capitalism was a necessary
evil. Where was the son who had confounded street thugs with well-
placed quips? Why were the two brothers trying to defy such powerful
political bullies? Cabrera Infante, of course, had grown up and had

us than an angry scowl or a funny
and intellectual freedom. He and
er, provoking among governmental
Dracula confronting the Cross. The
joyed did not help matters—at its
printed and the general population
ty-eight, an obvious indication that
he gang of irreverent intellectuals at
esthetic or political authority; it was
als to imagine themselves the object

Guevara, was transformed into a
ritten in Brussels in December 1962
e of *Mundo Nuevo*. Originally con-
npublished novel "Cuerpos divinos"
ailar el chachachá" ("A Felony to
versation between the narrator and a
Restaurant in Havana. The story deals
stic creations through the prism of
mber of witty barbs at his inquisitor
discouraged him by his clever appeals
fanaticism prevails six months later
eeds in engineering the closure of the
e narrator's bitterness is tempered by
in his life and he finds comfort in her
há" is a story of political disillusion-
rrated in a style similar to that of the
ed Tigers. Both texts contain a self-
he reader in the creative process and
Other similarities include wordplay,
ular culture, a mixture of playful mis-
n to graphics. Puns such as "William
works.

he story to the editor of *Mundo Nuevo*,
entified the models for several of the
evara as the commissar and Miriam
tionally indicated that a blank space in
e, an old-time party member who had

played a prominent role in the denunciation of *Lunes de Revolución*. He also spoke of "a certain political vacillation" in the story that speaks more to his own attitude toward his creation than the content of the work itself. Nearly four years passed before he submitted the story for publication and, according to his letter, only Miriam Gómez and three friends (Juan Goytisolo, Antón Arrufat, and Juan Arcocha) had seen it. Even Rodríguez Monegal thought it prudent to delay publication because of its antirevolutionary slant and the story did not appear until two years later.

Cabrera Infante's hesitation in sharing or printing the work is indicative of the painful disintegration of his political beliefs and his reluctance to make an overt break with the revolution, especially before the publication of *Three Trapped Tigers*. He also realized that political passion could contaminate artistic endeavors, an issue he has wrestled with throughout his career. His feelings on this matter were eloquently expressed in 1968 in a letter to Jorge Edwards dated March 6th: "I also have the translation of the prologue of what will possibly be my next book, 'Divine Bodies,' of which I have written 1500 pages, most of them discardable, and which confronts me, like my other projects, with the almost insolvable problem of finding an artistic form, not to elevate Cuban speech to the category of language, but my political thought, my political experience during the insurrection against Batista, during the Revolution, in the diplomatic service and now in exile, capable of expressing me freely, anarchically and expansively, in the always narrow confines of political norms."[15] Eventually, political concerns would be relegated primarily to his essays and interviews.

Cabrera Infante's editorial career was not the only thing that ended in shambles during the first years of the decade. He had become estranged from Marta Calvo, their marriage disintegrated, and they were divorced in early 1961. It had not been a happy union. His attitude toward the marriage from the beginning was one of physical and psychological flight, and he now regards most of his actions during those years as irresponsible. Like his father, he began to wander. For her part, Marta was not the most attentive of mothers and much of the responsibility of rearing their two daughters fell to Zoila. The marriage became a quarrelsome test of wills and finally ended in divorce in early 1961. For him the change brought a sense of relief, but for her it became an extended lament, although she succeeded in remarrying before he did.

Guillermo had met Miriam Gómez, a successful actress and model, a few years earlier. Like him, she was originally from the provinces, in her case the small town of Taguasco, with fewer than two thousand inhabitants, in the Escambray area in the central part of the island. A striking woman of a soft and gentle beauty, she conveys in portraits of that period a combination of delicacy and strength—she embodies Zoila's generosity and emotionalism and Guillermo Cabrera senior's perseverance. Although she did not respond with similar interest or enthusiasm to Cabrera Infante's infatuation with her, his persistence, which was encouraged by his future mother-in-law, eventually prevailed. Their marriage in late 1961 was an auspicious event in his life.

The shutdown of *Lunes* marked the end of Cabrera Infante's editorial career. He left behind the organized chaos of newsrooms struggling to meet deadlines, but the experience, along with his other journalistic activities, ingrained habits that still prevail. Like the film critic who returned to the offices of *Carteles* to compose reviews late at night or the editor who worked until dawn at *Lunes,* he still prefers to work into the early hours of the morning. He can easily adjust to a normal day's routine, but his first choice is that of a denizen of the night, late to bed and late to rise. He also has an unusual tolerance for noise and interruptions. He and Miriam have transformed three rooms of their London apartment into one spacious expanse that consists of a living room, study, and kitchen area. Each end of this section is framed by very large windows that complement the fifteen-foot ceiling. The back window has no covering, and the three front windows only have shades, which are seldom used. A large tropical plant, a Monstera deliciosa, has nearly overwhelmed the area in front of the bay windows and threatens to invade the living room. Its massive bulk is supported by a horizontal steel bar. The greenery softens the light that streams through the windows and screens the apartment from the noise and prying eyes of a busy street. Miriam Gómez occasionally mentions the possibility of trimming back the greenery, but her husband resists the idea—he has grown fond of his plant and does not want it mutilated, a lingering influence of his years in Gibara when he was surrounded by lush tropical vegetation. This ample area with its generous windows provides the combination of visual space, bright illumination, and auditory intimacy favored by many Cubans and creates a tropical ambience in a city where winter days only have six hours of light.

Guillermo works at his typewriter in the middle of this area, attuned, yet oblivious, to what is going on around him. Visitors, telephone
conversations, television programs, recordings of music, Miriam singing
or clanking around the kitchen, the arrival of communications by fax—
that vast array of intrusions seemingly created for the sole purpose of
thwarting writers—all leave him unfazed. If an interruption merits
attention, there may be a conversation. Occasionally a discussion becomes animated and passionate, bursting forth and dissipating with the
alacrity and intensity of a summer storm. The only thing that invariably
propels him like a shot out of his desk chair is a breaking newscast on
television. He and Miriam Gómez remain passionately committed to
current events.

In addition to influencing his work habits, the experience he gained
during his fourteen-year journalistic career in Cuba enabled him to
acquire skills that have contributed to his survival in exile. Out of
economic necessity, Cabrera Infante has become an excellent essayist,
and he publishes widely in the European and Spanish American press on
a variety of subjects. In this respect, he has followed in the footsteps of
another distinguished Cuban writer, José Martí, who spent many years
of his life in exile working for the independence of Cuba from Spain.
Some of Cabrera Infante's finest writing is buried here and there in
journals and newspapers. Another influence is more indirect and tenuous, yet important: there is no avoidance of the actual in Cabrera Infante's
writings. He prefers to deal with life as it is rather than as he would like
it to be, and he eschews wishful thinking or sentimentality in his works.

The last issue of *Lunes de Revolución* was dated 6 November 1961.
The *PM* affair had left the journal demoralized and subject to the whims
of censorial vigil—on one occasion a program on jazz planned for
television was prohibited because the saxophone was declared an impe-
rialistic instrument. After the closure of the review, Cabrera Infante
remained unemployed well into 1962. He could have remained on the
payroll of *Revolución,* but he thought it inappropriate and Carlos Franqui
agreed. Fortunately, Miriam's success as an actress provided sufficient
income for them to live on, although she was becoming disenchanted
with her profession as she found herself more frequently involved in
tedious, propagandistic productions. Cabrera Infante used his spare time
to write, working on *A Twentieth Century Job,* segments of *Three Trapped
Tigers,* and other fragments. Stung by the reversals in his career, he

responded in typical fashion once he had regained his equilibrium, with humor and renewed vigor. He has usually rebounded from disaster by reviving or initiating projects, a not unreasonable response to adversity. Although jobless, Cabrera Infante used his time as well as he could under the circumstances. Eventually, he was assigned to the position of cultural attaché in the Cuban Embassy in Brussels, Belgium, an indication that he still had influential friends in the government. He left for his new assignment in Europe in September of 1962 with Miriam Gómez and his older daughter Ana, less than two months before the missile crisis of October.

The Apprentice Storyteller

OF ALL CABRERA INFANTE'S ACTIVITIES IN THE 1950S, CREATIVE writing was the least consuming and the most casual. His first story, which was born of an idle boast and a dare, was successfully published and richly compensated for, a fortunate circumstance for such a young writer. Although that initial attainment undoubtedly stimulated his interest and confidence, if for no other reason than for the financial reward he received, it is perfectly human to distrust success when it comes too easily. He was, of course, in the process of finding his own voice by experimenting with different forms and by adapting various narrative styles, and between 1947 and 1960 he composed some twenty stories and submitted several of them to national literary contests. Many of these works appeared in journals like *Bohemia, Carteles, Ciclón,* and *Lunes de Revolución,* but his career as a creative writer at that time was random and unfocused. This was not the case in the film reviews he wrote for *Carteles* during the same period—there the reader finds a more assured and confident voice. In the movie criticism there is a direct relationship between productivity and the evolution of a personal aesthetic sensibility.

Cabrera Infante's first book, *Así en la paz como en la guerra,* is a collection of fourteen stories and fifteen vignettes written between 1949 and 1960. Thirty-three years would pass before the English translation, *Writes of Passage,* appeared, and when it did the vignettes were expunged from the text.[1] He has repudiated the Spanish edition on several occasions and would prefer that it receive the kind of perfunctory greeting accorded an infrequently seen acquaintance, politely acknowledged and quickly forgotten. Critics who tarry too long with this collection are usually accorded a response similar to that extended to Dr. Frankenstein after his resurrected creature had run amok among his neighbors. Cabrera Infante regards the form of the collection as too consciously artistic and contrived, a position difficult to counter. Several of these works would be only first drafts if he were composing them today.

He has declared *Así en la paz como en la guerra* "a book I disown: a Sartrean book. Not the content of the book (a few stories and vignettes) but its form, even if apparently influenced by Hemingway, was inspired, if I may use this verb, by Sartre's tenet on realism. There was more of *Qu'est-ce que la littérature?* than of *In Our Time* in this slim volume of mine."[2] Like Mario Vargas Llosa, he has rejected his early enthusiasm for Sartre. Cabrera Infante's comments on form concern the interweaving of vignettes on the political struggle against Batista with stories about other aspects of existence. Interestingly, this format was used, and in due time abandoned, in the first drafts of *Three Trapped Tigers.* The vignettes in that manuscript eventually provided the basis of another text, *View of Dawn in the Tropics.* In the "Prologue to English Readers" of *Writes of Passage,* Cabrera Infante declares: "My writing . . . springs up not from life but from reading."[3] This claim, which is reminiscent of Borges, carries more weight without the presence of the vignettes, those intrusions of unsavory realities into the realm of the imaginary.

Cabrera Infante also condemns the social realism that inspired his first book: "As a matter of fact, I am not so much against socialism as I am against realism: the creepy-crawlies on the blank page are symptoms of the delirium tremens suffered after having drunk two pints of the milk of human kindness spiked with a dash of hope, a pinch of faith and a spoonful of charity, stir well while adding some salt of self pity."[4] In these remarks he is expressing an abhorrence of sentimentalism, particularly when combined with political doctrines that provide accurate diagnoses of societal ills, but disastrous and sometimes fatal remedies. Cabrera Infante always has guarded against sentimentality in his works, precisely because he is given to that emotion. His remarks also reveal a strong distrust of committed literature. On another occasion he declared: "The worst thing about the book is the fact that my attitude when I wrote it was very negative. I was completely under the influence of Sartre, because I accepted the premise that a book should be a comprehensive critical act. So not only did I have to include reality, which is an idiotic pretension, but I also had to have criticism of reality and of the work itself."[5]

In spite of the author's reservations, *Así en la paz como en la guerra* enjoyed considerable success. By 1964 it was in its fourth printing in Cuba and had appeared in France and Italy in translations published by Editorial Gallimard and Editorial Mondadori. It has done equally well in Seix Barral editions published in Spain. The fifteen vignettes in the collection deal with the brutality and moral corruption of the Batista regime, and most were written in 1958. Surprisingly, he attempted to publish some of them in *Bohemia* and *Carteles,* but the editors had the good sense not to jeopardize their own security and his safety. The vignettes are effectively rendered in a laconic and realistic style. Seymour Menton has commented that "what makes most of the vignettes so effective is the Hemingway-like objective use of the third-person point of view. Sentences are relatively short, the preterit predominates, and there is no editorializing. In fact, the only vignette that clearly violates this last general principle, number 14, is undoubtedly the weakest of all."[6] However, the vignettes in this collection are devoid, for the most part, of the irony and humor found in *View of Dawn in the Tropics,* and there is little variety in their content. As soon as the reader becomes attuned to their substance, the reaction is apt to be a resigned shrug as yet another killing appears in the text.

One of the few exceptions is number 10, in which an officer reports to his superior about a successful ambush made possible by an informer. In what is cast as a telephone conversation, a technique that would be used with great success in *Three Trapped Tigers,* the officer finds himself caught between his contempt for the traitor and his general's decision to reward the informer with a major's commission. The officer reveals his true feelings about the betrayer, whom he considers a coward and a homosexual, as well as his abject subservience to his superior. The one-way telephone conversation (we only hear the officer's voice, a technique most likely garnered from film or radio) exposes the distortion of values and the corruption of basic decency that characterized the Batista dictatorship. Although violence is not the main focus of the vignette, there are enough details of the ambush, including bullets hitting flesh and the informer vomiting after seeing scattered brain tissue, to remind one again of the cruelty of the regime. Many readers are attracted to the vignettes in *Así en la paz como en la guerra* because of the historical immediacy they convey—these brief narrations are the product of moral indignation, and their macabre motifs provide ample justification for the revolution. The author's commitment to revolutionary change and his desire to cast off the past also are expressed in the introduction to the collection.

Cabrera Infante's debt to Ernest Hemingway is most apparent in the stylistic rhythm of some of the stories, especially in the mixture of long, descriptive sentences with brief, staccato statements. This influence is most apparent in "Mar, mar, enemigo" ("The Sea Changes"), in the stylistic rendering and in the portrayal of the ocean as both an adversary and an ironic symbol of freedom and death. In this work a woman, who had been educated in a convent, awaits the arrival of a man she has been involved with for ten to fifteen years. She is on an island and knows that he is carrying out an illegal activity that he believes will be lucrative. When he never arrives, she reluctantly concludes that he has failed and is most likely dead. Her religious background and his subversive endeavors provide an ethical counterpoint reminiscent of the contradictions in the author's family. The story may articulate, in a vague and indirect manner, a desire to exorcise a negative paternal influence.

In the September 1956 issue of *Ciclón,* a cultural and literary journal, Cabrera Infante published an amusing account of a gala affair held in the gardens of a brewery and sponsored by the producers of Hatuey beer and Bacardí rum to celebrate Hemingway's winning of the Nobel Prize. The commentary reveals his knowledge of Hemingway's works and the sardonic humor that would later characterize his own creative writings. The narration begins with a brief quotation from a terse and factually based newspaper report that conveys little about what really went on. In

Cabrera Infante's account, Hemingway is portrayed as gracious but bewildered and harassed by the aggressive antics of his enthusiastic admirers, many of whom have not read his works. They embrace, jostle, and torment him with their excessive attention. Publicity hounds crowd into picture-taking sessions, trying to grasp a moment of fame in the shadow of the celebrity. Everyone seems to want an autograph on the special pamphlets prepared for the ceremony. The gaudy mementos contain a photograph, which Hemingway detests, of the writer in a bathing suit and quotations from his works that mention Hatuey beer. The commercialization of literary fame is conveyed by a pun in the article's title, "El viejo y la marca" ("The Old Man and the Seal"). The playful rendering of the name of Hemingway's novella transforms "sea" into a commercial label.

In a song sung by Amelita Frade, the Nobel laureate is characterized as "a 'tiger' writing," which evokes the title of Cabrera Infante's first novel. Hemingway's announcement that he is going to donate his Nobel Prize medal to Cuba's patron saint leaves some observers nonplussed, wondering about the origins of such sentiments in a writer whose works are anything but religious. Hemingway's disclosure is the ultimate incongruity in the bizarre affair. The portrait of Hemingway and his tormentors brings to mind a laconic observation in Jorge Luis Borges's "Pierre Menard, Author of the Quijote" that "fame is a form of incomprehension, perhaps the worst."[7] In many respects, Cabrera Infante's remarkable account foreshadows, more than the stories of *Así en la paz como en la guerra* do, the future course of his work, and it demonstrates that he is at his best when responding to real events and people. Of course, in the process he transforms them into something uniquely his own.

The fourteen stories in *Así en la paz como en la guerra* are notable for their variety of techniques and content. Some are elaborate and long, close to being mature works. Others are brief and function as literary jokes, directed either at one of the characters, as in "Jazz," or at the reader, as in "Cuando se estudia gramática" ("Grammar's for the Birds"). In the first-mentioned work, a character toys with a friend, offering him some marijuana. When the cigarette is declined, the tempter refuses to acknowledge whether the offer was a subterfuge or not, slyly retreating into an ambiguous play on words. "Grammar's for the Birds" relates what happens between a young man and woman during a study session. At one point he asks her to disrobe and she willingly complies with his request. After staring at her for a while, he tells her to put her clothes back on and they resume their studies. An examination of the workings of language turns into a similar inspection of human anatomy—all theory, no practice. Occasionally a story relies excessively on a surprise ending; in "Abril es el mes más cruel" ("April is the Cruellest Month"), a young woman unexpectedly jumps to her death during her honeymoon. The dramatic and theatrical ending made it attractive for adaptation to a television program directed by the author, photographed by Orlando Jiménez and featuring Miriam Gómez.

The social panorama of the characters in the collection is extensive and includes, among others, a wealthy businessman, an unfortunate seamstress, a lonely mortuary worker, a callous bordello madam, destitute children, cane field workers, an actress, and a writer. Narrative technique also varies greatly. "Un rato de tenmeallá" ("Gobegger Foriu Tostay") consists of a thirteen-page sentence narrated by a six-year-old child who barely understands that the family's impoverishment is compelling an older sister to sell her virginity. The narrative is reminiscent of Joyce's Molly Bloom and Faulkner's Benjy in its portrayal of the flow of consciousness and its ability to combine an aura of innocence and degradation. The introduction to the volume relates this story to the author's personal experience in a room in a tenement, most likely 408 Zulueta, and mentions the small quarters and days without food.

More obvious personal associations appear in "El día que terminó mi niñez" ("The Day My Days as a Child Ended"), written as a Christmas story for Carteles. Many elements in the story parallel the author's life. These circumstances include references to a town by the sea, an absent father looking for work in a distant city, a younger brother, an uncle who expects children to ask for a blessing during a visit, and a mother who gives her oldest son instructions on how to behave in the presence of the aloof relative. However, as in much of Cabrera Infante's autobiographical writing, factual truth is less important than the persuasiveness of the account. A completely different narrative mode, one with several literary connections, is evident in "La mosca en el vaso de leche" ("A Fly in a Glass of Milk"). This work is a naturalistic portrait of the eroding sanity of a desperate seamstress. Her descent into madness is conveyed by the way her mind fastens on bizarre details in her environment. The portrayal of solitude recalls other characters tormented by estrangement and loneliness in Flaubert's "Un Coeur Simple" ("A Simple

Heart"), Faulkner's "A Rose for Emily," and Enrique Labrador Ruiz's "Conejito Ulán" ("Little Bunny Ulán").

The most accomplished pieces in *Así en la paz como en la guerra* are "Josefina, atiende a los señores" ("Josefina, Take Good Care of the Señores") and "En el Gran Ecbó" ("The Great Ekbo"), one of the most anthologized stories from the collection. In the first work, which was published in *Ciclón* in May 1955, a woman who runs a brothel talks about her establishment, attempting to pass herself off as a compassionate entrepreneur, devoted to the well-being of her girls and clients. She addresses the presumed listener in a colorful oral language, full of colloquialisms and trite sayings, and in the process she reveals herself as completely insensitive to the sordidness that surrounds her. In fact, she can be accused of being thoroughly alienated from humanity's finer qualities. This becomes distressingly evident when she tells the story of her most popular girl, the one-armed Josephine, who became a prostitute unwillingly through the manipulations of a lover. Josephine's ineffectual attempts to rebel against her situation include an attempted suicide and drug addiction. Her physical deformity is a sign of the emotional damage that is being inflicted on her. Josephine's desperation is only matched by her employer's greed and indifference. What makes the story so successful is the author's ability to use vernacular language effectively. The narrator betrays herself and her occupation with her own words. "Josefina, Take Good Care of the Señores" indicates that Cabrera Infante was learning one of the essentials of narrative art, the importance of showing rather than telling.

"The Great Ekbo" is the finest and most sophisticated story in the volume. Two lovers spend part of a rainy day in Havana together, dining and then attending a *lucumí* religious ceremony of African origin ("Ekbo" refers to a religious gathering of all the saints). The man tries to be cavalier and ironic in an attempt to resist the melancholy guilt that is seeping into their relationship, but his efforts do little to counter the remorse of his lover, an actress. Her guilt is intensified by photographs of his family, which he carries in his wallet, and by an unknown black woman's admonition at the ceremony that she stop living in sin. There is little action in this story, which depends on fine description and the evocation of mood for its success. In the introduction to the volume, Cabrera Infante remarks that the main character "is an upstart . . . it's as if the Silvestre of 'The Doors' and 'A Nest' had purchased an English sports car."[8]

Although the male protagonist in "The Great Ekbo" is unidentified, it is of more than passing interest that he should be associated with other characters named Silvestre. Indeed, that name is used in five of the stories in *Así en la paz como en la guerra* and it is, of course, the designation given to the author's alter ego in *Three Trapped Tigers*. The Silvestre in the novel and the main character in "The Great Ekbo" share an obsession with time: they both look at events in the present with an eye to how they will be remembered in the future. Although the central character in the story is anonymous, there is a playful reference to his identification in two lines that allude to the origin of his name in Cabrera Infante's experience with popular culture: "Delante, a la izquierda, por entre la lluvia fina, apareció deslumbrante un pequeño cementerio, todo blanco, húmedo, silvestre. Había en él una semetría aséptica que nada tenía que ver con la corrupción y los gusanos y la peste."[9] ("Ahead of them, to the left, a small graveyard shone all white and wild through the rain. Its sterilized symmetry belied any thoughts of maggots and foul corruption").[10]

In the narrator's mind, the cemetery is associated with a denial of death and corruption because he is most likely thinking of "a wry, adult comic book hero," the "back-from-the-dead criminologist Denny Colt," better known as the Spirit.[11] Created on 2 June 1940 by Will Eisner, *The Spirit* was a "weekly seven-page feature, part of a comic book Sunday supplement."[12] The words "cementerio" and "silvestre" in the original version of the short story are oblique references to the Spirit's hideout, Wildwood Cemetery, which appeared in Spanish editions as "Cementerio San Silvestre." This is the fanciful origin of the name of one of the three memorable characters of *Three Trapped Tigers*.[13] The young Cabrera Infante was particularly intrigued with the artistic quality of *The Spirit,* an admiration he maintains to this day, and its incorporation into his narratives is an acknowledgment of a passion from his adolescent years. Silvestre is an illuminating example of Cabrera Infante's utilization of an element from popular culture, one of an abundant number of such references in his works. It also speaks to his playful disposition as well as to the circuitous nature of the creative imagination.

Looking back at the original episodes of *The Spirit,* it is not difficult to see why he was so intrigued with Eisner's work. An episode published in 10 August 1941, for example, begins with a quotation from Michel de Montaigne and concerns a scientist who has successfully condensed time into a liquid element. Through a series of chance occurrences, an unsuspecting individual is able to see the future consequences of his criminal actions. Michael Barrier, in *A Smithsonian Book of Comic-Book Comics,* quotes John Benson, who has commented that " 'like Alfred Hitchcock, Eisner *shows* his stories instead of telling them. And Eisner's pictorial sense, like Hitchcock's, is so integral to his sense of narrative that it's often overlooked: the type of story favored by the artist is more likely to be recognized—the "Hitchcock story" or the "Eisner story".' "[14] Benson also points out that Eisner was a master of indirect portrayal and showed the result or reaction to an act rather than the action itself. Cabrera Infante would make ample use of this technique in *Three Trapped Tigers,* especially in the psychiatric sessions of Laura Díaz.

Although Cabrera Infante is not fond of *Así en la paz como en la guerra,* the book does indicate some of what was to come. The collection demonstrates, for example, his capacity to employ a variety of narrative styles, ranging from the purely objective to the intimate rendering of a flow of consciousness. His ability to re-create vernacular language as well as his successful assimilation of various influences, like that of Hemingway, also are evident. Even early in his career, it was apparent that he had a natural gift for imitation. A less satisfactory adaptation is the interweaving of highly different narrative modes, particularly the mixture of the stories with the vignettes. That strategy was most likely acquired from Faulkner's *The Wild Palms,* a work whose success is equally debatable. Cabrera Infante's first book attempted to accommodate contradictory tendencies, political commitment and a will to fragmentation, and it is fair to observe that this accounts for the book's deficiencies as well as his dissatisfaction with it.

Several of the characters evoke others who would follow. The actress and her lover in "The Great Ekbo" are suggestive of Laura Díaz and Silvestre of *Three Trapped Tigers.* "Un nido de gorriones en un toldo" ("Nest, Door, Neighbours") contains a child-woman whose penchant for role-playing leads her and those around her into labyrinths of illusion and deception, much as the formidable Amazon of *Infante's Inferno* and Laura Díaz of *Three Trapped Tigers* do in those novels. The superficial and cynical Solaún of "Ostras interrogadas" ("Oysters Helping with Their Inquiry") appears briefly in *Three Trapped Tigers.* These and other elements, such as stories cast in an autobiographical mode, point to the future, but they do not foretell it. It would be a mistake to claim that the major themes and strategies of his artistic maturity can be found in these first works, but it is fair to say that the collection contains experimental variations that enabled Cabrera Infante to explore options during his search for his own voice and that some of these variants would appear again. With the exception of two or three outstanding stories, the volume can be termed a collection of readable works, most likely to interest readers intrigued with historical referents or specifically concerned with Cabrera Infante's career.

Although he is an author who works from fragments, writing segments and eventually expanding them into texts, Cabrera Infante has not produced many short stories, at least in the contemporary understanding of the term. It should be mentioned, however, that many pieces, such as the portrait of Pepe Castro, "My Unforgettable Character," are conceived as stories by Cabrera Infante. He uses such a classification because he feels that once something disappears into a text, it becomes a fiction. For that reason, even works that purport to be historical accounts are fictions, a position that undoubtedly causes some readers difficulty. The fine line between the imaginary and the real is often a problematic distinction in Cabrera Infante's works—what we read is undoubtedly an illusion, but at the level of meaning there is frequently authenticity. Despite the author's misgivings, the stories and vignettes in *Así en la paz como en la guerra* are acceptable works, not equal in quality to his later writings, but undeserving of oblivion.

Citizen
Cain

WHILE *ASÍ EN LA PAZ COMO EN LA GUERRA* HAS BEEN ACCORDED the treatment of an illegitimate offspring by its creator, *Un oficio del siglo veinte,* 1963 (*A Twentieth Century Job,* 1991), is a favorite child. The later work is his first in which the organization depends on norms generated from within the text rather than on any externally imposed notion of structure. *A Twentieth Century Job* is postmodern in its celebration of contradiction, inconsistency, and error; in its use of devices such as lists that mocks attempts to organize reality rationally; and in its foregrounding of ontological issues. In the narrative sections of the text, a central concern is which self is telling the story. It is also remarkable for the challenge it poses to authority, even that of its own creator, whose aesthetic norms are undermined as soon as they are created. A deceptively innocent book that at first glance appears to be merely a collection of film reviews written between 1954 and 1960, *A Twentieth Century Job* is transformed into something more than criticism as the author, the critic (Cain), and films continually merge and separate in a cultural dialogue of change and identity. The book provides a depository of fragmentary sensations that are intensified by the random remarks of a self-consciously flippant Cain. In many respects, this collection prepared the way for Cabrera Infante's most widely acclaimed achievement, *Three Trapped Tigers*.

The aesthetic stance adopted by Cabrera Infante in his second and third books is due in part to those works being formed during the first years of the Cuban revolution. *A Twentieth Century Job* and *Three Trapped Tigers* affirm values that eventually would be considered anathema by the revolutionary government, particularly irrational spontaneity, popular culture from the capitalistic world, and disrespect for authority. The Cuban revolutionary movement was decidedly not postmodern, and, in fact, during the first years of the decade it was well on its way to turning its back on modernity. It was actually a reaction against the modern and an affirmation of nineteenth-century utopianism tinged with Rousseauistic romanticism. In the popular imagination, it is the bearded ones who descend from the mountain, that is, from nature, to bring rejuvenation to a weary and corrupt civilization. Despite its revolutionary rhetoric and identification with the new and radical, the movement was in essence a glorification and imposition of the old. It did embody radical transformation, but it was change desiring to embrace the past rather than the future. In a society in which jubilant enthusiasm had adopted the rhetoric of condemnation, few could grasp that fact. No one seemed to notice that the engine of history had slipped into reverse.

Cabrera Infante made every attempt to adjust to the transitions that were sweeping his country, but it was a schizophrenic endeavor that pitted affirmation, hope, and rationality against denial, doubt, and intuition. He had taken risks during the struggle against Batista and at first he could rationalize the necessity for governmental excess but, as power flowed into fewer and fewer hands, he began to have doubts. Cabrera Infante had spent the first decades of his life celebrating the new and glorying in the technology of popular culture—the comics, music, radio, the movies. Its energizing vitality and affirmation of plurality appeared more out of place each day in the new political climate. But trusted and well-intentioned old friends like Carlos Franqui and Alberto

Mora were still enthusiastically pursuing revolutionary goals. What was wrong? What essence was he missing? Could he turn his back on the lifelong endeavors of Zoila and Guillermo senior?

On the other hand, other close acquaintances conveyed doubt through apathetic looks and condemning silences. Antonio Ortega departed with a resigned shrug—he had seen calamity coming before in Spain and knew the futility of trying to convey that knowledge to others. The madcap Pepe Castro visited Cabrera Infante in his offices at *Lunes de Revolución* and asked embarrassing questions about the crusade against illiteracy. When he replied to his maternal great-uncle's questions with some of the stock governmental assertions, Pepe Castro let out a sigh and then lapsed into the stunned silence of someone who has seen it all before. Jesse Fernández just left, alluding to greener pastures in New York. And what could be made of Lino Novás Calvo's seeking asylum in the Colombian Embassy? That ironic radical had become so jaded over the old social and political order and its indifference toward artistic endeavors that he had abandoned his own literary career and had taken to advising young writers to expend their energies elsewhere. Why was he leaving now that things were changing? Had the innovative writer who had articulated the despair of society's most unfortunate members become a reactionary? In Novás Calvo's case, as in those of Antonio Ortega and Jesse Fernández, there was a similar connection— they had been in Spain during the tragedy of the Spanish Civil War and had gazed directly into the face of totalitarianism. Despite his doubts, Cabrera Infante yielded to the dictates of hope and accepted a new government position when it was offered in 1962, but the internal tension generated by his inner doubts found expression in two remarkable intuitive outbursts, *A Twentieth Century Job* and *Three Trapped Tigers*.

The journey toward the creation of *A Twentieth Century Job* began in 1948 when he published his first film criticism in *Nueva Generación*. His commitment to commenting on the movies lasted considerably longer than the journal, which only published a few issues. In the following year, he won a contest sponsored by the newspaper *El Mundo* with an article on *The Snake Pit* (1948), the terrifying black-and-white film about the harrowing experiences of a patient in a mental institution. Directed by Anatole Litvak and starring Olivia de Havilland, the motion picture sparked considerable public interest and the reform of laws covering psychiatric hospitals. The portrayal of the brutality of early electroconvulsive therapy was especially disturbing to contemporary audiences. It is difficult to forget the images of mouths being stuffed to stifle screams and the convulsions of bodies going into shock.

The prize won by Cabrera Infante was a summer scholarship to study cinema at the University of Havana, a course he completed in 1949. During that time he met Germán Puig and Ricardo Vigón, founders of the Havana Film Club, an organization that exhibited films in the Royal News on Trocadero. That street, with the homes of Antonio Ortega and Lezama Lima, the offices of *Bohemia*, and numerous brothels, became a veritable Yellow Brick Road in the life of the young Cabrera Infante. After *Bohemia* purchased *Carteles* in 1953. Antonio Ortega declared one day: "'Infante' (he called me Infante because I signed my stories Guillermo C. Infante, since I was always worried about the length of my name) 'I want you to take over the movie page.'"[1] Another reason for the modification of his name was to avoid confusion with his father. He started his new assignment the following year, initiating a fruitful period in his career.

Although his stint as a critic for *Carteles* was relatively uneventful, there were some difficulties. A review of *I'll Cry Tomorrow* (1955), a film about alcoholism, nearly cost him his job because one of the magazine's major advertisers, Bacardí and Company, was offended by the last line, which praised Susan Hayward's performance: "It is she—more than the certainly professional Eddie Albert and Van Fleet—whom one has to thank for this so effective effort to put on each bottle of rum a skull and crossbones warning."[2] There was also an interview with a government functionary, Captain Castaño, who spent most of his time shuffling papers in an anti-Communist police and research bureau, an event related in the first version of the movie script "The Lost City." According to Cabrera Infante, the meeting was innocuous and the only demand made of him was a polite request by a secretary that he not smoke in the official's office, but considering what had happened in 1952 and his clandestine support of the revolution, being summoned to the interview must have been intimidating. Evidently, Castaño had little interest in his guest and was going through the motions of conducting an investigation. After the triumph of the revolution, Captain Castaño was condemned to death by a tribunal headed by Che Guevara.

Cabrera Infante stopped writing movie reviews in 1960 after *Carteles* ceased to exist and Antonio Ortega went into exile. Since Ortega had been responsible for his appointment as a critic at *Carteles,* there was a hint of symmetry in the decision. He could have continued publishing criticism in other publications, including *Revolución* and *Verde Olivo,* since he had many outlets, but a number of things persuaded him not to take that course. Cabrera Infante realized that the routine of producing reviews had become a fatiguing burden and that in some respects he was no longer functioning as a critic. He found himself going to movies knowing what he would write about the films before viewing them. What was worse, the demands of constantly evaluating motion pictures had markedly diminished his enjoyment of cinema. In addition, his new journalistic and editorial duties at *Revolución* and its affiliate publications were demanding more of his time and energy.

Cabrera Infante also realized that there was a disturbing decline in the variety and quality of films being shown in Havana. There were fewer American movies but an increase in films from the socialist bloc. Although the latter were frequently of poor quality, it was impossible to criticize them because of ideological considerations. The final straw was a minor but dangerous controversy generated by one of the last American pictures he saw in Havana, *The Wonderful Country* (1959), with Robert Mitchum, Julie London, and Pedro Armendariz. A standard Western about a gunman's adventures in the Texas Rangers, the film provoked the Pavlovian attack of an ideologically inspired critic because of the appearance in the movie of "two Mexican bandits who were named the Castro brothers."[3] Political commentators such as Javier de Varona praised the vigilant critic for exposing the perceived slur against the national leadership, leaving anyone who had published favorable notices on shaky ground.[4] Although he had not written a review of the film, Cabrera Infante was so dismayed by the mindless and irrational assault that he wrote a response: "I then wrote an epitaph for Cain which I did not publish, at the request of Carlos Franqui, director of the newspaper *Revolución,* and that was the origin of *A Twentieth Century Job*."[5]

The controversy generated by *The Wonderful Country* took place in the middle of 1961 and *Lunes de Revolución* ceased publication in November. Cabrera Infante worked during that fall and into February of the following year on his collection of film reviews and other projects, pecking away at a typewriter in his three-finger style in the lofty heights of his apartment on the twenty-third floor of the Retiro Médico Building on La Rampa. That lodging also became a gathering place for individuals who were disgruntled with the direction the country was taking.

Assembling the volume was a relatively easy task, since Marta Calvo had kept copies of all of his reviews (the book acknowledges the cooperation of Marta Calvo and Miriam Gómez). He worked on three new sections that were integrated into the text. Two ("Portrait of the critic as Cain" and "Requiem for an *alter egotist*") operate as a prologue and epilogue, while another ("Nondescript manuscript found in a bottle......of milk") is placed in the middle of the book. In these added segments a dialogic exchange takes place between Cabrera Infante and his alter ego, Cain, although it should be noted that at times it appears that Cabrera Infante is the alter ego of Cain. During this process Cabrera Infante and Cain are transformed into fictional entities and the text becomes a requiem for the demise of a critical sensibility. In a society surrendering to ideological extremism, criticism could only take place in an imaginary realm.

The reviews in *A Twentieth Century Job* are organized chronologically according to their original date of publication in *Carteles* and *Revolución*. There is one marked difference between the notices published in the two journals. Having decided to come out of the critical closet of feigned objectivity, Cabrera Infante shifted from the use of the third person in the reviews published in *Carteles* to the first person in those in *Revolución*. The chronological organization gives a semblance of order to the collection, but in essence it is a re-creation of the random and haphazard process of writing reviews—there is no arrangement in the text according to the generic concerns of theme, technique, or any other categorization. This strategy, which appears logical and innocent at first glance, conforms well with the thematic thrust of the volume, a vague apprehension that eventually everything is going to collapse into the absurd. The compiler of the collection, presumably Cabrera Infante, introduces each review with a short commentary that frequently consists of a brief retrospective assessment of Cain and his judgments, that is, of humorous critiques of the critic and his criticism. In these quips consciousness turns back on itself, exposing contradictions and inconsistencies as well as its own failings.

The Cuban edition of *A Twentieth Century Job* is replete with graphics, including drawings and cartoons, and one of these becomes a central motif and a key icon. Many of the reviews are preceded by the figure of a headless statue (which now graces his desk in London), a reproduction of a sculpture Cain keeps on a table: "He had on his desk an ironclad statuette whose head was missing. It was a fencer and this made the accident into a metaphysical occurrence."[6] In a passage worth quoting at length, the compiler offers an explanation of the "metaphysical occurrence" by relating what he was told by Cain:

> He recalled the difficult times of the Dictatorship, the messages from a policeman very interested in the performing arts, censorship, and finally fear. He believed that the elegance of certain sentences, some few daring turns of phrase and almost direct allusions allowed him to confront destiny with weapons as effective as the sporting rapier or the fencing sword: the blunt épée. But the contender wielded an enormous sabre, capable of decapitating the most audacious as well as the pusillanimous. "Machiavelli said," said Cain, "that the world belongs to cold spirits," and continued; "but cold spirits can end up as cold cuts before the enemy grinder." I understood, I think, then. The dandy can remain calm, courteous, elegant, but that doesn't prevent the enemy from cutting his head off and making of him a most excellent corpse. Thus the small statuette acquired for him an allegorical and thereby exemplary meaning. Just like the Oscar. "I call it Victory in Reverse Gear," he told me. He terminated his monologue with a sentence, which, if not ambiguous, was at least obscure: "Cynicism is the dandy's art of fencing." (6)

The critic then remains headless after his encounter with authority during the dictatorship, a mindless entity forced into cynicism in order to survive. This would seem at first reading to refer only to his difficulties under Batista in 1952, but he was never deprived of a forum in those days—he never lost a journal. But the reference to the previous regime permits him to slowly shift political commentary into a veiled criticism of the present government. The mention of the performing arts can be taken as an allusion to the *PM* affair. He even slipped in a direct mention of that film in another passage in the Cuban and Spanish editions by cleverly locating the title next to a day of the week so that it appears to be a reference to time, but the use of capital letters reveals the significance of the reference. Other comments make the historical context of the added segments of the book more apparent, since they adapt contemporary revolutionary rhetoric:" 'Self-criticism is the order of the day,' said Cain to me. I gathered (that's the verb) then that the only form of self-criticism which he permitted himself was eulogy: flattery will take you to the leader" (21).

Considerable tension is generated in the give-and-take relationship that exists between the compiler and Cain as each becomes the butt of the other's jokes and vies for the reader's attention. Cain is portrayed as a dandy so affected by his profession that he sees the world and existence as a film, that is, as a realm of make-believe. We are told that "there was nothing sacred for Cain when the hoax sickness attacked him: history, economy and geography were converted into pieces of a lame puzzle, which, once assembled, turned out to be a one leg pull" (10). As self-conscious commentary goes, this is an apt description of much of the text; the exchanges between Cain and the compiler, while amusing, have serious purpose. And what kind of a hoax do Cain and the compiler make of history?

In *A Twentieth Century Job,* the concept of history as a progressive enterprise moving toward a utopian future is ridiculed along with the intellectual strategies that claim to unlock its workings. In a section entitled "Who Killed Hegel Valdés?" the compiler declares: "I, for my part, tender a declaration which I can dispatch by a dialectical path: it can successively be hypothesis, thesis, and antithesis. Here it is: this history is not the truth nor is it a lie but quite the contrary" (4). This passage mocks Hegelian dialectics by applying them and reveals that Cabrera Infante is, as he has often indicated, a confirmed Marxist of the Marx Brothers persuasion, with a little bit of Lewis Carroll thrown in.

For his own part, Cain claims in a note to the compiler that history is essentially a confusion of facts and that in the distant future "all our present will be confused with our historic past and with our immediate future (he had put, bull's-eyes of the subconscious, fruit instead of future), in an infinite ocean of errors: history will fold in upon herself like a telescope and in that enormous accordion the facts that today stand out in some relief will disappear" (19). The substitution of "fruit" for "future" reveals a repressed realization that historical consciousness has become a farce. Although these statements can be regarded as the histrionic babbling of an iconoclast, they are actually more insidious than that because they undermine the authority of those who claim to possess history. If a society's understanding of the past is based on "an infinite ocean of errors," what validity do political and economic reorganizations have whose authority depends on historical interpretation? Why surrender power to those who foster such programs? Cain the hoaxer undermines the intellectual pretensions that are used to conceal Machiavellian machinations—in this regard, the book is a parody of modern life. If history is a machine, it must be a jalopy coming apart at the seams as Cain and the compiler, the Laurel and Hardy of the critical set, race it down the road to oblivion.

Many of the techniques used in *A Twentieth Century Job* appear in the pages of *Three Trapped Tigers* and, in many respects the former was a training ground for the latter. Compared to the grimness of *Así en la paz como en la guerra,* Cabrera Infante's second book is an explosion of humor, a creative outburst that spills over into his third creation. Satire, self-mockery, and parody are among the elements used extensively in both works, and spontaneity and irreverence energize the two books. They share a delight in wordplay and some specific phrases, such as "matrimony" rendered as "martyrmony," appear in both of them.[7] Names also are distorted and at times related to vernacular expression, as in a list of occupations in *A Twentieth Century Job* that includes "moby dicks" (26) or the transformation of Buffalo Bill into "Bunny Bill" (10). The banter between Cain and the compiler is replicated in *Three Trapped Tigers* in the dialogues between Silvestre and Arsenio Cué. Written while Cabrera Infante was going through the emotionally draining process of working through his ambivalent attitudes toward the Cuban revolution, *A Twentieth Century Job* and *Three Trapped Tigers* functioned as antidotes to the despair that was seeping into his life. They were like the ballast that keeps a sailboat on an even keel.

The three sections written during 1961 and 1962 allowed Cabrera Infante to articulate a subversive stance, while the original reviews provided a veneer of conformity and respectability. The commentaries reflect the evolution of his cinematic sensibility as well as many of his concepts about film and literature. Both the contents of the reviews and the relations between his movie criticism and literary expression have been studied elsewhere, but it is significant to note that as the years dedicated to evaluating films passed, Cabrera Infante demonstrated more interest in literature.[8] Many of the movie evaluations became, in fact, pretexts for literary discussions, and these reveal what he was reading during those years. There are many mentions of Herman Melville and

James Joyce along with comments on Sherwood Anderson, Arthur Miller, and Tennessee Williams, as well as references to classical Spanish authors such as Francisco de Quevedo. He was especially intrigued with *Moby Dick* and his interest in Hemingway and Faulkner continued unabated.

In a review of the Warner Brothers' film, *The Old Man and the Sea,* he recognized Hemingway's work as a classic but declared *The Sun Also Rises* his favorite (a character in *Three Trapped Tigers* would later remark that the sun is the only thing that rises in that novel). He justified this preference by explaining that "the talent of Ernest Hemingway is merely the talent of a storyteller, of a short story writer who was able to find a different style and combined it with a strange ability to make the most false and unreal conversations in all literature—by a miracle of graphics, because typography is still an obscure craft—be read with an easiness and a sense of immediacy that left a sensation of natural ease and randomness, when they were really the work of tenacity and artifice" (258). The remarks on the creation of a sense of immediacy and randomness are revealing, for they are elements that he has assiduously cultivated in his own art. He went on to condemn the film and had harsh things to say about the casting of the main character: "Tracy is the worst of actors for this folly, with his flabby face, his cynical mouth and his mocking air" (261). Biting but accurate criticism of a film that failed to capture successfully the drama of the book.

After completing the draft of *A Twentieth Century Job,* Cabrera Infante worked on other projects, and from March to August of 1962 he prepared and presented a series of lectures on film that were published many years later in *Arcadia todas las noches,* 1978 ("Every Night Arcadia"). When he departed for Europe in September 1962, he left the task of reading the galley proofs of *A Twentieth Century Job* with his father, who made some minor changes of a moral nature by cleaning up the language. Most likely remembering the fiasco of 1952, Guillermo senior was trying to protect his son from a similar reaction. Along the way, a review or two disappeared, such as one of *Animal Farm.* The manuscript was in the hands of Ediciones R, another creation of Carlos Franqui that Cabrera Infante formerly had managed, and its new director, Virgilio Piñera. Piñera was of two minds about publishing the book. He had no qualms with the artistic quality of the collection, but he was no fool and recognized the subversive nature of the text. He did not favor censorship, but he was a fearful man easily given to morbid thoughts. The decision to publish became a struggle between his professional ethics and his paralyzing fear. Cabrera Infante did what he could to help his manuscript, but from Europe it was difficult.

To Piñera's everlasting credit, he overcame his justifiable apprehension and dread and the book was published in an edition of four thousand volumes, a small printing by Cuban standards of that time. The text was so ingeniously subversive that it was assumed that many would miss its intent, and the modest edition ensured that it would not have an extensive distribution. There never was another Cuban edition and it was the last book that Cabrera Infante published in his native country. Before his departure for Brussels, he saw José Lezama Lima on two occasions, and when he told the great poet of his new assignment, Lezama commented: " 'In dark times the best disguise for the wolf is to become a sheep. Don't abandon that disguise'."[9] The transformation of Cain into a fictional entity in *A Twentieth Century Job* foreshadowed the fate that eventually would befall Cabrera Infante in the cultural life of Cuba—he would disappear. Ultimately, his books were banned and his name was expunged from reference works. Citizen Cain became a nonentity.

The Elusive Tiger

WHEN CABRERA INFANTE LEFT HAVANA FOR BRUSSELS IN SEPTEMBER 1962, he completed a move from a high-profile position as editor of *Lunes de Revolución* to that of cultural attaché in an embassy of secondary importance. Although the editorship had provided national and international prominence, the flight into obscurity was not entirely unwelcome after months of unemployment and the glaring publicity of the *PM* affair. Since he was now a member of the diplomatic corps, he was not entirely free of the long reach of Havana's paranoia, but at least he was on its periphery and in a post not apt to attract much attention. As luck would have it, he would eventually run afoul of a security agent assigned to the embassy, one who would seriously complicate his life when he returned to Havana in 1965, but for the time being he could look forward to a relatively peaceful sojourn in Europe.

However, the abrupt change was not without serious emotional strain. Cabrera Infante felt isolated and alone in Brussels and was very homesick, so much so that he started to grumble about returning to Havana. In a letter dated 30 December 1962, Virgilio Piñera set him straight on that matter. "We are all alarmed with your 'sighs' about returning. Guillermo, it would be a great folly . . . here you will not have the peace you need in order to write. . . . Think it over carefully; take into account that you are better off than I am." And Piñera ended his letter with a flourish and an admonition directed at Cabrera Infante's pride and his commitment to writing: "Well, Guillermo, hang on, don't give in, write, write, write, write . . . William the Conqueror, remember your ancestors."[1] It was a frank and frantic appeal that attempted to exploit every vanity and weakness in the homesick writer's emotional armor and it was very effective. Cabrera Infante persisted in his efforts to leave Brussels, but the object became a transfer to a more interesting city, such as London or Rome, where he could speak the language. He hung on in Belgium, hoping that Carlos Franqui could somehow work a miracle for him in Havana.

Although he did not know it at the time except perhaps on an intuitive level, his departure from Havana in 1962 marked the end of a twenty-one-year love affair with that city. Much of what happened during those years was to reverberate throughout the remainder of his life. Not only was there his linguistic transformation into a resident of Havana who had cast off his Oriente accent and mannerisms, there was also his acquisition of English and other languages; the formation of friendships with Antonio Ortega, Carlos Franqui, and Alberto Mora; the termination of one marriage and the initiation of another; the joys and responsibilities of two daughters; and his full-fledged entrance into the artistic and intellectual life of the city. In addition, he had accumulated an intimate knowledge of Havana and had learned most of its secrets, acquiring in the process an intuitive feel for a time and place that would nourish his creative imagination throughout his career. When he returned in 1965, the city he had known, and still cherishes, had ceased to exist.

Cabrera Infante passed his first year in Brussels living in the Kraainen section of the urban center and the next two in the Uccle area. He had left behind in Havana a comfortable apartment overlooking the sea and a sports car, and he now found himself and his family living in cramped quarters with little money or clothing. Although he was paid in dollars through checks issued by the Narodny Bank of Moscow, there was barely enough to live on in Brussels, one of the most expensive cities in Europe at that time.[2] After the exhausting turmoil of the initial period of the revolution, with the demanding editorship and trips abroad to North and South America, Eastern Europe, and Russia, he and Miriam were relieved to be out of the eye of the storm. A trip with a group of journalists to the Soviet Union in 1960 had left him impressed with the poverty he saw in that country and the degree of state control of everyday life. He was surprised to discover that the prostitutes who worked the hotels were KGB agents and, therefore, property of the state. He had participated in a meeting the delegation had with Premier Nikita Khrushchev but had declined the chance to visit the crypts of Lenin and Stalin. His roommate, Alfredo Viñas, gave him a vivid account of what could be seen of those former leaders and reported that Stalin's remains were particularly impressive. Zoila and her husband must have been disappointed that their son, demonstrating his typical aversion for things touching on death, had missed out on such an opportunity.

The group also visited a collective near Kiev, and Cabrera Infante and Viñas were amused when a party official mistook advertising jingles they were singing for Cuban folklore. Other points of interest during the trip included a visit to the Chekhov museum and a meeting with the widow of Bertolt Brecht in East Berlin. He found the cigar-smoking Elena still attractive despite her age, and he inadvertently angered her when he commented that the best version of *The Three Penny Opera* he had seen was a New York performance with Lotte Lenya. He later discovered that there were personal reasons for her reaction, since she and Lenya had feuded for years. Cabrera Infante was also experiencing the shock of something entirely new to him—the extreme cold for which even his visits to New York City had not prepared him. Small details remembered after so many years clearly convey the unwelcome sensation—seeing frozen clothes, for example, on a clothesline during the visit to the Chekhov museum. While in East Berlin, he spent several days in his hotel room with a miserable sore throat, and he recalls hearing on the Voice of America the announcement of John Kennedy's election to the U.S. presidency in November 1960. Although he was taking in the sights of the Communist bloc countries, he was not cutting off sources of information from the Western world.

Three years later, in November of 1963, he took a different type of trip from Brussels to London with Miriam Gómez while on holiday, and he was not overly impressed with the rainy city. Little did he suspect that within a few years he would become a permanent resident of the English capital. He and Miriam also had the pleasure of a long stay with Zoila, who spent several months in 1963–64 visiting her sons in Belgium and Spain. Miriam accompanied her on excursions to France and Spain and Carola to England while the diplomat toiled away at the embassy. Zoila's photographic record of her travels now resides in Cabrera Infante's London apartment, each snapshot carefully described by quips he had written to accompany them. One of the photographs shows her viewing snow for the first time from the warmth of their apartment in Brussels, but she is contemplative rather than excited.

Although there are many brave smiles in her snapshots, Zoila appears subdued and pensive in several of the pictures. There was a lot to think about. Zoila had been the emotional center of her family for most of her married life and had expended considerable time and energy nurturing those around her. Now she was facing the bleak realization that her sons and grandchildren were living in exile and would not return— she herself had advised Guillermo not to contemplate going back to Cuba. She had been an incurable romantic all of her life and now was facing the consequences of some of her most cherished illusions. When she returned to the island, she became reclusive and seldom left home. It was as if she had a premonition that the end was near or was mourning a loss of innocence. Guillermo senior's satyriasis did not help matters, particularly when a mistress took to phoning him at home. Zoila's visit in Europe was the last time that Cabrera Infante saw her alive.

Zoila's trip had been made possible by Comandante Alberto Mora, whom Cabrera Infante had known since 1950 when the two men were twenty years old. His father, Menelao Mora, had coordinated the 1957 attack on the Presidential Palace and was killed in the operation. After the fall of the Batista government, a lurid photograph of Menelao Mora's corpse appeared in the 11 January 1959 issue of *Bohemia*.[3] Even in death, he barely looked old enough to have a son in his twenties. Undaunted by his father's violent end, Alberto Mora kept active in terrorist activities against the government. During one period of time, he hid in Zoila and Guillermo senior's Vedado apartment for several months while being hunted by governmental authorities. Mora's need of a refuge provoked discord in the family. Guillermo senior, following the Communist Party's policy of keeping a discreet distance from violent groups such as the Directorio Revolucionario, was opposed to granting him asylum. Guillermo and his father locked horns over the matter and Zoila decided the issue by siding with her son, a not unusual occurrence when the two Guillermos clashed. With his plastic-rimmed glasses and boyish face, Mora hardly had the appearance of a terrorist. After the triumph of the revolution, Mora worked for Che Guevara and became minister of foreign trade. Heberto Padilla has written that "Alberto Mora was genuinely an intellectual politician. I have met few Cubans to equal his in-depth knowledge of literature, philosophy, and music. In his last years at the ministry, he traveled frequently to Europe and sought out his old friends."[4]

It was through Mora's influence that Zoila was able to obtain the much cherished privilege of traveling abroad and Cabrera Infante was allowed to move about fifteen of his books to Europe. After Che Guevara "fell from grace in Cuba, Mora ceased to be Minister. He then drifted into increasing obscurity, until the famous Padilla case, when he wrote personally to Fidel Castro to protest the treatment given Padilla, who was jailed and made to confess. As a result of this letter, he was sentenced to hard labor on a farm. . . . But rather than go, he decided to kill himself."[5] Mora's death occurred in September 1972, a decidedly bad year in Cabrera Infante's life because he was in the midst of his own emotional breakdown when Mora shot himself with a pistol his father had given him.

The figure of Mora appears in several of Cabrera Infante's works, including two unpublished manuscripts, the film script "The Lost City," and the autobiographical novel "Itaca vuelta visitar" ("Ithaca Revisited"). In the first-mentioned work, Mora appears as a decisive and ironically intelligent revolutionary, and in the second as a sensitive and concerned colleague helping a friend (Cabrera Infante) during his difficulties with the revolutionary government. Although he is not named, Mora also appears in one of the vignettes of *View of Dawn in the Tropics*, which narrates his demise. Interestingly, Cabrera Infante has written about Mora by beginning with his death in the 1974 *View of Dawn in the Tropics* and progressively working back in time in the unpublished manuscripts. The first draft of "Ithaca Revisited" was written in 1973 and narrates events that took place in 1965. Mora appears in the third draft of

"The Lost City," dated 24 April 1991, in the course of the struggle against Batista and during the first years of the revolutionary government. The film script also contains the 1957 attack against the Presidential Palace. Mora operates in Cabrera Infante's creative imagination as a metaphor for the revolutionary process in Cuba. Like so many movements of its kind, the revolution has diligently consumed its own children, despite Fidel Castro's early assurances that such a thing would never happen in Cuba.

Alberto Mora is one of two people to whom *View of Dawn in the Tropics* is dedicated. Although the portrait of Mora in this work is characteristically unsentimental, it is obvious that Cabrera Infante felt deep affection for his friend. He wrote:

> THE COMANDANTE GAVE HIM A STORY TO READ. In it a man would go into the bathroom and spend hours locked inside. The wife worried about what her husband was doing in the bathroom for such a long time. One day she decided to find out. She climbed out of the window and walked along the narrow ledge that went around the house. She slid up to the bathroom window and looked in. What she saw stunned her: her husband was sitting on the toilet and had a revolver in his hand with the barrel in his mouth. From time to time he took the barrel of the gun out of his mouth to lick it slowly like a lollipop.
>
> He read the story and gave it back to its author without further comment or perhaps with an offhand comment. What makes the story particularly moving is the fact that its author, the comandante, committed suicide seven years later by shooting himself in the head. So as not to wake his wife, he wrapped the gun in a towel.[6]

The technique of a story within a story underscores the tenuous relationship between fact and fiction in the vignette. At the same time, the procedure paradoxically creates distance and intimacy as the narrator struggles with the desire to remember and his wish to forget. A hint of remorse is introduced into the vignette when the friend (presumably the narrator) returns the comandante's story to him in an almost indifferent fashion: "He read the story and gave it back . . . without further comment or perhaps with an offhand comment." Evidently unimpressed with the literary quality of the work and unsuspecting of its personal implications, the friend hands back the comandante's account in an evasive and uncommitted manner. Theory precedes practice when the comandante writes about a deed before carrying it out. The phrase "what makes the story particularly moving" undercuts the narrator's feigned objectivity as the vignette closes with a concrete occurrence rather than a theoretical abstraction. The vignette's impact is as shocking as the deed that inspired it.

Although this vignette was composed in the early 1970s, style and content in it is similar to many of the segments originally included in early drafts of *Three Trapped Tigers* and eventually published in *View of Dawn in the Tropics*. Organized generally around two narrative lines, the first drafts of *Three Trapped Tigers* attempted to combine dissimilar texts into one work, as had been done in *Así en la paz como en la guerra* and *A Twentieth Century Job*. He originally planned to include narrations about the revolutionary struggle with others concerning nightlife in Havana. The latter constituted a continuation, in effect, of the subject matter of the film *PM*. Fortunately, this plan was eventually discarded, although he persisted with it for some time.

The attempted blend reflected aesthetic as well as psychological concerns as Cabrera Infante struggled to reconcile his commitment to and doubts about the revolution. With his customary sense of duty, he tried to do his best at his new diplomatic post, and he encouraged all the outstanding performers he encountered to travel to Cuba as participants in cultural exchanges. Despite his misgivings about the political changes taking place in Cuba, he was not ready to break with his country and its new government. A sign of this was the decision to allow his daughters to accompany their grandmother when she returned to Cuba from Europe in 1964. It is highly unlikely that he would have allowed Ana and Carola to travel to Havana with Zoila if he had been entertaining living in exile. He was, in fact, during the first years in Europe, decidedly homesick, and this was a motivating factor in the writing of *Three Trapped Tigers*.

The evolution of the work took place in three cities, Havana, Brussels, and Madrid, and spanned several years. A consideration of the way Cabrera Infante goes about writing and assembling a text can shed light on the manner in which *Three Trapped Tigers* evolved into its final form. He maintains notebooks where random observations and descriptions are kept, and Miriam Gómez also retains her own that record any of her husband's remarks she feels are worth keeping. They often use stenographer's notebooks for this purpose and several usually are scattered around their living quarters. He frequently writes fragments with no set plan or work in mind. In this fashion, a fragment can develop into an article or a story and such segments in turn into a larger text. Frequently, the pieces are published as independent entities, so it is not unusual to find segments of a book scattered in journals years before or after its appearance. A classic example is "Meta-Final" ("Meta-End"), a conclusion not used in *Three Trapped Tigers,* but published in a journal three years after the appearance of the novel.[7]

Once he begins to work on a book, Cabrera Infante may write different sections without making a determination as to how they will all fit together until an extensive number of pages exist. A manuscript in this stage of development often will consist of hundreds of typed pages with penned notations, mixed in with an occasional handwritten sheet and source materials. Although such a collection is frequently unnumbered, Cabrera Infante moves through the accumulation with considerable ease, an indication of his extraordinary memory. If he decides to assemble a text based on autobiographical materials, he may write an early draft in linear fashion and with numbered pages, but with an eye to submitting them to considerable rewriting at a later date. Although at first glance this method may seem haphazard, it responds, in fact, to its own internal logic—the procedure is decidedly organic. Most of his manuscripts go through multiple drafts and extensive revisions despite the spontaneity many of them convey. Because of the way he writes and the many transformations that can occur in a text on its journey to publication, precisely dating the composition of a manuscript is at best a relative endeavor. It is equally difficult to ascertain how many drafts of a given book actually existed.

Although Cabrera Infante created segments before 1961 that were incorporated into the final version of *Three Trapped Tigers,* it was in that year that he began to consider writing the book. The event that initiated the process was the death of the singer Fredy in Puerto Rico during the first months of 1961. Cabrera Infante was on duty as a member of the militia guarding the offices of *Lunes de Revolución* on a six-hour shift when he heard the news at approximately seven in the morning. The only thing he had with him at the time was a rifle, so he requested pen and paper and began to write "Ella cantaba boleros" ("I Heard Her Sing"). Since he usually composes at a typewriter, it was an unusual occurrence in strange circumstances, but the writing flowed effort-lessly—it might have been an antidote to the boring task of having to assume the role of man-at-arms. Thus began one of the most successful and engaging sections of *Three Trapped Tigers* and the creation of one of the novel's most formidable characters, the gargantuan Estrella Rodríguez or La Estrella.

Cabrera Infante had seen Fredy several times and Miriam Gómez knew two friends who had taken Fredy under their wing and had allowed her to live with them. They soon became the victims of their guest as she took over their apartment and became the monster of the house. In life she was as unusual and bizarre as the character in the novel. Cabrera once described Fredy as "one of the ugliest women I have ever seen" and as "a walking monument."[8] The segment he initiated that morning was published in the 23 October 1961 issue of *Lunes de Revolución* in a version of approximately five thousand words. The introduction to the selection announced the intent to create a book: "'I Heard Her Sing' forms part of a novel in progress, 'La noche es un hueco sin borde' ('Night Is a Limitless Void'), a continuous narrative of a string of inci-dents that occurred in the nocturnal past, in Havana."[9] The labored title was soon abandoned, but the commitment to writing a novel about the activities of pleasure-seekers of the night is clearly indicated, along with the notion of producing the work as a continuous narrative. In the last months of 1961, the novel was still in a seminal stage, and he was preoccupied with other things, especially the closing of *Lunes de Revolución*. Most of the following year was devoted to a lecture series, the completion of *A Twentieth Century Job,* and the move to Belgium. Once he was settled into Brussels, he returned to working on the novel.

Cabrera Infante has described the writing of *Three Trapped Tigers* in Brussels as "a kind of narrative explosion."[10] It was clearly an effusive emotional period and many sections of the novel were created in that city.

> It was really there that *Three Trapped Tigers* came into being. I could not stop the avalanche of memories that came over me each evening which kept me from sleeping, and to exorcise them I began to write all the first part of the book that is called "Beginners," and then the chapter about Bustrófedon and "Mirrormaze," which I completed in very little time. I continued "I Heard Her Sing," which remained a linked *suite,* as I had planned from the beginning. I also wrote the

psychiatric sessions and, almost at the start, the "Prologue," and found by sheer luck among the papers brought from Cuba, that confession of the crazy woman in the park which forms the "Epilogue."[11]

Since he still had not resolved his ambivalent feelings about the revolution, he persisted in the plan to combine two dissimilar texts into one. "I conceived the completely mistaken idea to confront all the characters in *Three Trapped Tigers* with some from *Así en la paz como en la guerra*."[12] He came across a postcard in the basement of the embassy with the descriptive phrase "View of Dawn in Tropics" and decided to use that as the title of his manuscript. The basement provided another inspiration when he found *Tratados en La Habana* ("Treatises in Havana") by Lezama Lima and came across a sentence that sounded like Trotsky's last words in an entry entitled "From *Orígenes* to Julián Orbón." The sentence reads in part: "I feel too close to Julián Orbón to be able to pronounce his elegy without trembling from head to toe, *like one possessed who has just been penetrated by a soft hatchet. . . .*" (my emphasis).[13] It provided the inspiration for a parody included in "The Death of Trotsky as Described by Various Cuban Writers, Several Years After the Event— or Before." He was like a vigorous, bubbling spring.

In 1964 he submitted the manuscript to a literary contest in Spain and won the coveted Joan Petit Biblioteca Breve Prize awarded through the publishing house Seix Barral. The members of the jury included Carlos Barral, José María Castellet, Gabriel Ferrater, Luis Goytisolo, José María Valverde, and Mario Vargas Llosa. Some of the jury suggested breaking up the manuscript into more than one text, but plans were evidently made to publish it intact, although there were reservations about mixing the heroic struggle against Batista with the pleasures of the night. Meanwhile, at the embassy, other important and sinister developments were taking place. Intrigue and backstabbing were afoot as a member of the staff attempted to undermine the ambassador, and a security agent began to look into the matter.

Cabrera Infante describes the investigator in "Lives of a Hero": "Regardless of whether he was called Pablo or Agustín Aldama, he was genuinely impressive. He was bony, black and about six feet, six inches tall, with long hard hands and blind in his right eye."[14] The agent boasted of being a stuntman in Mexico for Robert Mitchum in, of all things, *The Wonderful Country*, but the bragging ceased when he learned about the controversy the film had provoked in Havana. When Cabrera Infante had previously encountered a one-eyed being, it was a librarian who located the writings of Homer for him, but this time the initiation would be into the dangerous labyrinths of paranoia. The spy terrorized the embassy staff and Cabrera Infante did everything he could to have Polyphemus summoned back to his cave in Cuba. The security agent eventually was recalled to Havana, but not before making veiled threats. On his return, he apparently sowed fear and distrust back home. It was a dangerous game to see who had the most powerful friends in Havana. Among the changes that took place was the recall of Ambassador Gustavo Arcos to Cuba for a consultation in the middle of 1964.

Arcos, a devout Catholic, had reluctantly participated in the rash attack on the Moncada Barracks in Santiago de Cuba on 26 July 1953. He had been badly wounded and was lucky to survive. He was left partially paralyzed for a time and has had trouble with one leg ever since. He was with Castro in Mexico and generally was in the midst of most of the struggle against Batista. His fall from grace within the revolution was a gradual and unspectacular process, but, in the end, he was incarcerated and has been in and out of prison ever since. Recently, he has become a human rights activist. Through the years, Cabrera Infante has made numerous unsuccessful efforts to obtain his release when Arcos has been incarcerated.[15] As a result of the return of Arcos to Havana in 1964, Cabrera Infante had to assume more responsibilities in the embassy, and he was, in effect, the chargé-d'affaires when he received an important communication from home.

On 2 June 1965, Carlos Franqui called Cabrera Infante from Havana. The news was grim—Zoila was ill and her condition was terminal. Cabrera Infante immediately called the minister of foreign relations, Raúl Roa, to explain the situation and to ask for permission to return. Since the management of the embassy was in disarray and there was no one to leave in charge, Cabrera Infante was reluctant to depart without clearance. Also, he may have had a premonition of what was awaiting him in Havana. Roa responded without hesitation and authorized the trip. Cabrera Infante was soon off by plane to Havana, as best and as quickly as he could under the circumstances. He arrived in Cuba just in time for the funeral services. Zoila's illness was sudden and unexpected; an ear infection had developed into cerebral meningitis through medical negligence. When Marta Calvo visited Zoila in the hospital, she was so alarmed by Zoila's deteriorating condition and lack of care that she called Alberto Mora. The comandante hurried to the hospital and his appearance jolted the medical staff into action. Doctors, including a specialist, were summoned, but it was to no avail; her infection had reached an irreversible stage.

When Cabrera Infante arrived at the funeral home with Carlos Franqui immediately after reaching Havana, Gustavo Arcos was there. He and Zoila had become good friends during her visit to Europe. Arcos complained to Cabrera Infante that Carlos Franqui was convinced that he (Arcos) was being followed by the sinister spy who had terrorized the embassy in Brussels, an assertion that Arcos found ridiculous. Numbed and in a state of shock over Zoila's death, Cabrera Infante paid scant attention to Arcos's indifference to danger and Carlos Franqui's worried concern about their friend. The next day he reported to Minister Roa and was informed that he was to be promoted to ministerial status, that he would take charge of the embassy on his return, and that he should leave as soon as possible. Roa also asked some casual questions about Arcos. Although he would see the foreign minister on a few other occasions from a distance, it was the last time that Cabrera Infante spoke directly with him.

On 13 July 1965, just fifteen minutes before his flight was to depart from the Havana airport, Cabrera Infante received a call from the vice minister of foreign affairs, Arnol Rodríguez, informing him that Roa wanted to see him and that he could not leave. He returned to the city with his two daughters and all the family members and friends who had accompanied him to the airport to see him off. Although there were the usual reassurances of some mistake having been made, everyone knew that the signs were foreboding. He made several attempts to talk with Roa but never succeeded in doing so, although he did catch glimpses of Roa scurrying out of his sight on two occasions. "Like one of Kafka's characters, I had been called to the castle to be interviewed by the Lord who could not see me."[16] He slowly realized that he had slipped through the cracks of respectability and into the limbo of someone under suspicion. He was now under the wing of State Security and had become a leper in his own land.

In Brussels, Miriam Gómez carried on the duties at the embassy, which included deciphering diplomatic communications and instructions. One of the directives she decoded ordered the embassy not to share any confidential materials with her husband. Things were not much better in Havana. Living with his father, Cabrera Infante was forced to borrow money from friends, and he started to sell off some of his possessions to pay his debts. Marta Calvo arranged for someone to purchase his collection of jazz records for a 10 percent commission, and his father sold his record player to a friend for five hundred pesos. The sale of the record player was difficult because it reminded him of a happier time in early 1961 when Miriam Gómez started living with him. Both he and Miriam became alarmed when she was informed that a ticket for her return to Havana was being sent to Brussels. This only increased Cabrera Infante's determination to leave Cuba with his daughters, but the prospects looked bleak. The more insistent he became, the more his friends worried about him.

The entire episode is narrated in the unpublished "Ithaca Revisited," a manuscript of 314 typewritten pages. "Ithaca Revisited" is a straightforward factual narration of the death of his mother and his trip to Cuba. The manuscript opens with a quotation from Henry James: "but history is also allowed to represent life." In the foreword to the text, the author declares: "All the characters are real. Their names are those of real life. The story really occurred. So, only the book—these white pages with black imprints, the paste of the spine, the garish cover—only the book is fictitious." As previously noted, Cabrera Infante maintains that anything within a text is fictitious, a reasonable position for someone whose works depend so richly on personal sources. Having a writer in the family has its disadvantages. Shared experiences and memories become part of the public domain and are subject to simplistic and naive interpretations as reality and signification are confused. For such a writer, the issue of referential slippage is acute.

The narration in "Ithaca Revisited" is in the third person, but the focalization is through the eyes of Cabrera Infante, a technique used in some of the vignettes of *View of Dawn in the Tropics*. Written in 1973 when he was working his way through a serious depression, the book helped him reconstruct and exorcise memories of the past. It is a fascinating and engaging read, but Cabrera Infante feels that the style is too direct and should be denser. He says, "I am not content with the narration of this book. I want to change it. But the question is when. How do I buy time?"[17] One also suspects that there is a reluctance to return to a painful period of the past when everything was at risk and so much was lost. It is like other manuscripts that languish unpublished in his London apartment, particularly "Divine Bodies" and the engaging film script based on the Malcolm Lowry novel of the same name, "Under the Volcano." But the movie script has disturbing associations, and he prefers not to publish it. He once discharged a literary agent, Carl Brandt, for allowing visitors from Hollywood to leave his office with a copy of "Under the Volcano." Cabrera Infante takes some satisfaction in the fact that the agent's father had been fired by Raymond Chandler.

In addition to being pleasurable reading, "Ithaca Revisited" is a cultural and historical slice of a crucial time in Cuban history. Many family members appear in its pages, including the unforgettable Pepe Castro in a state of shock over Zoila's death, Marta Calvo and members of her family, Miriam Gómez, and close friends such as Carlos Franqui, Rine Leal, Alberto Mora, and Gustavo Arcos. Writers and critics who appear or are discussed include Alejo Carpentier, Humberto Arenal, Oscar Hurtado, Pablo Armando Fernández, Ambrosio Fornet, Nicolás Guillén, Jaime Sarusky, Virgilio Piñera, and José Lezama Lima. Among the political leaders are Carlos Rafael Rodríguez and President Dorticós. It is enough to make a Cubanist weep. Most of these, of course, are not central characters. They flit in and out of the text as they appeared in the life of the author during his restless search for a solution to his dilemma or comfort from the strain. The latter endeavor involved him in intimate relationships, and during one amorous adventure, when a feared pregnancy proves a false alarm, the narrator expresses the desire to celebrate in his lover's menses like an avenging Dracula. The impressive episode recalls Camille Paglia's observation that "sex is sloppy and untidy, a return to what Freud calls the infant's polymorphous perversity, a zestful rolling around in every body fluid."[18]

During his four months in Havana, Cabrera Infante received a letter from Carlos Barral, the editor of Seix Barral, informing him that his presence was needed in Barcelona for the editing of his manuscript. This provided a convenient argument for his return to Europe. Alberto Mora carried the initiative through the governmental bureaucracy and arranged for a meeting with Carlos Rafael Rodríguez, "the most flexible of the old Communists, Castro's oldest friend among them."[19] Mora and Cabrera Infante met with Rodríguez and during their conversation the subject of Alejo Carpentier came up, in particular that writer's publication of "El año 59." Within that context, Rodríguez made a comment to the effect that they did not want to have a case like Pasternak's in Cuba. Cabrera Infante understood the remark as an oblique reference to his own situation. Rodríguez took up the matter with President Dorticós and permission was granted for Cabrera Infante to leave the country.

He then found himself in the process of getting new and nondiplomatic passports for himself, his daughters, and Miriam Gómez. The only photograph he could find of Miriam was one taken when she was seventeen or eighteen years old, which must have raised the eyebrows of more than one immigration official. On 3 October 1965 at 10:10 P.M., his flight departed Rancho Boyeros Airport, but he did not breathe a sigh of relief until the plane had passed the halfway point of its journey and he knew it was no longer possible to return to Havana. He left Cuba with his two daughters, manuscripts he had worked on during his stay, and a few books, among them a first edition of Raymond Chandler's *The Big Sleep* and Lino Novás Calvo's *La luna nona y otros cuentos* ("The Ninth Moon and Other Stories"). He had made the decision to go into exile; from this point on there would be no turning back.

His brother had also received permission to travel to Madrid to put his affairs in order before returning to Cuba. He too remained in exile and, in fact, announced his decision in Europe long before his older brother. For their father, back in Havana, the one black sheep of the family was being transformed into two. Sabá has been a cautious and invisible exile and disappeared into private life in New York City. For his own part, Cabrera Infante did not publicly explain why he had left Cuba until the summer of 1968, when he did so in spectacular fashion in a declaration published in the form of an interview in the 16 August issue of *Primera Plana,* which was recently republished in *Mea Cuba.* It was the last act in a slow and painful process akin to a river bank's sudden collapse after years of gradual erosion. Doubt had finally overwhelmed hope and his schizophrenic accommodation to the revolution came to an end. Sabá reacted to that event with advice worthy of their father, counseling his older brother to refrain from making controversial declarations for his own safety. Cabrera Infante did not accept the unsolicited admonition, and on several occasions he has followed Zoila's inclination to take a stand on important issues in spite of the risks. Eschewing his father's caution and reserve, he opted instead for Zoila's courage and rashness.

After his return to Europe, Cabrera Infante discovered from his publisher that "View of Dawn in the Tropics" had not been approved for publication by Spanish censors. Carlos Barral told him there was no recourse except to change the title and to rewrite the book. The rejection was a blessing in disguise. During the process of rewriting the manuscript, he decided to go back to an earlier title based on a tongue-twister and to remove the historically based vignettes. The resolution of his relationship with the revolution enabled him to untangle troublesome issues in his text. One section of the work, "Seseribó," appeared in Cuba in the September–October 1965 issue of *Casa de las Américas,* and he had started working on "Bachata" during the four months he had spent in Havana. The location and time of writing helps explain the nostalgia and sense of loss that permeates that section of the text.

In November 1965 while on a trip to London, he was advised by the Cuban Embassy in Paris that he should not associate himself with a new journal that was about to be published under the editorship of Emir Rodríguez Monegal because, the Cuban authorities asserted, it was funded by the CIA. Shortly after that, Alberto Mora visited him in Madrid and conveyed a personal message from President Dorticós that his brother's defection did not prejudice his own case and that he was welcome in Havana. Although he had wandered from the fold and was in danger of losing his way, he still was not considered a lost cause. Having decided not to return to Ithaca for a second round of turmoil and anxiety, Cabrera Infante and his family remained in Madrid. The two links in the message of reconciliation would perish tragically under similar circumstances. Several years later, Dorticós had his own difficulties and committed suicide after falling from power.

Cabrera Infante's time in Spain was confusing, but not without successful interludes. He began to work intensely on the revision of his manuscript in Madrid, and he experienced a burst of creativity similar to that in Brussels. Since he was unsuccessful in finding work in Spain, all of his energies went into the revision and expansion of the book, which grew by leaps and bounds. They lived off savings provided by the sale of their car in Havana and ten thousand dollars from the Seix Barral prize. In April 1966 he took the final draft by train to Barcelona along with an extensive selection of photographs taken by Jesse Fernández in Cuba. One of that photographer's pictures of some musicians playing at a beach was used on the dust jacket of the first edition. Unfortunately, Cabrera Infante did not have negatives of many of the photographs and, naively placing too much trust in his publisher, did not make any copies of the last draft. All of those materials eventually disappeared.

In November 1966, Severo Sarduy took Cabrera Infante to meet Emir Rodríguez Monegal in the Paris apartment of the Uruguayan editor of *Mundo Nuevo*. It was the beginning of a professional association and friendship that lasted until Rodríguez Monegal's death on 14 November 1985. The symmetry in the chronology of their relationship (the warning, first meeting, and death all took place in the month of November) must have reinforced Cabrera Infante's faith in coincidence and chance. *Mundo Nuevo* provided a source of income during an economically difficult period in Cabrera Infante's life, and Rodríguez Monegal, along with Juan Goytisolo, helped persuade Carlos Barral to publish *Three Trapped Tigers*. A fervent supporter of the Cuban revolution, Barral had lost his enthusiasm for Cabrera Infante's work and was dragging his heels in regard to its publication. He probably thought it impolite for the author to have buried, in his text, references such as "fidel fiasco" and "psicocastro."

Barral reacted violently to Cabrera Infante's August 1968 declarations in *Primera Plana* and denounced the action in a letter to him dated 25 October 1968 in which he asserted that Cabrera Infante's arguments might impress the readers of *The Reader's Digest* and the bourgeoisie of Topeka, Kansas, but they wouldn't move his friends. Misspellings of Topeka and *The Reader's Digest* add comic flair to the letter and are indicative of the writer's wrath. Barral had the good sense and courtesy to send a copy of his letter to *Casa de las Américas* in Havana, undoubtedly to preserve his revolutionary credentials. Although *Three Trapped Tigers* was a spectacular success, no further printings were produced until Carlos Barral's departure from the publishing house in 1970.

Of course, 1968 was not an auspicious time for antirevolutionary proclamations. Emmanuel Carballo first informed me of the interview in *Primera Plana* in his home in Mexico City in August of that summer, and the affable Mexican critic brushed it off as the inarticulate ravings of a lunatic. Cabrera Infante soon discovered that even in London he had acquired an embarrassing ideological disease. Cordiality frequently disappeared as soon as he mentioned that he had broken with the revolution. His incredulous listeners either would lapse into stunned silence or would begin to mumble about the need to fulfill a pressing obligation somewhere else. He started wondering if he should put on a scarlet letter, but after careful reflection he concluded that even in a city accustomed to eccentrics, the neighbors might become alarmed. He decided the best thing to do was to tell the truth as he saw it, and he began to point out, without any particular plan or schedule, that the Prince in Havana was not wearing any clothes. However, deeply distrustful of patriots and wary of opportunists, he has steadfastly refused to become involved in politics and, in fact, has provoked the wrath of all extremes of the political spectrum. Nevertheless, his independent stance has not restrained others from using his name without authorization in the pursuit of pet political causes.

In late 1966 things were looking bleak for the young writer and his family. They were denied residence visas in Spain as Cabrera Infante's eternal difficulties with government bureaucracies continued unabated—first Batista, then Castro, and now Franco. He had begun working on scripts for the British film industry in 1966 and England appeared as one of the few avenues open to him. His acquisition of English in the 1940s was beginning to pay desperately needed dividends. His initial contact in London was Joe Massot, an American whose mother was Cuban. They had met in Havana in connection with the Cuban Cinematic Institute and Massot had visited him in Brussels. Massot arranged the funding for a trip to London from Madrid, and Cabrera Infante soon found himself involved in the production of film scripts, including "The Mercenary," "On the Speedway," and "Wonderwall."

When he first moved to London, Cabrera Infante and his family lived with friends, he and Miriam at one location and the two daughters at another. By the end of 1966, the family was living in a damp basement apartment in the back of the building at 18 Trebovir Road. Located under a hotel and next to the Earl's Court subway station in an area of seedy gentility, it was not a quiet or desirable location, but at least the family was together again and no longer scattered throughout the city. They moved in after Christmas amid the lingering hope and despair of the season. Mario Vargas Llosa and his family lived in similar circumstances in very close proximity to the Cabrera Infantes. Continuing a family tradition established by Zoila, the modest Trebovir Road apartment became a social center and gathering place for many friends, including Carlos Fuentes and Mario Vargas Llosa. The Cuban writer Calvert Casey and a male companion visited in December 1966, and he and Juan Arocha sent money to Cabrera Infante from abroad to help him demonstrate to the British Home Office that he had income from royalties. Having eluded the worst traps of three dictatorships, he was now discovering the joys of democratic officialdom.

Casey did not adjust well to exile. Consumed by a vague and persistent sense of guilt, he took his own life, dying in Rome on 14 May 1969. It was a grievous and painful blow for Cabrera Infante in London, and he slipped into a period of sedatives and sleeping pills. He most likely took it, at a visceral level, as a metaphoric premonition of disaster. Miriam lit a candle in memory of Casey in Brompton Oratory, the church where the marriages of Stepháne Mallarmé and Alfred Hitchcock, two other figures highly esteemed by her husband, were performed.

With funds produced by the movie script "Wonderwall," the Cabrera Infantes moved in October 1967 to a much more satisfactory apartment, at 53 Gloucester Road in South Kensington. It was located on the ground or first floor in more spacious quarters, and they no longer had to hear and feel the rumble of subway trains at Earl's Court Station. Their apartment is a few minutes' stroll from the Gloucester subway station near the intersection of Cromwell and Gloucester Roads, an area with many embassies and close to Kensington Palace. Their street is lined on both sides by stately five-story buildings, many of brick construction. A three-columned portico leads to the entrance of their residence, which is located in a building constructed in the 1830s. They live a few doors from the church where T. S. Eliot served as churchwarden for twenty-five years and around the corner from the poet's former residence at 3 Kensington Court Gardens as well as from the apartments of Henry James and Robert Browning on De Vere Gardens. It is probably coincidental that Cabrera Infante's publisher in London, Faber and Faber, is the editorial house where Eliot worked. But what really tickles Cabrera Infante's fancy is residing in the vicinity of what once was Alfred Hitchcock's third-floor apartment at 153 Cromwell Road, a dwelling that has not yet been marked with one of London's distinctive blue plaques.

Since the music for *Wonderwall* had been written by George Harrison, Cabrera Infante had the opportunity to meet the Beatles during the opening night of Apple. Unimpressed, he wrote in a description of the encounter: "The worst was John Lennon; the least offensive, Paul McCartney. Ringo did not even know his instrument."[20] He was now in the midst of swinging London, pop musicians, mini-skirts, and all. Early in 1967, the Cuban government notified him that his reentry visa was no longer valid because of his collaboration with *Mundo Nuevo,* but that was the least of his worries. The publication of *Three Trapped Tigers* was spectacularly successful and his work in the movie industry was generating good income. In addition, he had acquired acceptable living quarters for his family, and they were able to send their daughters to a convent school. He and Miriam realized that a proper education was indispensable in a society in which a verbal accent is destiny.

Persistent visa difficulties continued unabated and they both experienced health problems during 1967. Hesitant to declare himself a political refugee, Cabrera Infante found himself committed to an unsatisfactory course of action. The Home Office was reluctant to extend his visa for more than a few months at a time and at one point even seized the family's passports. On several occasions he attempted to prove he was financially solvent, a feat that required imagination because of the unreliable nature of his income. Certification as a steady collaborator on *Mundo Nuevo* was useful as well as his success as a scriptwriter. It was a game of cat and mouse and he was the prey. The whole ordeal did little to calm his shaky nerves, but he was never expelled and eventually prevailed, although many years later. He and Miriam spent less than an hour at a New Year's Eve party in the apartment of the Vargas Llosas, where Cabrera Infante chatted briefly with García Márquez. They judiciously talked about myths and superstitions rather than politics. All in all, the year turned out satisfactorily. The elusive tiger had found a safe lair.

CHAPTER SEVEN

A Nocturnal Rhapsody

DURING THE 1960S CUBA PASSED THROUGH ONE OF THE MOST tumultuous periods in its history as it underwent radical social and political transformation, and these events had a profound effect on Cabrera Infante's life and career. The evolution of *Three Trapped Tigers* into the text that was finally published in Barcelona in 1967 reflected the author's gradual disillusionment with the political process that was sweeping his country, and it is not surprising that such profound change found expression in his novel. It is true that much of his early enthusiasm and later discontent were relegated to omission and silence as the politically inspired vignettes were expunged from the manuscript, but *Three Trapped Tigers* contains elements of ideological subversion and plays on a broader cultural stage than Cuba.

Cabrera Infante has always been attuned to changes in mass media and popular culture. In addition, his travels in the United States and

Europe as well as the creation and elaboration of *Three Trapped Tigers* in Havana, Brussels, and Madrid exposed him to a variety of dynamic influences. His radically innovative work breaks with a number of traditions and initiates several new trends, probably best expressed in what critics refer to as the transition from modernism to postmodernism. In this respect, *Three Trapped Tigers* represents a cultural fault line, a radical shift in artistic expression. The different parts of the text radiate like fissures throughout the surface of the old, exposing a world that is passing away as another is coming into existence. The disintegration of the past and the creation of the new is most apparent in two sections located near one another in the center of the novel, the contradictory stories of the adventures of Mr. Campbell and the supposed Mrs. Campbell in Havana and the literary parodies that stylize several narrations of the death of Trotsky.

The tourist weekend in Havana appears in the section of the novel entitled "Los visitantes" ("Vae Visitors"), with the subtitle of "Historia de un bastón y algunos reparos de Mrs. Campbell" ("The Story of a Stick, with Some Additional Comments by Mrs. Campbell"). The original version was written in Belgium and began as a story based on an adventure that befell Cabrera Infante's friend Nestor Almendros while on a trip.[1] When Cabrera Infante finished a first version of the story, he sent it to Almendros in Paris, and was surprised by Nestor's critical reaction. Essentially, Almendros felt that Cabrera Infante had made a number of mistakes and had gotten it all wrong, and he proceeded to make corrections and annotations to the story. Cabrera Infante's response was to transform his friend's criticisms and objections into the opinions of Mrs. Campbell, and he added this duplication and contradiction of the original story to the text.

To complicate matters further, another rendering of both versions is included, with footnotes and revisions. Much later in the novel it is revealed that these are translations with corrections from the original English carried out by Rine Leal and Silvestre. As Suzanne Jill Levine has explained:

> Mr. Campbell, a buffoonish avatar of Hemingway, has supposedly published the story in *Beau Sabreur*, a fictive American magazine, and "GCI" has found it and wants to publish it in the Cuban magazine he works for, *Carteles*. The story is first literally translated by a real life

friend of GCI, Rine Leal, whose last name ironically means "loyal." A letter from "GCI" to Silvestre (474) explains that the second "translation" of the Campbell story . . . is actually the first, Rine's awkward translation. Typically, this literal "translation" is a more elaborate version than Silvestre's, with more details, footnotes, and allusions. Its rhetoric is more mannered, and comically unidiomatic; it is indeed a *cuento,* a short story, as opposed to a *historia,* a narration of events.

The supposedly original English version will never be seen, however, since the translations are in reality parodies of what a prejudiced American tourist would write about La Habana and of what happens when English texts are translated into Spanish. These translations mock Lino Novás Calvo's translations, but Cabrera Infante parodies the strategies and mistakes of translations to show that all writing suffers from betrayal.[2]

This confusion emphasizes, among other things, that fiction and translations are misreadings.

All of the section on the Campbells evolves around what really happened and the differences between illusion, reality, and error become both humorous and problematical for the reader. In this respect, the reader is forced to deal with problems of knowing, that is, with epistemological concerns. The origin of this fine mess, Nestor Almendros, was surprised and at first even annoyed to find his earnest comments transformed into Mrs. Campbell's version of events. This indirect parody, which does not mention origins, is closely followed in *Three Trapped Tigers* by another section that explicitly identifies models.

"The Death of Trotsky as Described by Various Cuban Writers, Several Years After the Event—or Before" is presented in the novel as parodies carried out by Bustrófedon orally and recorded on tape. At the time of publication in 1967, all of the seven writers imitated except one, José Martí, were alive, and that particular selection is in the manner of Martí but as if written by the Cuban critic Juan Marinello, who specialized in Martí.[3] "The Death of Trotsky" inspired a good deal of pique among several of the authors whose writings, personalities, and attitudes toward literature and the world are parodied in this masterful section. Several reactions drifted in indirectly; many were offended, among them Alejo Carpentier, but a few, like Lydia Cabrera and Virgilio Piñera, were delighted with the results. One of the authors parodied, Lino Novás

Calvo, was more concerned with criticisms made by Silvestre in the end of "Bachata" of his translation of *The Old Man and the Sea.*

Lino Novás Calvo fired off an angry letter to *Mundo Nuevo* in Paris in 1967, and Emir Rodríguez Monegal forwarded it on to Cabrera Infante in London and asked if he wanted to respond in some fashion in the pages of *Mundo Nuevo,* perhaps in a reply to the letter. Cabrera Infante thought it best not to answer the impetuous attack. He had too high a regard for the works of Novás Calvo to become involved in a public dispute with him.

Cabrera Infante, who professes to view parody as the result of attentive readings and as a form of homage, claims to have been puzzled by the negative reactions, a position that Dwight Macdonald would view with sympathy, since he has written that "most parodies are written out of admiration rather than contempt."[4] But why the death of Trotsky as rendered by several Cuban writers? It is all related to the murky and mysterious role that Trotsky's assassin, the man known as Ramón Mercader, Jacob Monard, or Frank Jacson, and his family played in Cuban affairs. In his 1990 interview with Nedda G. de Anhalt, Carlos Franqui explained that he and a group of collaborators from *Revolución,* including Cabrera Infante, expressed their concerns to Fidel Castro in 1960 when they discovered that Mercader was scheduled to pass through Cuba on his way to Czechoslovakia after being released from a Mexican prison.[5] Ramón Mercader walked out of jail on 6 May 1960 and Franqui believes that he actually spent time in Cuba until his recent return to his native Spain, and that he and a brother served as advisers to state security. The Mercaders were active in Communist activities in Spain until the fall of the Republic, and Ramón had been trained in Moscow.[6]

According to Franqui, Ramón's mother, Caridad Mercader, was employed at the Cuban Embassy in France in 1962 and he, Marta Frayde, and Juan Goytisolo complained about that assignment. In his 1970 interview with Rita Guibert, Cabrera Infante describes seeing Caridad in the Cuban Embassy in Paris in 1965. He also expresses the belief that Caridad Mercader was Cuban and that Ramón had been born in Santiago de Cuba: "The parodies of Trotsky in *TTT* were derived from this fact."[7] He gives more details about the Mercaders in the recent *Mea Cuba* and asserts his belief that Ramón is buried in Cuba.[8] Whatever the specifics of the case, there is no doubt that the Mercaders moved between the Communist and Hispanic worlds and that they had significant contacts in Cuba. And, of course, the most important factor is what Cabrera Infante thought of the matter at the time he wrote the novel. Robert Payne, in his 1977 biography of Trotsky, gives a detailed description of the lengthy process of uncovering the identity of the murderer, which included a definitive match of fingerprints and a subsequent interview with the assassin's father, Don Pablo Mercader, in Barcelona. According to Payne's synthesis of the work of several investigators, Caridad del Río was indeed Cuban, but her second son, Ramón Mercader del Río, was born in Barcelona on 7 February 1913.[9] Caridad emerges in his version as a passionate and unstable Cuban beauty who attempted suicide on several occasions and who became the mistress of a general in Soviet intelligence. She received the Order of Lenin from Stalin after the spectacular success of her son.[10]

Unlike the section about the Campbells, the segment on Trotsky involves no doubts as to what happened. Epistemological problems are not the main concern of this part of the text. Rather, the focus is on essence and being, as much about the nature of violence, which Cabrera Infante detests, as the dispositions of the authors who are parodied and the victim of the crime. Brian McHale argues that a shift from an epistemological focus to an ontological one is a primary characteristic of the transition to postmodernism. In this regard, the center of Cabrera Infante's text contains sections that highlight first epistemological and then ontological concerns, signaling the cultural shift from one focusing component to another. McHale has pointed out that "there is a kind of inner logic or inner dynamics . . . governing the change of dominant from modernist to postmodernist fiction. Intractable epistemological uncertainty becomes at a certain point ontological plurality or instability: push epistemological questions far enough and they 'tip over' into ontological questions. By the same token, push ontological questions far enough and they tip over into epistemological questions—the sequence is not linear and unidirectional, but bidirectional and reversible."[11] This is precisely what happens to the reader who confronts "Vae Visitors" and "The Death of Trotsky" in the middle of *Three Trapped Tigers;* the bridge between these two sections is "Rompecabeza" ("Brainteaser"), Códac's narration about a character who wallows in the playpen of language—Bustrófedon.

"Brainteaser" begins with a series of ontological questions: "Who was Bustrófedon? Who was/is/will be Bustrófedon?"[12] The text never answers these queries explicitly, but it does offer a compelling and humorous portrait of the mad antics of Bustrófedon and his games with language. He delights in playing with words and on occasion extends a part of his own name to everything he sees. More than any other character, Bustrófedon represents the incarnation of the word into a living reality, and the text implies, through Bustrófedon's actions and his influence on other characters, that creativity is the only answer to questions concerning the nature or essence of being. It seems the only way to fill the void created by time and death, and in *Three Trapped Tigers* creativity is synonymous with being. Bustrófedon is an absent presence in the novel, since he is dead and lives on in the memories of the other characters and through the recordings. This gap between his physical absence and symbolic presence underscores the referentiality of all language and its proclivity to error once it is removed from its original sources. In this regard, particularly as related to Bustrófedon, language becomes a contradictory metaphor for creativity and death. As Roberto González Echevarría has observed: "Malformation and error are the gaps between the self and the world and between the self and its own intended representation in language. All the distortions of language in *Three Trapped Tigers* issue out of this double negation of lesion and death. The novel is sad because of the realization that logos as ontology is at best this marriage of error and death. The novel is a kind of wake for Bustrófedon, and in this sense it has a profound affinity with *Finnegans Wake*."[13]

It is significant that Bustrófedon is Cabrera Infante's favorite character, and some of this creation's characteristics can be related to two of the author's most cherished relatives during the years in Gibara, the unconventional and madcap Pepe Castro and the reckless and devil-may-care Cándido Infante Espinosa. These were not necessarily conscious models, but his great-uncle and grandfather were inspirational figures in his youth. Pepe's cultivation of oral language and zany inventiveness and Cándido's ability to counter adversity with humor left their mark. Of the two, Pepe is undoubtedly the dominant figure; even his interest in science is reflected in the figure of Bustrófedon. The appearances of some of his relatives' characteristics in Bustrófedon constitute an acknowledgment of the creative vitality of the maternal side of the family. "Brainteaser," "Vae Visitors," and "The Death of Trotsky" embody important cultural changes and mirror their creator's own movement from revolutionary certainty to antirevolutionary doubt. The shift from epistemological uncertainty to ontological plurality is accompanied by an affirmation of the sort of creativity that delights in flirting with chaos. It is an enterprise in which relativity increasingly becomes the norm in a random universe. Bustrófedon was Cabrera Infante's answer to his text's slide into the ontological abyss.

Bustrófedon shares with many of the characters in *Three Trapped Tigers* a propensity to resist established norms and to challenge authority. Cabrera Infante sees him as a "literary anarchist" who uses parody to attack tradition and prestige.[14] The other raw creative force in the novel, La Estrella, is equally anarchistic and rejects all limitations imposed by others, to the point of engaging in willful lying and self-destructive behavior. La Estrella is so confident of her abilities that she even refuses to be accompanied by an orchestra and disdains attempts to foster her career through the modern wonders of publicity. Unlike her opposite, the opportunistic Cuba Venegas, who is devoid of talent and who uses sex to further her career, La Estrella depends only on her marvelous voice. Another character, Magalena Crus, declares her independence in a vulgar carpe diem directed at her grandmother and announces her intent to go off and enjoy life. She stomps out of her past, acting like Bette Davis and affirming her intention to be a dancer. In fact, most of the characters who spend their lives meandering from one nightclub to another are resisting a social order they detest. Their nocturnal wanderings embody their restless search for freedom as well as pleasure.

One of the more engaging and subtle figures in regard to the subversion of authority is the neurotic Laura Díaz, a Penelope figure for Arsenio and Silvestre, who weaves and unweaves confusing tales. In early manuscript versions of *Three Trapped Tigers,* some sections begin with an indication of the name and age of important characters. The difference in age between Laura (twenty-eight) and Arsenio (twenty-two) explains some of the pathos in their relationship and his feeling that she is unattainable. The fanciful and atrocious stories she relates, sometimes to her psychiatrist and on occasion to her husband, Silvestre, undermine patriarchal structures. Laura, like many of the characters in the novel, subverts visions of the world established by tradition and authority. And, of course, the most iconoclastic voice in *Three Trapped Tigers* is the monologue that closes the novel, the random ravings of a madwoman on a park bench who vents her rage at unnamed forces. She can be termed the feminine side of Bustrófedon's unarticulated nightmares. Both react instinctively to the imposition of ideology in any form and respond to utopian dreams with horror and disgust.

To a certain degree, both characters can be considered avatars of the authorial self to the extent that they resist the imposition of ideology. Cabrera Infante shared with his family and associates a hatred of Batista and early enthusiasm for the revolution. However, the institutionalization of the Cuban revolution was the beginning of an extended nightmare for him, although for Zoila and Guillermo senior it was the fulfillment of a lifelong dream. The keeper of the family's ideological archive was, of course, Guillermo senior, and this is one of the sources of the text's resistance to patriarchal tradition.

Within a national cultural context, *Three Trapped Tigers'* undermining of prestige and power can be associated with "choteo" (literally, "jeering" or "mocking"), the Cuban tendency to subvert authority or level hierarchies through disrespectful humor. Gustavo Pérez Firmat, in his intelligent discussion of Jorge Mañach's classic *Indagación del choteo* (1928), adds an important distinction to the concept, seeing choteo "as a movement toward, or assault from, the margins."[15] Since many of the characters in *Three Trapped Tigers* are creatures of the night, they can be thought of as existing on the fringes of society, and many of them, especially the women, live on the periphery of power. This displacement from centers of authority recalls what happened to Cabrera Infante when he tumbled from the editorship of *Lunes de Revolución* into unemployment and then on to what he regarded as an obscure post in a remote embassy. He was physically and emotionally exiled from Havana and he has been filling that void ever since through his writings.

Within an international cultural context, the challenge of authority can be linked to postmodernism's fragmentation of form, the erasure of distinctions between high and low culture, and the subversion of literary norms. Creations from the mass media are incorporated into the book to such a degree that it is difficult to distinguish the boundaries between fictions generated inside and outside of the text. McHale points out that *Three Trapped Tigers* calls attention to itself as a book and as a physical presence in the world of the reader through devices such as the use of blank pages and the manipulation of print.[16] Titles appear as if they are headlines, to indicate that individual sections of the book can stand on their own as independent entities. Cabrera Infante's incorporation of his own initials in a memo to Silvestre concerning the translation of the

Campbell story, his use of the names of actual friends such as Rine Leal and Matías Montes Huidobro, and other devices highlight ontological boundaries and tensions.

Cabrera Infante's attention to graphics is related to his early interest in comics, film, and photography; his appreciation of visual devices; and his experience on *Carteles* and *Lunes de Revolución*. He never forgot the impact that the photographic essay "The Beauty of the Bomb" had on the readers of *Carteles,* and *Lunes de Revolución* was noted for its daring artistic displays. The model for the character Eribó in *Three Trapped Tigers* was a graphic artist for *Lunes de Revolución* who had once been a musician in the orchestra of Beny Moré, one of Cuba's most renowned singers. Sometimes such figures from the past reappear in Cabrera Infante's life. Another source, the basis for the impetuous and delightful adolescent Vivian Smith Corona, recently wrote Cabrera Infante. He was pleased to hear from her and to know that the original inspiration for his literary creation is now living in Chicago.

Three Trapped Tigers is so intimately connected to all of the arts and to many intellectual traditions that the consideration of sources is an endless subject. He has remarked, for example, that the novel owes more to Martin Gardner's *The Annotated Alice* than to Lewis Carroll's work.[17] *Three Trapped Tigers* recognizes the mesmerizing power of popular culture as well as the interconnected nature of all artistic expression. Cabrera Infante is well aware that his work is a part of a fabricated tradition from which he takes considerable inspiration. He acknowledges many of these sources in his text and in commentaries and interviews, and considered over the span of many years, the total number of references is so extensive that one wonders if he is not parodying a cherished practice of literary criticism. As his readings have become more extensive over the years, so have his literary antecedents, in good Borgesian fashion. His best interviews are rendered in written form (sometimes he even asks the questions), and given his propensity for playing with language and concepts, it is not surprising if a name or two (or three) is dropped in for linguistic or aesthetic effect. His ability to imitate in speech or writing anyone he pleases further complicates the matter.

Suzanne Jill Levine summarizes many of the literary sources in sentences as succinct as the following: "An anglophile like Borges, Cabrera Infante took as his models Lewis Carroll and Joyce in turning words inside out, in discovering neologisms, while Hemingway, Mark Twain,

Raymond Chandler, and S. J. Perelman served as his Virgils in translating spoken speech into written language."[18] The comments on language are important because one of the singular achievements of *Three Trapped Tigers* is Cabrera Infante's creation of a version of Cuban Spanish that is effective and convincing. The language, while unique, does not detract from a sense of reality and this is a considerable accomplishment. Part of this success is due to his ability to create contexts in which the language of the characters seems natural. *Three Trapped Tigers* successfully integrates oral and written language and captures the spontaneity of orality. The concentration on orality explains the diffuse nature of the work, its emphasis on sound, and the favoring of atmosphere over action. As Walter Ong has pointed out: "Present day de-plotted narrative forms are part of the electronic age, deviously structured in abstruse codes . . ."[19]

Since the novel was written with an eye to being read aloud, it is partially a performance. Anyone with acting experience can take a scene from the novel and know how to present it, as many professors and students have done in class. In this respect, *Three Trapped Tigers* recalls Cabrera Infante's early literary interests—his fascination with the works of Homer, specifically the *Odyssey*. His creation shares with such antecedents sections suitable for recitation at one time. One of the highlights of the Eleventh Puterbaugh Conference on Writers of the French-Speaking and Hispanic World at the University of Oklahoma in March 1987 was a reading by Cabrera Infante of selections from the work, particularly excerpts from the "Death of Trotsky" section. He even successfully mimicked the voices of the authors parodied.

In an interview with Alfred J. Mac Adam, Cabrera Infante acknowledged that Chandler's *The Long Goodbye* was "one of the models for TTT."[20] Since one of the few possessions he took with him when he left Cuba in 1965 was a copy of the first edition of *The Big Sleep,* there is no doubt about his interest in that author. The most direct borrowing from the first-mentioned novel, which is one of Chandler's best, appears in *Three Trapped Tigers* in the reference to "Tinkers & Evers (& Chance)" in a list of "Authors of Poperas."[21] The pop opera in question is baseball and the names belong to a trio of record-breaking double-play artists from the Chicago Cubs who started playing together in 1903.[22] The reference appears in *The Long Goodbye* in a comment by Philip Marlowe: "Back in my dog house on the sixth floor of the Cahuenga Building I went through my regular doubleplay with the morning mail. Mail slot to desk to wastebasket, Tinker to Evers to Chance."[23] The addition of an "s" to Tinker and the playful inclusion of one of the last names, Chance, within parentheses highlight Cabrera Infante's fascination with randomness even in a realm of favorable probability and, perhaps, the haphazard way the trio was brought together.

When Terry Lennox tells Philip Marlowe in *The Long Goodbye* that all he can do in life is act a part, it is as if he is setting the norm for the actions of many of the characters in *Three Trapped Tigers* for whom appearance rather than essence is everything. The relationship between Marlowe and Lennox oscillates between friendship and antagonism much like that of Arsenio Cué and Silvestre. Other possible connections include literary intertextualities, the appearance of a text within a text, metaliterary references, ironic humor, a singular lack of sentimentality, and key scenes in nightclubs. In both works, when sentimentality appears, it is simply mocked.

As far as literary sources are concerned, if Cabrera Infante's private library in London is any indication, James Joyce is one of his most abiding interests. Although raw numbers are a less than satisfactory indication of intertextualities and an unreliable one, they at least reveal authors and subjects that fascinate him. There are forty-six books by and about Joyce in a collection of slightly fewer than two thousand volumes.[24] Cabrera Infante is most partial to *Dubliners* (translations into Spanish by him appeared in 1972 and 1973) and *Ulysses*, but he does not care for *A Portrait of the Artist as a Young Man. Finnegans Wake* simply defeats him and he can only read two or three pages of that hermetic work in a sitting. Another indication of his regard for Joyce is a visit he made to Joyce's tomb in Zurich in Spring 1993. He was impressed with the bronze sculpture of the writer and was moved by the experience. Since he usually avoids cemeteries and regards individuals who frequent such places with suspicion, it was an exceptional excursion. Although he has lived in London since 1966, he has never visited the grave of Karl Marx. When Guillermo senior journeyed to London, his granddaughter Ana took him to Highgate Cemetery.

A sampling of other authors in Cabrera Infante's library and the number of books by and about them include Jorge Luis Borges (thirty-seven), Truman Capote (six), Lewis Carroll (twenty-two), Raymond Chandler (ten), William Faulkner (ten), Ernest Hemingway (twenty), Homer (five), Malcolm Lowry (seven), and Laurence Sterne (three).

The library also contains a complete collection of the works of Charles Dickens. Although few in number, the books by Homer (there are four versions of the *Odyssey*) are significant because of their early influence on him and their connection to Joyce. A major part of the library is dedicated to literature, with nearly seven hundred volumes covering works from Cuba, Latin America, and Spain. There are close to four hundred volumes on North American and English literature. Some sixty-five books concern art and photography and there are nearly one hundred fifty on film.[25] Cabrera Infante's library also includes an extensive collection of movie videos.

Three Trapped Tigers is a nocturnal rhapsody on Havana. The work is rhapsodic in its irregular form, improvisation, emotional intensity, and ironic inversion of ancient epics. Its characters struggle as much against themselves as against the world around them. Their restless wanderings throughout the city indicate their desire to find freedom and to overcome internal as well as external limitations. They contend with circumstances beyond their control just as the work itself resists the tyranny of novelistic form. Silvestre and Arsenio Cué's random movement throughout the city, especially in the "Bachata" section of the novel, reflects a restless search for being. In *Three Trapped Tigers,* despair is often masked by laughter, but witty banter is so effectively integrated into the work that it has unleashed an explosion of humor in Spanish American fiction. Humor is now a legitimate part of Spanish American narrative as works such as Mario Vargas Llosa's *Captain Pantoja and the Special Service* or *Aunt Julia and the Scriptwriter* amply demonstrate. In *Three Trapped Tigers,* humor also has a leveling effect, reducing all of its victims to the same category. As Bakhtin has remarked: "Laughter demolishes fear and piety before an object, before a world, making of it an object of familiar contact and thus clearing the ground for an absolutely free investigation of it. Laughter is a vital factor in laying down that prerequisite for fearlessness without which it would be impossible to approach the world realistically."[26]

Three Trapped Tigers is a portrait of a society reluctant to face the truth and incapable of comprehending that it is on the road to ruin. In such a work, humor becomes an antidote to illusion. For some of the characters, like the emcee whose inane chatter opens the novel, comedy is an evasive tactic, a way of attempting to avoid or disguise reality. In that remarkable scene in the Tropicana Nightclub, the glaring light of the spotlight introduces the reader to many of the characters just as the double-edged humor begins to expose the superficialities of a foolish world. Written during a period of dramatic change in Cabrera Infante's life, *Three Trapped Tigers* captures a time and place that has become a distant memory, but that has not been allowed to fade away.

CHAPTER EIGHT

Lowry's Ghost

ONE DAY IN THE SUMMER OF 1967, WHILE CARLOS FUENTES AND Cabrera Infante were strolling back from a visit at Mario Vargas Llosa's apartment on Philbeach Gardens in London, Fuentes asked if Cabrera Infante had ever read Malcolm Lowry's *Under the Volcano.* When Cabrera Infante replied that he had not, Fuentes recommended that he read the novel and added that Luis Buñuel wanted to film the story. At that time, Carlos Fuentes was staying at a hotel near Cabrera Infante's residence, and he frequently came by the Gloucester Road apartment in the morning to use the typewriter. They talked of working on a script together, but, as so often happens in the film industry, the project eventually fell through. Lowry's account of a man's descent into self-destruction may well hold the all-time record for inspiring movie projects that never reached fruition. Cabrera Infante has pointed out, in his revealing "Un guión para la locura" ("A Script for Madness"), that Lowry himself wrote a film version of his book and that others who have taken on the task include Jorge Semprún, Dennis Potter, Melvyn Bragg, and Gabriel García Márquez.

As so often happens in such cases, when *Under the Volcano* finally made it to the screen in 1984 in a version involving none of the individuals mentioned above, it was a dismal disappointment. Leslie Halliwell summed it up well: "A subtle novel has on film become a drunken monologue, fascinating as a *tour de force* but scarcely tolerable after the first half-hour."[1] Even Albert Finney's considerable talents could not save the film. Little did Cabrera Infante suspect that his name would join the legions of the disappointed, but in a project with the American director Joseph Losey in 1972 rather than Luis Buñuel in 1967. Neither could he have guessed that the consul's dissolution in *Under the Volcano* would parallel his own descent into irrationality.

Between 1966 and 1968 other scripts, including "El Máximo!" "The Mercenary," "Birthdays," and "The Jam" were completed but never filmed, not an unusual circumstance in the movie industry. As far as Cabrera Infante was concerned, the important thing was that his efforts were generating badly needed income. "El Máximo!" of 8 August 1966 presents a sardonic view of political events and was inspired by the Cuban practice of referring to Fidel Castro as "El Máximo Líder" ("The Supreme Leader"). Although the work contains several allusions to Cuba, the script is a satirical farce based on a composite of the ludicrous characteristics of several dictators. It is a humorous compendium of megalomania in which the Supreme Leader even commands his wife to stop dreaming. The title page refers to the work as a "Marxist film" according to the philosophy of Groucho, and the script as a whole reflects Cabrera Infante's early disillusionment with the leadership of the Cuban revolution.

"The Mercenary" (1966), later titled "Universal Soldier," was based on an original story by Derek Marlow and Joe Massot, and Cabrera Infante and Joe Massot collaborated on the screenplay. In this work two hardened mercenaries spend three weeks in London and become involved with a young woman who is associated with a gang of bikers. She falls in love with one of the mercenaries, but her new lover finally realizes that his profession makes a permanent relationship impossible. She wants to accompany him on his next assignment, but he recognizes the danger and futility of the situation and declines the opportunity. The two men leave London on a Spanish ship appropriately named *Sierra Maestra*. "The Gambados" of 4 July 1967, a forty-one-page film treatment, represents a venture by Cabrera Infante and Joe Massot into the Western genre. In this satire, an unlikely trio of men seek their fortune on the North American frontier. The combination of an African American gambler, a Mexican cowboy, and a Japanese dressed as a samurai seems more appropriate for the multicultural 1990s than the divisive 1960s.

"Birthdays" (1968) was written with the cooperation of Carlos Fuentes and was based mainly on the Mexican author's short story "Tlactocatzine, del jardín de Flandes" ("In a Flemish Garden"), but elements were also culled from the novella *Aura*. Cabrera Infante finished the tightly written script of less than a hundred pages in September 1968. The story takes place in London during the same year and involves a man whose identity belongs as much to the past as the present. "The Jam," also completed in 1968, was a close rendering of Julio Cortázar's "Autopista del sur" ("The Highway to the South"). The script went through several stages and revisions. The first version, dated December 1966, was entitled "On the Speedway" and consisted of 59 pages. A revised draft under the name "The Jam," marked 11 February 1968, contained 105 pages, and another version the same year increased to 122 pages. The final draft consisted of 89 pages and also was dated 11 February 1968, but another date, handwritten and underlined in black ink, was added: May Day 1968.

Cabrera Infante worked enthusiastically on the adaptation of the Cortázar story and the result is an accomplished piece of writing that amply demonstrates his rapid mastery of the art of creating screenplays. "The Jam" presents a vision of modern life collapsing into the absurd when a massive traffic jam endures for months and becomes the norm of daily existence. It is a black comedy in which cars seem to multiply more rapidly than people. During the indefinite lull on the highway, a truck loaded with autos is turned into an apartment building and one individual is even buried in his vehicle. In its use of the absurd, "The Jam" captures the spirit of an earlier work, *A Twentieth Century Job*. There are inserts in "The Jam" from Laurel and Hardy's *Two Tars*, in which a car driven by Edgar Kennedy bumps into that of Laurel and Hardy. The minor jolt sets off a series of gradually escalating confrontations that eventually evolve into mayhem and chaos. There are a number of references to other movies and cinematic personalities in "The Jam" that make the script a film buff's delight.

Cabrera Infante and Julio Cortázar maintained a correspondence over several years, and many of their letters dealt with the frustrations involved in filming the venture. Cortázar was pleased with Cabrera Infante's faithful rendering of his story, but the producer and director, John Barry and Joe Massot, eventually made other plans. Cortázar was anxious to allow some Italian producers to film the script for a movie for television, but the contract he had signed complicated the matter. Cabrera Infante did what he could and even wrote an angry letter to John Barry: "Once more I beg of you, John (as I begged in the past both you and the infamous Joe Massot, . . .) to send Cortázar at least a letter explaining how things are going and his real contractual situation as of now."[2] However, he had essentially no leverage and accomplished little. Although the production was announced by an advertisement in the 10 April 1968 issue of *Variety,* it was never filmed, much to Cabrera Infante's distress and embarrassment. Cabrera Infante's relationship with Cortázar went well as long as he avoided politics (Cortázar admonished him on one occasion to avoid the topic), but once the practical reason for the contact ended, they drifted apart and became dedicated foes. Given Cortázar's commitment to Marxist regimes, first in Cuba and later in Nicaragua, the breakup was inevitable. It can be noted in this regard that Cabrera Infante has distinguished himself by having worthy adversaries.

Another script completed and filmed in 1967 and released the following year was a more satisfactory experience in that a movie was actually made. However, Cabrera Infante was less than pleased with the results, which he has termed an "unfunny, funny film."[3] Based on a story by Gerard Brach, the script for *Wonderwall* was created by Cabrera Infante and Joe Massot. The film was directed by Massot and featured Jack MacGowan, Jane Birkin, Irene Handl, and Richard Wattis. As he did in all of his scripts of that period, Cabrera Infante used the pseudonym G. Cain. The work is a charming screenplay full of wit and whimsy that strikes deep psychological chords even as it amuses. That is, it is a comical farce about serious emotional conflicts. In it Oscar Collins, an eccentric scientist who is about fifty years of age, devotes himself to the study of insects. In the annotated script dated 21 March 1967, Oscar is described as "a cross between Mark Twain—and Einstein. But, when excited, he *is* Ben Turpin, cross-eyed and all."[4] Oscar's placid existence of scholarly study begins to unravel when an attractive young woman moves into the apartment next to his.

Oscar is first disturbed by loud music and then by an image that is projected into his apartment through a crack in the wall that separates the two dwellings. Drawn to the opening, Oscar discovers that he can observe his stimulating neighbor. She appears to his excited eyes like the image of his favorite insect, a pink praying mantis. Oscar's worldview is tempered by what he sees through his microscope and the script blends his unusual perspective with the reality presented to the viewer/reader. From this point, Oscar becomes a voyeur and gradually opens larger and larger holes in the wall separating the two apartments. The wall symbolizes what he must overcome in order to participate fully in existence. Obstacles to Oscar's desire to establish a relationship with his beautiful neighbor include his timidity, her boyfriend, and his mother's ghostly influence.

Instructions in the script indicate that the same actor should play the parts of Oscar and the ghostly apparition of his mother. When she appears, she is in a wheelchair and is covered with cobwebs, indications of her emotionally crippling power. One by one, Oscar overcomes these obstacles, and he succeeds in banishing the psychological tyranny of his mother by defending the memory of his father. This affirmation of the paternal enables him to overcome his claustrophobic existence. The film ends with Oscar interested not only in his neighbor, but in all women. She introduces him to the excitement of erotic splendor. There is much humor in this presentation of an introverted professor tormented and transformed by his discovery of a femme fatale who looks like "*the Columbia Pictures trade mark.*"[5]

Some of the elements in "Wonderwall" point to future works, especially *Infante's Inferno* and "The Voice of the Turtle." The screenplay anticipates the subordination of all concerns to eroticism and the presentation of woman as temptress and femme fatale so prevalent in *Infante's Inferno*. However, one of the images in the film script is not carried to its logical conclusion. The female praying mantis is known for devouring its mate after the love embrace, but this fate is avoided by Oscar. This theme is broached, however, in the final section of *Infante's Inferno* when the narrator disappears into the vagina of an intended lover, and in "The Voice of the Turtle" when the violation of a sexual taboo results in death. But "Wonderwall" swerves away from such concerns in its delightful affirmation of eroticism.

Cabrera Infante was involved in the filming of *Wonderwall* and this experience was useful to him in another project. In 1969 he began working on a screenplay that eventually became the successful movie *Vanishing Point* (1971). Directed by Richard C. Sarafian and starring Barry Newman, the 20th Century Fox film was financially lucrative and has become a minor cult classic. The main character, Kowalski, seeks freedom in speed as he drives a car from Denver to the West Coast. Along the way, Kowalski becomes involved in a dangerous and reckless duel of hide-and-seek with the police in several states. His rash ways attract the attention of the authorities during his flight from reality, a journey that reaches a violent conclusion when he hurls his car into a police roadblock formed by bulldozers. During preparations for the film, Cabrera Infante traveled throughout several areas of the West and Southwest, from Death Valley to Taos and the Utah Salt Flats, looking for suitable filming locations.

Cabrera Infante left London on 15 February 1970 on a TWA flight for the United States after a three-month delay. His eternal difficulties with governmental bureaucracies continued unabated and now his adversary was the U.S. State Department. He still must present an application each time he journeys to the United States, and the issuance of a visa in London is no guarantee that he will not be detained and harassed at his point of entry. Although he became a British citizen in 1979 and was quoted by George Bush by name during the presidential campaign of 1988, as of 1992 he still remained on the State Department's infamous blacklist. His problems with the Home Office in England came to a close, as far as a visa was concerned, after he engaged a solicitor and was advised that his biggest mistake had been not to declare himself a political refugee from the beginning. He started the process of applying for British citizenship in 1972, but he was turned down and no reason was given. He initiated the procedure again in 1976 and eventually was granted citizenship in 1979. Miriam Gómez became a British citizen in 1980, a year after her husband, and they marked the occasion with a festive party. If there is an international association of bureaucracies somewhere dedicated to complicating the lives of individuals, Cabrera Infante is undoubtedly on one of its lists.

When he arrived in Hollywood, Cabrera Infante stayed at the famed Chateaux Mormont Hotel on Sunset Boulevard and signed himself in as Guillermo Cain and G. Cain on separate occasions. On the one hand, Cain had slipped out of the pages of *A Twentieth Century Job* and was reborn as a screenplay writer striving for more lucrative recognition. On the other, the variations in the signature indicate a wavering of identity or the playing of roles to diminish his uncertainties. Cabrera Infante said in his interview with Rita Guibert of October 1970 that "my film criticisms are signed G. Caín, pronounced Cah-ín. The scripts by Guillermo Cain as in Kane."[6] The variations reveal his tendency at that time to split his personality into different personas, harbingers perhaps of things to come. The evolution of the signatures is evident in the different editions of *A Twentieth Century Job*. The Cuban and Spanish editions of 1963 and 1973 feature both G. Caín and Guillermo Cabrera Infante on the title page, but the English version of 1991 uses only G. Cabrera Infante. Another significant change is the addition of a quotation from the film *Citizen Kane* in the epigraph of the English edition to underscore the connection with the Cain in the text. Clearly, the integration of personas is more complete in the most recent version. On an ironic level, *Cain* in both Spanish and English also suggests the biblical figure who was condemned to roam the earth as a fugitive.

In Hollywood, Cabrera Infante was discovering another type of curse, for although the financial rewards were considerable, there was less autonomy for a writer. The creation of a film script is a truly collaborative endeavor; producers, directors, advisers, and sometimes even actors involve themselves in the process. There are constant demands for revisions, particularly from those who would be unemployed except for the lucrative business of rewriting scripts. At times the texts of suggested changes rival in length the original screenplays. The writer who finds his or her cherished work being set upon by an endless horde of official and self-appointed critics requires great patience and considerable tolerance of frustration. There are times when it seems that everyone has a finger in the text, as artistic and commercial interests clash. The one-and-all approach to scriptwriting intensified when Cabrera Infante started working in an office in the Old Writers Building on the grounds of 20th Century Fox.

Cabrera Infante labored over the revisions and other aspects of the production and made the social rounds of the industry. Highlights included meeting the unforgettable Mae West during a filming. He had a satisfactory conversation with the aging star, who was waging a valiant but losing battle against time and fading beauty, but Cabrera Infante found her voracious sensuality and singing voice surprisingly intact. He also had dinner at the home of Robert Wise, whose credits include the film editing of *Citizen Kane* and the direction of *The Set-Up* and *The Sound of Music*. Many consider *The Set-Up* (1949) "the best boxing drama ever filmed."[7] A longtime admirer of Wise's work, Cabrera Infante was anxious to talk to him about his accomplishments, but Wise wanted to talk about Cuba. Each found the other's memories more fascinating than his own. The chat was a classic example of two curious individuals conversing at cross-purposes.

Cabrera Infante escorted Mrs. Norman Spencer, the wife of the producer of *Vanishing Point,* to the 1970 Academy Awards and discovered that the glitter and overstatement of Oscar night were predictably disappointing. More rewarding for him that evening were encounters after the ceremonies and elsewhere with two actresses, heroines of his youth, Marie Windsor and Myrna Loy. Every time he turned around, it seemed he was running into his past. He met Myrna Loy at the end of the evening in an elevator at the Chateau Marmont. Best known for her role as Nora Charles opposite William Powell in *The Thin Man* (1934), a movie that launched a series of highly successful sequels, Myrna Loy responded with gracious charm when her fan wished her a good evening. Her cheerful demeanor opened a floodgate of pleasant memories. It was an enchanting moment during a splendid visit. His stay was going well enough for him to engage as his agent in Hollywood George Litto, the man who also represented Joseph Losey. Litto negotiated a lucrative contract for him to write the script for a spy thriller. Another sign of success was the replacement of a stodgy, rented Volkswagen with a flashy, fast Lotus borrowed from the props for the movie—Arsenio Cué and Silvestre were footloose and fancy-free in Hollywood.

Cabrera Infante left Los Angeles on 13 April and spent four days in New York City before returning to London. He visited Jesse Fernández in New York and was dismayed to find him not doing well, physically or financially. He found "an absolutely God- and fortune-forsaken Jesse, devoid of teeth, living in a room filled with cats and old photos. He'd lost everything except his camera, a Leica, of course. With it, he took a memorable New York picture of me, as if we were still in 1957: I look petulant and confident. Jesse, in victory or defeat, was a consummate portraitist—the finest I ever knew. His masterpieces are the best proof: the portrait of Borges dominated by the presence of his mother, both of them sharing a Freudian sofa. Hemingway simultaneously swaggering and melancholy—you can see suicide in his face; Lezama Lima, aspiring to the condition of gourmet in a crummy cafe . . . Carlos Fuentes as doubtful dandy . . ."[8] Cabrera Infante honors Jesse with his verbal portraits, and the adjectives he uses to describe himself ("petulant and confident") reflect the glow of his successful stay in Hollywood.

Back in London he waited nearly a year before *Vanishing Point* was released, working on film scripts and a manuscript, "Cuerpos divinos" ("Divine Bodies"). After his return from Hollywood, he wrote two spy thrillers, "The Salzburg Connection" for 20th Century Fox and "A Taste for Larceny," based on a novel by Eric Ambler. Another thriller, "The Hero" was also completed during the early 1970s. *Vanishing Point* was released in 1971, a year in which he also enjoyed a Guggenheim Fellowship for creative writers and received France's Prix du Meilleur Livre Étranger for *Three Trapped Tigers*. In 1971 he also met Jorge Luis Borges and John Kobal. The latter was an accomplished film historian and critic and the author of works such as *A History of Movie Musicals, Gotta Sing, Gotta Dance,* which was first published the year they met. Kobal was the owner of a world-class collection of movie stills, probably the best in existence. In fact, the photograph of Groucho Marx that graces the cover of the Faber and Faber edition of *Holy Smoke* came from the Kobal collection. They remained close friends until Kobal's death on 27 October 1991 from complications due to AIDS. Although he was greatly distressed to see his friend withering away before him, Cabrera Infante kept in close contact with Kobal until the end. My wife and I met Kobal in Cabrera Infante's apartment on 1 August 1991, and although he was obviously a very sick man, he maintained his passion for life and film and expended a great deal of energy in animated and brilliant conversation. Although he left exhausted, he intended to see the movie *Backdraft* that evening. Kobal clung to life tenaciously and fought his illness until its bitter conclusion. Although he is not religiously inclined, Cabrera Infante attended Catholic services for Kobal with Miriam Gómez after his death.

When Cabrera Infante attended a private showing of *Vanishing Point* in a Fox theater in Soho Square, he was disappointed to discover that his script had been turned into a chase film and that the complexities of the main character had disappeared: "But I clearly wrote a film script about a man with problems in a car and Sarafian made a movie about a man in a car with problems."[9] A comparison of the unpublished script with the film reveals significant differences. The motives for Kowalski's behavior are lost in the movie or are so obscured that they hardly are recognizable. In the script Kowalski uses speed to flee from a world he cannot tolerate as he struggles with contradictory internal impulses to survive and self-destruct. Moving through space at great velocity is a way of calming his inner tensions. "Speed seems to disintoxicate the driver's soul."[10] When Kowalski drives his car into the roadblock formed by bulldozers in the movie, he does so without any hesitation or doubt, but in the script he has a moment of indecision, brakes his car, and turns it sideways in a desperate effort to avoid his fate. A complex personality struggling with inner demons is transformed in the film into a rebel without a cause.

In spite of the unsatisfactory changes, *Vanishing Point* was a box office success and did very well in the English-speaking world and in foreign countries. Alberto Moravia was particularly intrigued with and favorably disposed toward the film. In parts of Mexico slang terms such as "he pulled a Kowalski" are directly related to the actions of the main character in the movie. By the end of the decade a film that had cost $1,300,000 to produce had taken in over thirty million dollars. Since Cabrera Infante has rights to a percentage of the income, it was a fortunate venture.

The script for *Vanishing Point* contains a significant technical innovation in its use of music, which is only partially realized in the movie. Instead of using a musical sound track to comment on the action, music is generated from within the action of the film through broadcasting stations, radios, and PA systems. The purpose of this approach is clearly indicated in the foreword of the script: "Our intention is to create (or rather *to try*) a new form, the true *melo*-drama—a musical drama using pop songs as Wagner used opera. Thus the function of lyrics and tunes will be not only to comment on the action but to control it, and furthermore, to *generate* film-action. . . . For instance, in all the sequences on the highway the car-radio will become a real though disembodied presence, all invisible 'passengers' linking the driver to the remote DJ who is his guide through the maze of patrol cars, police forces, barricades." The creation of a blind DJ (Super Soul) who communicates with Kowalski through his broadcasts was a stroke of genius and one of the most dynamic features of the film.[11] Through his exuberant and hyperbolic language, Super Soul attempts to give direction to Kowalski and to save him from the inner and external forces that are moving him toward destruction. The DJ's blindness is a metaphor for Kowalski's lost soul.

The dynamics of the struggle between the impulse to live and the impulse to die have concerned Cabrera Infante since his first twelve years in Gibara. During that time, he learned firsthand of a bizarre method of death by one's own hand. Among the Cuban lower classes, in general, and women, in particular, suicide by self-immolation is not an uncommon practice. He personally remembers three such cases in Gibara "in a town as small as ours."[12] One was a young prostitute under sixteen, who responded to a threat of imprisonment by soaking herself in gasoline and setting herself on fire. She ran through a part of the town located on a hill, startling the residents with a streaking and self-consuming column of flame. In 1938 a close friend of Zoila took her life in the same manner, and Cabrera Infante remembers seeing her body in a casket with the face and neck badly burned. On another occasion, in Havana, he visited a hospital ward for women who had survived attempts at self-immolation. All were badly disfigured and many were naked, since they could not stand to have anything touching their skin. Some were in beds surrounded by mosquito netting that gave a surreal appearance to the macabre scene.

In addition to the figure of Kowalski in *Vanishing Point,* suicide appears in a story in *Así en la paz como en la guerra,* in vignettes in *View of Dawn in the Tropics,* and in the third draft of the film script "The Lost City," dated 24 April 1991. Also, in an early draft of *Three Trapped Tigers,* a character named Petra, who becomes the object of malicious gossip in the first episode of "Beginners," committed suicide by self-immolation. But the episode was deemed too melodramatic by Miriam Gómez, she and Guillermo argued over it, and in a moment of pique he simply changed it to Petra moving away. The modification is still a delicate subject in the Cabrera Infante household. The change removed an explanation for a nightmare suffered by the guilt-ridden Laura Díaz in which a dog is consumed by fire. The use of a canine in flames as an emblem of guilt is reminiscent of the dead dog rolling in the surf in James Joyce's *Ulysses.* What cultural, social, and psychological factors have converged to motivate individuals in Cuba to manifest psychic distress in such a spectacular fashion is open to question, but in Cabrera Infante's texts suicide is usually related to guilt, failure, or a fear of loss. On a personal level, he has indicated in some of his writings that Zoila was given to suicidal inclinations. Cabrera Infante's interest in this subject may have been an important factor in his attraction to Malcolm

Lowry's *Under the Volcano,* which is, among other things, the narration of an individual's inept search for oblivion.

Cabrera Infante first met Joseph Losey in February 1972 in Rome, an ironic encounter since both were living in exile in London at that time. To circumvent Guillermo's documentation problems, Miriam removed a page that contained the visa expiration date from Carola's passport and sewed it into her husband's. An American from the Midwest, Losey (1909–1984) was a casualty of the hysteria of the McCarthy era in the United States. "Losey was in Italy in 1951 shooting *Stranger on the Prowl,* an American/Italian co-production, when he learned that he had been summoned to testify before the House Un-American Activities Committee after being identified by a witness as a former Communist. Unwilling to interrupt his filming schedule, he returned to Hollywood after the completion of the shooting, only to discover that he had been blacklisted by the industry in the interim. Unable to work in America, he settled in England."[13]

However, as the McCarthy era faded in the United States, Losey stayed on in England for other reasons. According to his biographer, David Caute, "Losey's 'second exile' from Hollywood was commercial, not political. He would dearly have liked to work in America again. But Losey offered a fatal combination: irascibility and box-office failure. Bertrand Tavernier comments that the blacklist became, in the end, his alibi."[14]

Losey had been impressed with *Vanishing Point,* especially its innovative use of music, and he was interested in having similar techniques incorporated into his next production. When Cabrera Infante met Losey in Italy to discuss the writing of the movie script, the director unexpectedly and surprisingly declared: "'I was a Stalinist and I don't regret it.'" Although he was startled by Losey's candor, he was not at a loss for words and immediately replied: "'I was a Trotskyite and I don't regret it either.'"[15] On the basis of these defiant declarations, that mixed confession and challenge, a friendship was forged. Since Zoila and Guillermo senior were Stalinists and Cabrera Infante had previously waved his Trotsky banner on the pages of *Lunes de Revolución* and in *Three Trapped Tigers,* the situation was not new to him. On an emotional level, his first encounter with Losey must have had the feel of an old shoe that had never quite fit. Interestingly, among Losey's many film credits is *The Assassination of Trotsky,* an Italian-French production of 1972. According to Cabrera Infante, Losey's only shortcoming as a filmmaker was his lack of humor, but the director apparently did not require that attribute in daily life. It was Losey who first informed Cabrera Infante in a birthday greeting that the Cuban author shared his birthdate with Vladimir Ilyich Lenin.

Losey wanted the script to follow the original novel as closely as possible, and Cabrera Infante accepted the challenge, plunging himself wholeheartedly into the project for an intense three months. He read the novel six times and researched Mexican culture to capture the setting. The cultural attaché at the Mexican Embassy in London, Hugo Gutiérrez Vega, even gave him an empty mescal bottle so he could be in touch with a major cause of the consul's alcoholic downfall (the bottle still sits on a bookshelf of Cabrera Infante's London apartment). His diligent preparation is reflected in many details in the script such as a reference to the transparent Aztec skull that now resides in the British Museum and the use of the musical composition "Homage to Lorca" by Silvestre Revueltas. The script of *Vanishing Point* consisted of 128 pages, but the Lowry project was considerably longer and more complicated. When an initial draft was completed in May of 1972, it consisted of 247 pages.

Significantly, the title page gives a specific date for its completion— May Day. On one level, the mention can be regarded as an acknowledgment of Losey's interests, since that day is important in the Communist world. However, on a personal level, that particular date has a specific connection to one of the most traumatic episodes in Cabrera Infante's life, the arrest of his parents on May Day Eve in 1936. Rendered as "Mayday," it is, of course, an international distress call. Whether intentional or not, it is an unusual conjunction of telltale signs, remarkably expressive of the emotional chaos that was overtaking Cabrera Infante as he was finishing the script. During that period in 1972, Cabrera Infante was overwhelmed with fatigue; he was, in fact, physically and mentally exhausted and well into his own period of darkness and despair. Like the Day of the Dead in Lowry's text, May Day marked a reckoning with disagreeable and frightening forces as rational distinctions between time and space were replaced by dismay and confusion. Significantly, a photograph dated May Day 1888 was used in the film script "Birthdays" as a device that reveals an intimate connection between the present and the past. Also, the script of "The Jam," a project that ended in much personal embarrassment for Cabrera Infante, has scrawled in black ink on the title page "*May Day 1968.*"

Cabrera Infante's version of Lowry's novel is an engrossing and powerful screenplay, linguistically and technically complex. There are numerous takes in the first fourteen pages that introduce the reader-viewer to the narrative shifts that will transpire, and dialogue is skillfully handled. At one point the consul reveals his stubborn fatalism when he asks: "'What's the use of escaping from ourselves?'"[16] In another exchange, between the consul and a filthy man in a bar, degradation is captured by linguistic confusion. When the consul simply asks the unknown man what time it is, he receives a surprising reply: "'Sick. Sick of the cock./ You mean six o'clock?/ Yes, sí señor. Sick on the cock'."[17] One of the screenplay's more remarkable features is the astute manipulation of point of view, a challenging cinematic enterprise considering the complexity of the original work.

Since the novel is a story within a story, Cabrera Infante utilized flashbacks and flash-forwards to present the world as experienced by some of the major characters. In the introduction to "Un guión para la locura," which appeared in *Cambio 16,* Weiland Schulz-Keil is quoted as commenting: "The memories of Laurelle and the internal monologues of the consul were, respectively, treated by *flashback* and by *flash-forward.* Other passages, more descriptive, were presented by means of a camera-narrator outside of the story. Unfortunately, the script, the result of a long and detailed effort, was three times longer than a normal screenplay, and it could not be cut without losing the virtues that distinguished it."[18] All of these observations are well taken, particularly the allusion to the organic unity of the script. In this specific case, the script may well be superior to the original. Since one page of text usually translates to one minute on the screen, the length was problematic. The 247-page script would have required a four-hour movie.

In contrasting this work with the earlier *Vanishing Point,* Cabrera Infante has written: "*Vanishing Point* is the narration of an external persecution, *Under the Volcano* is the story of an internal hunt. The two protagonists are, nevertheless, incarnations of the tragic hero. *Vanishing Point* was informed by pop music and literature, *Under the Volcano* by great literature. That is, poetry from Homer to Dante to Christopher Marlowe and, at times, up to John Donne and William Blake and also, of course, James Joyce."[19] The range of intertextual references reflects the ambitions of the screenplay and the richness of the sources. The pattern of employing popular culture in one work and elite sources in another parallels what he did in *Three Trapped Tigers* and *Infante's Inferno*. He conceives of the first-mentioned work as being similar to a bolero from Cuban popular music and the latter as a classical composition. The fusion of popular culture with experimental literature in *Three Trapped Tigers* and high culture with sexuality in *Infante's Inferno* indicates that all of his works are informed by a concept of conjuncture.

When he completed the project, Cabrera Infante delivered it personally to Losey in Cannes. Although Losey found it too long, he was convinced that revisions would make it a filmable script. Losey was also pleased that Richard Burton was interested in making the film with him. Under the terms of Cabrera Infante's contract, he had received an advance of twenty-five thousand dollars, with a similar amount to be paid after the completion of the screenplay. After his return to London and while in the midst of serious mental problems, he received a letter from his English agent informing him that the French producers of the project were reclaiming the advance he had received, for breach of contract. Misjudging the severity of a conflict between the producers and the director, Cabrera Infante unwittingly had wandered into the no-man's-land between the warring factions and had delivered the script to the wrong party. He soon discovered that he indeed had broken the terms of the contract and that there was no recourse except to return the money. All he had to show for his months of intensive effort was fatigue and exhaustion. Everything seemed to be coming apart around and within him.

His mental problems started during the writing of the script as he moved in and out of periods of intense agitation and suspicion accompanied by hallucinations. He was taking an assortment of medicines that had no effect. It was as if a symbiotic relationship were developing between the consul and Cabrera Infante. Suicide attempts by Natalio Galán, a former associate on *Lunes de Revolución,* and the secretary who was working with him on the preparation of the film script did not help matters. The secretary was saved by one of her neighbors from an overdose of sleeping pills just about the time the script was being finished. Cabrera Infante did what he could to help her, although it is open to conjecture as to which one was in more need of assistance. The former music critic for *Lunes de Revolución* was not so fortunate; he was seriously injured after jumping from a window of his home in Puerto Rico. The memory of Calvert Casey's suicide three years earlier in

Rome must have been casting a long shadow again in Cabrera Infante's mind as he felt himself slipping into psychic dissolution.

In April 1972 Miriam went to Miami to see her mother, who had recently arrived from Cuba and whom she had not seen in ten years. Guillermo had insisted that she make the trip and when she left, he was in good health and spirits. She planned to return in time for them to celebrate his birthday together. However, during her two-week absence, a complete transformation took place. When she returned, she found a man in a state of agitation who claimed to have discovered the solution to all their problems and those of the world in an episode of the television program *McMillan and Wife*. On another occasion, during a trip to Barcelona made after the visit to Cannes, he had the sudden revelation while dining with an editor that his daughters in London had become the victims of terrorists through his culpability, and a telephone conversation with Ana did little to calm his fears. The trip home became a dash for safety, with Miriam concerned about her husband's condition and possible difficulties with immigration officials, since they were traveling with Costa Rican passports valid for only one week but under Cuban citizenship. Back in England, consultations with a psychoanalyst of Indian-Pakistani background were equally disastrous; the bewildered doctor arrived at hasty conclusions after only three visits and offered no hope. He was so overwhelmed by the case and so anxious to bail out that he did not even charge for all his services. Finally, no longer able to cope with the accumulated weight of a lifetime of real and imagined traumas, Cabrera Infante collapsed into a catatonic state. "I ended up a classic vegetable. I had no visible reactions, neither ate or relieved myself or apparently heard anything said to me."[20] During this turmoil, one fortunate occurrence was the arrival of a substantial check for *Vanishing Point*.

The turning point and the beginning of the long road back to normalcy took place when their general practitioner recommended an English psychiatrist, Peter Dally. The new doctor was highly competent and the author of a book in his specialty, the medicinal treatment of emotional disorders. Dally had published *Chemotherapy of Psychiatric Disorders* just five years before meeting his new patient. Although an expert and an advocate of the use of drugs in psychiatric therapy, his publication demonstrates a healthy respect for the complications that such powerful medicines can produce. In addition to being a cautious practitioner, he is also compassionate and a literary man as well. A slender individual, Dally is gracious in manner and handles a partial paralysis with grace and good cheer. His demeanor conveys gentle strength, and a stranger immediately feels comfortable in his presence. The author of a book on Elizabeth Barrett Browning and an ongoing study of Virginia Woolf, Dally's literary interests provided a fortunate match with his patient's career.

One of the treatments recommended was electroshock therapy and this forced Miriam Gómez to face one of the most difficult decisions of her life. While effective, this treatment can alter memory, and Miriam was well aware of how much her husband's writings depend on his recollections of the past. She assented to the therapy but with considerable anguish and misgivings. In the course of his hospital stay and a period of recovery, Cabrera Infante received eighteen applications of this treatment in the clinic and in the office of his physician. During a five-year period, he also went through a series of five different antidepressive medications before settling into a routine of lithium, which he has taken since 1977 and now combines with Surmontil. Adjustment to the use of such powerful drugs has not been easy. Maintaining a proper dose, for example, can easily be jeopardized by going on a diet. However, with the help of Miriam's constant vigil he has returned to a normal life.

Cabrera Infante has faced this episode, which he considers the most traumatic of his life, with typical candor. He has made no attempt to hide it from the world and even has participated in a public forum in which he and other notables, including Susan Sontag, discussed their struggles against mental and physical illness. The shock of the truth has been the modus operandi of his life and work throughout his existence, a mode of operation that has caused him many difficulties. With characteristic honesty, he believes his illness originated within himself and his family line, and he does not blame exile, which could well serve as a plausible scapegoat. Of course, detractors have made mischief with his misfortune. On the other hand, close friends such as Emir Rodríguez Monegal and Victor Batista stood by him and some offered assistance, often without being asked, throughout his season of bitter harvest. He shares his misfortune with a number of other talented people. Kay Redfield Jamison, in her remarkable *Touched with Fire*, offers scientific evidence that mood disorders occur with greater frequency among highly creative people than among the general population as a whole. For some conditions, artists are ten to forty times as likely to suffer from such illnesses.[21] Jamison includes James Barrie, William Faulkner, Ernest Hemingway, Malcolm Lowry, and Virginia Woolf among those who have suffered a similar fate.

Cabrera Infante attributes his recovery to the skill of Dr. Dally and to Miriam Gómez's devotion and determination. It is reassuring testimony to the impact that individuals can have on human affairs that his doctor's knowledge and his wife's persistence made the difference they did. Cabrera Infante holds an affectionate regard for his physician, not his habit with doctors, whom he considers traumatized people. He could, of course, add his own joyful affirmation of life and sense of humor as important factors in his rejuvenation. It is an unusual patient, for example, who asks a nurse drawing blood whether Count Dracula should be invited to the festivities. Or who tells of hearing lions roaring in the night while hospitalized and wondering if Metro-Goldwyn-Mayer was after him. When he related the latter experience to a nurse the next morning, she laughed and informed him that he was not hallucinating. The hospital was simply located near a zoo next to Regency Park. The most difficult aspect of his illness was that while in the depths of despair he lost his sense of humor, his most effective weapon against tribulation and alienation. During the process of his recovery, his former wife called collect from Havana in the middle of the night to inform him that his difficulties were related to his abandonment of her.

Paradoxically, writing, which was a factor in his downfall, helped him to recover once he left the clinic. *View of Dawn in the Tropics, Infante's Inferno,* and the unpublished "Ithaca Revisited" are among the creative texts he worked on after his hospitalization. Creative writing has become such an ingrained part of his existence that it is difficult for him to imagine one without the other. "For me living and writing are now the same thing," he declared in a public forum at the Germán Sánchez Ruipérez Foundation in Madrid on 22 October 1990. Since imaginative endeavors are so important to him, it is not always easy for him to exercise restraint once he has committed himself to a project, and he is quite capable of extending an undertaking well beyond its planned length. His doctor must have realized this when he placed limits on the number of hours he can work each day, a directive that Cabrera Infante does not always follow to the letter, but one that Miriam Gómez can invoke when necessary. Miriam watches over her husband with great care. While it is true that she is a worrier, it is well to remember that individuals frequently marry partners who share a similar trait, but to a degree that makes one's own weakness seem somehow less significant.

Joseph Losey's association with Lowry's novel did not end in 1972, and, in fact, the project went through a gradual disintegration as slow and agonizing as the consul's death. Losey left a copy of Cabrera Infante's script with Carlos Fuentes in June 1972 and they both agreed that the script needed to be revised and shortened. Richard Burton remained interested, but there were problems with financing and acquisition of the rights to the novel. Rodolfo Echeverría, the brother of the then president of Mexico, was interested in committing government funds to the project, but the enterprise of bringing Lowry's novel to the screen became a scramble between a number of different interests. As far as Cabrera Infante's association with Joseph Losey on the project was concerned, the whole affair came to an ignominious conclusion in the summer of 1974 when Mrs. Malcolm Lowry signed a contract with others to avoid the strain of a lawsuit. The project had turned into a disaster for Losey almost equal to that of Cabrera Infante. The frustrated director indicated in a letter to Mrs. Lowry dated 10 July 1974 that he regarded losing the project as a loss of a piece of his own existence.[22] His statement could apply with equal validity to Cabrera Infante's nightmarish experience.

However, as matters changed and options expired, Losey persisted in his efforts to film the project, but not always with Cabrera Infante. David Caute has indicated that Losey received a new script from Tom Ropelewski in 1976 and forwarded it on to Mrs. Lowry with the claim that it was superior to Cabrera Infante's, but she rejected it. Caute also reports that Losey approached Harold Pinter in June 1978 about a possible collaboration: "With notable disloyalty to Guillermo Cabrera Infante—given the history of the project—Losey referred to the previous scriptwriter as 'somebody else.' . . . Pinter's initial response was encouraging but he changed his mind after reading the novel. 'I find the language dense and convoluted, to the point of being impenetrable.'"[23] In retrospect, Losey's request that Cabrera Infante's script closely follow the novel was, at best, careless, and, at worst, irresponsible, because it failed to take into account the nature of Lowry's work. And Cabrera Infante's mental collapse in 1972 further complicated matters.

Cabrera Infante regards Lowry's novel as a metaphor for that author's unfortunate life, and in his own imagination the film script has taken on a similar association in his personal existence. For that reason, he has been reluctant to return to the text and has responded negatively to offers to publish it.[24] He prefers to keep Lowry's ghost confined within the pages of his powerful and dramatic screenplay; he is wary of letting the genie out of the bottle. The journey was so painful that he does not wish to retrace any of its steps. Mental fatigue and physical exhaustion undoubtedly played major roles in his breakdown. Under the imperative of deadlines imposed by others, he produced the script in English within three months, working from a highly literary and challenging text. Considering his family history, the fact that he was an anxious child, his predisposition to periods of joy and despair, and the adversities he has confronted during his life, it is remarkable that he avoided a major misfortune as long as he did. In 1972, he was simply a man challenged beyond his capacity to resist.

Images
of
History

UNLIKE THE FICTIONAL WORKS THAT PRECEDED AND FOLLOWED IT, *View of Dawn in the Tropics* is a model of restraint. *Three Trapped Tigers* and *Infante's Inferno* are exuberant creations that extend stylistic and thematic concerns to their imaginative limits, but *View of Dawn in the Tropics* is remarkably concise and constrained. Assembled during a period of deep despair, *View of Dawn in the Tropics* is a collection of vignettes based on a melancholy and dark view of Cuban history. Cabrera Infante began work on the book in 1972 after his hospitalization, but many of the segments that deal with the revolution were originally written between 1962 and 1964, when they formed part of earlier versions of *Three Trapped Tigers*. Others had been composed at different times over the years, typical of Cabrera Infante's tendency to work intermittently on several manuscripts and to revise his texts frequently. Some of the sections of

View of Dawn in the Tropics were rewritten as many as four times, and different versions of the entire text were even typed in various colors.

In many respects, *View of Dawn in the Tropics* represents a return to the past, to Cuba's collective history and to former periods in the author's literary career—even the title was originally destined for *Three Trapped Tigers*. Stylistically, many of the vignettes in this collection are similar to those that appeared in his first book, *Así en la paz como en la guerra*. Significantly, as he reorganized and created new materials, he arranged them chronologically, avoiding an earlier preference for an atemporal ordering. While working on *View of Dawn in the Tropics* between 1972 and 1974, Cabrera Infante was reassembling a fragmented memory, an essential step on his own personal road to recovery. The movement from dispersion to unity in the text paralleled his private odyssey.

For many readers the generic classification of the collection is problematic. Emir Rodríguez Monegal compared the vignettes to the "takes" of a film and concluded that cinema has a decided presence in the work.[1] Matías Montes Huidobro, who worked with Cabrera Infante on a number of journals in Cuba including *Lunes de Revolución,* classifies the work as a historical novel and argues that *Citizen Kane* and the films of Alfred Hitchcock are a predominant influence, particularly in the conception of characters as agents rather than psychological entities.[2] David William Foster has pointed out that the text is based "on narrative fragments that are neither completely interdependent nor completely autonomous."[3] The interplay of autonomy and interdependency brings to mind another influence that from a textual perspective predates that of the movies, Cabrera Infante's long-standing interest in the comics.

The function of the segments in *View of Dawn in the Tropics* is similar to that of the frames in a comic strip; most of the vignettes are decidedly visual in focus and the collection can be described as an anthology of images. Individual frames exist as singular entities, but each has more meaning when associated with others—this segmentation is essential to the organization of a comic strip and to Cabrera Infante's text. In both cases, it is left to the reader to establish connections between the separate units and to form a story, to transform the segments into a cohesive whole.

What emerges from a reading of *View of Dawn in the Tropics* is a narration of some of the central themes of Cuban history. Although all the episodes except one are grounded in Cuban history, specific names are seldom used. The suppression of such information was carried out intentionally in order to ensure the universality of the text and the emphasis of patterns that could be repeated in many cultures. That is, the relationship between specificity and generality parallels the ambiguity between individual segments and the text as a whole; in both instances an aesthetic decision was made relative to the presentation of content. Although the Spanish version contains 101 vignettes, the collection achieves cohesion and unity through consistency in style, narrative technique, and thematic content: aesthetic strategies enable the narrator to impose order on the chaos of history, but the reader is left with an uneasy recognition of the irrational forces in human existence.

As Cabrera Infante ventures back into the past, he perceives history as an unavoidably heavy burden. He responds by casting his text into a modality of opposition; that is, he condemns history but adopts a guise of detached irony. *View of Dawn in the Tropics* suggests that an unrestrained will to power runs rampant throughout Cuban history. Cabrera Infante's book is a meditation on the cruelty of history and on one of its most pitiless instruments, violence. Many critics, who have taken a cue from Cabrera Infante's own comments on his creation, have seen violence as the central concern of the book, but I believe that the deep structure of the text is based on the cruelty of nature and human beings. It is the stylization of this brutality that gives the collection its aesthetic appeal and attractiveness.

The first segment in the book describes the creation of the archipelago that would eventually form Cuba. Its natural beauty is suggested by references to lush colors, but this impression is reversed by a reference near the end of the selection to "the thousands of keys, isles, islets" as "clots of a long green wound."

> THE ISLANDS CAME OUT OF THE OCEAN as isolated isles, then the keys became mountains and the shallows, valleys. Later the islands joined to form a great island, which soon became green where it wasn't golden or reddish. Islets continued to emerge beside it; now they were keys and the island turned into an archipelago: a long island beside a great round island surrounded by thousands of islets, isles and even other islands. But since the long island had a defined form, it dominated the group, and nobody has seen the archipelago, preferring to call the island "the island" and to forget the thousands of keys, isles, islets, that border it like clots of a long green wound.

There's the island, still coming out between the ocean and the gulf: there it is.[4]

The above quotation, from the translation by Suzanne Jill Levine published by Harper and Row in 1978, is a very accurate and close rendering of the original Spanish. When the Faber and Faber edition came out in 1988, it contained significant revisions by Cabrera Infante that intensified the contrast between beauty and cruelty. The new version of the above vignette contains references to Venus and the word "beautiful" is actually used, but the island also is portrayed as an area hostile to mammals. The mention of Venus suggests the visual attractiveness of the area, an allure that belies its innate danger. Another important addition is the comparison of Cuba's form with a cayman swallowing everything around it. In this rendering, the island is even more vividly associated with a devouring reality and nature is viewed as a dangerous force.

THE ISLAND CAME OUT OF THE SEA like a Venus land: out of the foam constantly beautiful. But there were more islands. In the beginning they were solitary isles really. Then the isles turned into mountains and the shallows in between became valleys. Later the islands joined to form a bigger island which soon was green where it wasn't reddish or brown. The island under the tropic of Cancer was a haven for birds and for fish but it never was good for mammals. The island was actually an archipelago: a longer island near a round smaller island surrounded by thousands of islets and isles and even other islands that later were called keys to the ocean and the sea. Since the long and narrow island had a defined form (curiously that of a cayman) it devoured the group geographically and nobody saw the archipelago. It is still there but the natives prefer to call the island the Island and they forget all about the thousand keys, isles and islets that glut the passage around the big island like clots in a green wound that never heals. There's the island, still coming out between the sea and the gulf, garlanded by keys and cays and fastened by the stream to the ocean. There it is.[5]

In both English versions as in the Spanish original, the key trope is the simile that likens the small keys that surround the main island to clots in a green wound. The second English version extends the comparison by adding that the wound "never heals," projecting into perpetuity the existence of the lesion. These modifications clarify but do not substantially change the meaning of the passage; they simply highlight, especially for English readers, the dichotomy of beauty and cruelty that underlies the entire collection. On another level, of course, the wound can be taken as a metaphoric allusion to exile.

It is of more than passing interest that the first segment stresses the deterministic forces of geography and nature. After his childhood days in Gibara, Cabrera Infante eschewed the natural order and embraced the city and civilization. There, specifically after the fall of Batista, he acquired the belief that individuals and nations are not completely bound to history and are capable of being the masters of their own destiny. To put it simply, he had caught the utopia bug. However, the turmoil of the revolutionary process, the loss of his country, and his dramatic illness blunted that view. In *View of Dawn in the Tropics,* he returns to deterministic forces, especially the aggression and conflict of nature, a topic he had previously approached in the movie script "Wonderwall," in the imagery of the praying mantis. He would pursue this concern further in the raw sexuality of *Infante's Inferno* and "The Voice of the Turtle." These writings reflect his growing awareness that the brutality of nature had followed him into the city and that culture and civilization offered scant refuge from cruelty and the will to power. This realization is conveyed in the laconic fifth vignette: "IN WHAT OTHER COUNTRY OF THE WORLD is there a province named Matanzas, meaning 'Slaughter'?"[6]

In other segments, like the seventh, the dichotomy between nature and civilization is intensified by a subtle inversion:

IN THE ENGRAVING YOU CAN SEE A BAND OF SLAVES. They are led, four abreast, by one slave driver at the head of the line, and another spurring them on with a whip. The slaves are joined by a clamp, usually made of wood. They are barefoot and half naked, while the slave drivers wear sombreros to protect them from the sun. One of the slave drivers smokes a cigar and doesn't seem to be in a hurry to take his band to its destination, while the other snaps the whip in the air. Behind the group you can see a palm tree and several banana trees, which give the rest of the engraving an exotic, almost bucolic touch.[7]

The engraving, of course, is a stylized version of reality, further filtered by the narrator's linguistic conceptualization. This double focalization through two artistic forms is employed in many of the vignettes to create an ironic effect and to expose the pretensions of ideologies alien to the narrator. The barefoot and half-naked slaves securely clamped together and the powerful sun's rays deflected by a hat imply that the creator of the engraving perceived the slaves as manifestations of wild nature under control. The narrator undermines this illusion by noticing in the last sentence "a palm tree and several banana trees, which give the rest of the engraving an exotic, almost bucolic touch." The key phrase, "almost bucolic," clearly suggests that all is not well in this scene and reinforces other elements in the description, especially the indifference of one slave driver, who casually smokes a cigar, and the cruelty of the other, who brandishes a whip.

In another selection that uses the same technique of an ironic reversal in the last sentence, the narrator describes an engraving of an escaped slave, trapped and surrounded by pursuing dogs. The hapless man tries to defend himself from the ferocious animals with "a long knife or machete":

> IN THE ENGRAVING YOU CAN SEE AN ESCAPED SLAVE, cornered by two bloodhounds. Barefoot, in threadbare clothes, the runaway clutches a long knife or machete. One of the dogs draws dangerously near his left, while the other closes in on his right. In the middle of the engraving there's an earthen cooking pot and a low flame. You can also see a palm-leaf or straw hat. Between the fugitive and the dogs there's only the space of the knife cleaving the air. The caption says: "The runaway slave, caught by the dogs, defends himself from them like a cornered beast."[8]

The description of the slave acting like a "cornered beast" is the signature expression of the selection, a metaphoric move designed to associate the unnamed man with untamed nature and to categorize him as less than human. This attempt to reduce another to the category of a beast has been an ideological strategy since time immemorial. The narrator counters this move with his own stratagem, exposing the cruelty of those who pretend that they are instruments of civilization. The engraving's attention to details like the cooking pot and flame and the artistic rendering of such a violent scene intensifies the cruelty conveyed by this fragment from the past.

View of Dawn in the Tropics gazes into the heart of darkness of history and strips the reader of any illusions about the benign tendencies of human nature. Like Joyce, Cabrera Infante regards history as a nightmare, and like Conrad, he sees evil at the center of human experience. The engravings in the above vignettes underscore his conviction that cruelty can appear in artistic expression and his belief that culture, as well as nature, can embody violence. Indeed, in these vignettes social and political institutions simply extend and formalize the innate brutality of nature. In *View of Dawn in the Tropics* history is not regarded as evolutionary but rather as cyclical, what Torres Fierro has termed Cabrera Infante's presentation of "the eternal return of the same."[9]

The narrator of *View of Dawn in the Tropics* uses and "reads" a number of real and imagined historical artifacts including engravings, photographs, songs, popular legends, a tape recording, and other texts. He empties these artifacts of meaning by exposing them to the cold glare of consciousness, subverting their underlying assumptions or conceptions of reality. Some of the engravings and photographs appear as fixed tableaux frozen in time; in such instances, he focuses on their defining essence or essential human quality. This is particularly true in the vignette "HE'S FALLING, BEHIND THE HILL,"[10] which describes Robert Capa's timeless photograph of a Loyalist rifleman during the Spanish Civil War at the precise moment he is wounded. Capa's "The Falling Soldier" was taken "on or shortly before Sept. 5, 1936" and in the photo a piece of the top of a soldier's head is peeling back as it is struck by a bullet or a piece of shrapnel.[11] As he falls backward, his extended right arm is losing its grip on his rifle.

Stylistically, Cabrera Infante's description flows in one extended sentence and several variations of the verb *to fall* are repeated. The photograph is transformed into an image of humankind's plunge into the abyss of hatred and violence, and there is a resonance, of course, of the biblical Fall from grace. In this regard, the vignette is a synecdoche of the human condition. In other selections, satire and irony are used to reveal unarticulated values and unsavory social and political norms. Frequently, the narrator undermines the ideology implicitly embodied in an artifact by accentuating some of the system's worst features. If there is any hope in this collection, it is found in the capacity of individuals to resist tyranny, and, perhaps, in art's ability to impose order on the chaos of history. The accentuation of the visual in the vignettes, especially in the descriptions of lithographs and photographs, creates the illusion of an objectified reality that is under scrutiny and control. This imposition of order must have been reassuring to a writer in the process of restoring emotional equilibrium to his own life.

Suzanne Jill Levine, in *The Subversive Scribe,* discusses many of the intertextualities in *View of Dawn in the Tropics,* especially the literary ones, and points out that "*View's* originality lies in its critical dialogue with other historical and literary texts, in its violation of the boundaries between history and fiction, between original and translation."[12] She comments specifically on Borges and Hemingway's *Green Hills of Africa,* not surprisingly in the latter case because of Hemingway's early influence on Cabrera Infante's work and his use of a particular passage from the mentioned book as a model for his last segment. Rodríguez Monegal, in his review of *View of Dawn in the Tropics,* saw a predecessor in Borges's *Historia universal de la infamia* ("A Universal History of Infamy"), particularly in the contradictory movement between a reductionistic style and the accentuation of certain qualities. But, undoubtedly, the primary sources are historical texts themselves, and the one most frequently cited by critics, since Cabrera Infante quotes it directly, is Fernando Portuondo del Prado's *Historia de Cuba.* A quotation from Portuondo's book appears at the head of the second selection in *View of Dawn in the Tropics,* and this inclusion emphasizes intertextuality.

Cabrera Infante used the sixth edition of the Cuban textbook as a source for his rewriting of the island's history, and occasionally the borrowings are direct but significantly modified. For example, the following account in Portuondo's text describes an early encounter in Cuba, and Cabrera Infante used it extensively. Since we are comparing two texts here, we will list first the Spanish originals, beginning with the Portuondo selection, and then the English renderings:

> Un deplorable incidente interrumpió la pacífica ocupación de la Isla. Al llegar a *Caonao,* pueblo no distante del lugar donde hoy se levanta la ciudad de Camagüey, los conquistadores encontraron reunidos unos dos millares de indios en una plazuela, todos en cuclillas, esperándolos con mucho pescado y casabe. Comenzó la acostumbrada distribución de vituallas a la tropa, cuando uno de los

españoles sacó su espada y se lanzó sobre un indio, acción que imitada por otros soldados produjo terrible matanza. Ésta resultó espantosa al penetrar los españoles en una casa de grandes proporciones donde estaban reunidos unos quinientos indios, de los cuales muy pocos tuvieron oportunidad de huir. "Iba el arroyo de sangre, como si hubieran muerto muchas vacas," cuenta el padre Las Casas, testigo airado de aquella inútil carnicería.

No fué posible entonces conocer el origen del hecho. Según Velázquez los expedicionarios tuvieron noticias de que nueve españoles desembarcados en Jagua al regreso de Darién habían sido muertos cerca de Caonao, y al llegar allí y ser recibidos amistosamente "pensaron que tanta cortesía de los indios era por les matar sobre seguro." Sea como sea, Narváez presenció impávido hasta el fin la matanza.[13]

And Cabrera Infante's revision:

AL LLEGAR A UNA ALDEA GRANDE, los conquistadores encontraron reunidos en la plaza central a unos dos mil indios, que los esperaban con regalos, mucho pescado y casabe, sentados todos en cuclillas y algunos fumando. Empezaron los indios a repartir la comida cuando un soldado sacó su espada y se lanzó sobre uno de ellos cercenándole la cabeza de un solo tajo. Otros soldados imitaron la acción del primero y sin ninguna provocación empezaron a tirar sablazos a diestra y siniestra. La carnicería se hizo mayor cuando varios soldados entraron en un batey, que era una casa muy grande en la que había reunidos más de quinientos indios, "de los cuales muy pocos tuvieron oportunidad de huir." Cuenta el padre Las Casas: "Iba el arroyo de sangre como si hubieran muerto muchas vacas." Cuando se ordenó una investigación sobre el sangriento incidente, se supo que al ser recibidos los conquistadores con tal amistosidad "pensaron que tanta cortesía era por les matar de seguro."[14]

The English versions, beginning with Portuondo's text, are as follows:

A deplorable incident interrupted the peaceful occupation of the Island. On arriving at Caonao, a village not far from what is now the city of Camagüey, the conquistadores found some two thousand

Indians gathered in a small square, all of them squatting, waiting for them with a lot of fish and cassava bread. The normal distribution of provisions to the troops began, when one of the Spaniards took out his sword and attacked an Indian, an action which imitated by other soldiers produced a terrible slaughter. The latter proved horrifying when the soldiers entered a house of great proportions where there were some five hundred Indians gathered, among whom few had the chance to escape. "There was a stream of blood as if many cows had been slaughtered," Father Las Casas tells us, an angry witness to that useless carnage.

It was not possible at that time to find out the cause of the incident. According to Velázquez, the expeditionary force had heard that nine Spaniards who landed in Jagua on their return from Darién had been killed near Caonao, and on arriving there and being received in such a friendly fashion "they thought that so much courtesy was intended to kill them for sure."

Whatever the reason, Narváez witnessed undaunted the whole slaughter.

And Cabrera Infante's revision:

UPON REACHING A LARGE VILLAGE, the conquistadores found some two thousand Indians gathered in the central square, awaiting them with gifts—a quantity of fish and also cassava bread—all of them squatting and some smoking. The Indians began to hand out the food, when a soldier took out his sword and attacked one of them, lopping off his head in one stroke. Other soldiers imitated the action of the first and without any provocation began to swing their swords left and right. There was even greater butchery when several soldiers entered a *batey*, a very large house in which over five hundred Indians had gathered, "among whom few had the chance to escape." Father Las Casas tells us: "There was a stream of blood as if many cows had been slaughtered." When an investigation of the bloody incident was ordered, it was found out that the conquistadores, receiving such a friendly reception, "thought that so much courtesy was intended to kill them for sure."[15]

Cabrera Infante's rewriting is briefer, contains more graphic details of the attack, and ignores the flimsy excuses offered by the Spaniards. Portuondo, in the typical fashion of a historian, tries to straddle the event. He includes explanations given immediately after the episode on one hand, but also uses condemnatory phrases such as "deplorable incident" and "useless carnage" on the other. Although Cabrera Infante avoids such evaluative expressions, his account captures the horror of the incident more vividly and this intensifies the reader's moral revulsion. There is no intent on Cabrera Infante's part to diminish or excuse the violent tendencies of the conquistadores. His evaluations are revealed as much in the details that are emphasized or excluded as in the style. Cabrera Infante's account also suppresses specific information concerning the site of the massacre and the names of participants except Las Casas. And the language flows and is not stilted like that of the historical source.

The first Spanish edition of *View of Dawn in the Tropics* contains 101 segments. Taking into account the needs of his American readers and responding to his impulse to tinker with his creations, Cabrera Infante expanded the vignettes in the first English version published in New York to 103. Two segments were added, one concerning the struggle for independence from Spain and the other the 13 March 1957 attack on the Presidential Palace in Havana. Also, the titles of two other vignettes were modified. When the second English version appeared in London in 1988, the number of segments had expanded to 117. The new selections included one episode during the Machado dictatorship, five under Batista, and eight in the Castro period. Although the names of none of the participants are mentioned, one of the additional segments concerns the visit of Jean-Paul Sartre and Simone de Beauvoir ("THE FRENCH PHILOSOPHER AND HIS CONSTANT COMPANION")[16] to Cuba in late February and early March of 1960 and their meeting with Comandante Plinio Prieto in the colonial city of Trinidad.

The Frenchwoman finds the comandante sexually attractive, but since she speaks little Spanish and he no French, he remains oblivious to her interest. Cabrera Infante writes: "What the Frenchwoman didn't know was that the comandante didn't care for sex, only for power." Six months after their meeting, Prieto participated in a rebellion against the government and was captured and summarily executed by firing squad in September. The vignette closes: "Years later, when the French lady writer published her memoirs of her visit to the paradise island, she mentioned the interpreter but she forgot all about the comandante."[17] In this segment, a discreet omission becomes the sign of an ideological commitment. The episode is significant because *View of Dawn in the Tropics* is dedicated to the memory of Plinio Prieto and Alberto Mora. An unnamed interpreter who appears in the vignette is the writer Juan Arcocha, and the many details of the encounter come from Cabrera Infante's recollections, since he participated in the meeting.

There are other revolutionary episodes in the collection in which the narrator-observer reflects the direct involvement of the author. For example, "THE SECOND COMANDANTE" deals with his travels with a group that accompanied Fidel Castro during a search for Camilo Cienfuegos, whose plane disappeared on 28 October 1959 during a flight from Camagüey to Havana. Cienfuegos was one of the most cherished revolutionary leaders in the country, a dashing and romantic figure whose popularity was second only to that of Castro. The general populace usually referred to both leaders by their first names, creating an aura of familiarity and intimacy between the national figures and the people. After spending a night at an expropriated ranch, the search group returned to Havana: "As the plane landed, the head comandante saw the second comandante's parents waiting anxiously. Until that moment the comandante-in-chief had been joking and talking trivia, but when he saw the anxious couple he suddenly looked remorseful and went up to them to embrace them in condolence. Tears almost came to his eyes."[18] The essence of this vignette is Fidel Castro's ability to tune in to the emotions of those around him, a talent that has made him such a successful and durable leader. Cienfuegos's plane was never found and the episode raised many suspicions about foul play.[19] Cabrera Infante believes that Cienfuegos was the victim of his own imprudence by insisting that his small plane depart during a storm.

A droll detail not mentioned in the vignette is Cabrera Infante's melancholy recollection of Castro smoking all of his cigars. The "confiscated cigars" caper is narrated in *Holy Smoke* (1985), but without any mention of the purpose of the trip and only in reference to the evening spent at the ranch watching a Western on television:

Castro came into the room to watch the show and immediately he asked: "Who has a cigar?" I had four Havanas in my shirt pocket, very visible in the moonlight of the prairie. So I said I had. I *had* to. I also had to give him a cigar. As he got involved in the yarn of singing cowboys and wagons and their masters, Castro asked for a second cigar. Then for a third. Fortunately I knew that *Wagonmaster* was Ford's shortest Western, barely ninety minutes long. It was soon over. Castro stood up, all uniformed and pistoled six feet of him, and commented: "Too many songs and not enough Indians." We all agreed. Our Prime Minister was our first film critic too. He was also the sole talker, as usual: he made us turn the room into a Cuban chorus. Fortunately he was tired that night and soon went to bed, followed by his bodyguards. But before leaving he turned to me and said: "I see we have one Indian left." He was pointing at my pocket and not my head: he meant my last cigar. He referred to it as if it were one more Apache. "Do you mind if I borrow it?" What could I say? Don't mind if you do, *Comandante?* I surrendered my last cigar. When he left with that borrowed Por Larrañaga that he never paid back, I turned to the TV set. It was off but around it on the floor were the other three *tabacos,* dead soldiers all but barely smoked. Obviously prime ministers make lousy smokers.[20]

Observing his prized possessions, four cherished Por Larrañagas, going up in smoke in the mouth of another man was not a highlight of Cabrera Infante's revolutionary career. The episode revealed the author's inappropriate notion of private property as well as his insufficient sense of social sacrifice. *View of Dawn in the Tropics* narrates a sardonic slice of the excursion and *Holy Smoke* a self-mocking and amusing one, but a sense of loss and deception prevails in both.

The manuscripts of *View of Dawn in the Tropics* at the Firestone Library of Princeton University contain many episodes that have never been published. One vignette concerns the Civil War in the United States and a subject that appears in several of the published segments, the tragedy of slavery. In this instance, a leader, Abraham Lincoln, is associated with the armies he directs. "Also moving is the verse that the slaves sang during the North American War of Secession. Advance, Lincoln, advance / for you are our hope." Another selection captures the essence of the entire collection and was perhaps omitted for that reason, that is, for being too direct: "When did it all happen? When power totally corrupted its possessors? When heroes turned out to be villains? When an ideal became a cause and the cause turned into fanaticism and a crusade? When so many hopes were wrecked by total deception? These are merely rhetorical questions but all should have an answer." The writing of *View of Dawn in the Tropics* during the early years of the 1970s enabled Cabrera Infante to begin to reassemble a shattered life and to reassess the fragmented history of his native country. His journey into the past was not an easy undertaking and was fraught with emotional danger. It is not surprising that many questions remained unanswered nor that he concluded that cruelty is a predominant norm of human existence.

The Vertigo of Memory

THERE ARE TWO IMPRESSIVE ARRANGEMENTS OF MOUNTED photographs on the walls of a long corridor in the London apartment of the Cabrera Infantes. The first, which is placed on a north wall and can be seen from the study–living room area, consists mainly of literary figures, including Alejo Carpentier, José Lezama Lima, and Virgilio Piñera, but there are also portraits of the photographer Jesse Fernández and his lifelong friend, the late Nestor Almendros. The second group, which cannot be seen from the main area of the apartment, is located next to the sleeping quarters on a south wall at the end of the approximately thirty-eight-foot hallway. Twenty-eight mountings contain individual and multiple photographs, mainly of family members from several generations. There is a large frame with various pictures of Miriam Gómez, a poster of Havana proclaiming the "magic of its music and monuments" featuring Miriam when she was an actress and model, and many photos of relatives and immediate family members taken in Brussels, Cuba, and London. There are two panoramic views of Gibara and one of Havana, and a large portrait of the irascible Pepe Castro. Cabrera Infante and his brother appear together wearing identical clothing in a photograph taken in Gibara in 1937. In two others Sabá is seen as a painter and as the pale and languid victim of tuberculosis, an illness he struggled with from 1947 to 1954. Offenbach the cat appears in three of the photographs, quietly proclaiming his proud Siamese heritage.

Tucked away in the lower left corner of the entire collection, a black-and-white photo of an attractive young woman is discreetly placed among pictures of Miriam Gómez and Cabrera Infante's parents and brother. The dark-haired woman is leaning against a large rock that occupies the left side of the photograph. She is in the center of the picture, the massive rock on one side and the sea on the other. A double-frilled blouse is pulled below her shoulders. She looks dreamily into the sky, a wistful look on her face. "The most beautiful girl in the world," Miriam Gómez declares in a confidential but matter-of-fact manner and goes on to relate that the woman still lives in Havana and recently suffered a mastectomy. I think of the marvelous and sensual character in *Infante's Inferno* who insists on making love to Debussy's "La Mer," and of the harried narrator's frantic efforts to satisfy her whim by transporting a borrowed record player by bus to his married lover's apartment. She is such a scorcher that one of the characters in the novel remarks that when she opens her legs, "green smoke emerges."[1] When I ask Cabrera Infante if the girl in the photograph is indeed the model for the character in the novel, he answers with a noncommittal "Perhaps," unconvincingly avoiding my clumsy attempt to link autobiographical eroticism and fiction. A year later when the photograph came up in another context, Cabrera Infante simply identified the striking woman as "Julieta Estévez," the name of the character in *Infante's Inferno*.[2]

This vacillation in identifying origins is understandable in regard to a novel as self-referential and erotic as *Infante's Inferno*. Critical commentary could easily become a reductionist exercise in embarrassing and fruitless comparisons and identifications. In efforts to protect the guilty as well as the innocent, Cabrera Infante has declared on a number of occasions that the erotic shenanigans in the work are not his own. However, sexual exploits aside, autobiographical elements cannot be simply disregarded, because there are so many of them in this extensive book. The novel opens on 25 July 1941, as the narrator climbs the stairs at Zulueta 408, the family's second address in Havana after the move from Gibara. The first address, Monte 822, and the third, on the Avenue of the Presidents and Twenty-seventh Street, are also extensively treated, along with other precise places such as the Maternidad Privada del Vedado on Twenty-third Street, where Ana and Carola were born, and a number of specific movie theaters.

For anyone acquainted with Havana in the 1940s or 1950s or desiring to know what the city was like during those decades, *Infante's Inferno* is an archive of information. The text operates like a map of the city with cinematic, cultural, erotic, geographic, and linguistic overlays. There is also an abundance of names of actual people, like Cabrera Infante's maternal cousin Infante the Kid, and friends such as Rine Leal, Carlos Franqui, Calvert Casey, and Virgilio Piñera. Although she is not named, his first wife appears, and some episodes could possibly be associated with his second. Indeed, a good deal of material about his first marriage, not all of it favorable, was expunged from the final version of the novel. Cabrera Infante's parents and their activities in the Cuban Communist Party, his father's and his own association with the newspaper *Hoy,* and his activities on the magazine *Carteles* are examples of an extraordinary number of autobiographical references. For Brian McHale, such elements operate as "a particularly heightened form of ontological boundary-violation: like travelers to or from other worlds in science fiction, these 'visitors' from the world of autobiography function as synecdoches of their place of origin, in effect carrying their reality into the midst of the fictional world and setting off a whole series of disruptive ontological repercussions."[3] Just where the autobiography ends and the fiction begins is difficult to ascertain, and it is doubtful that the author himself always knows. As the narrator of *Infante's Inferno* reflectively declares on one occasion: "I have to be faithful to my memory even though it may betray me."[4]

José Miguel Oviedo has commented that "Cabrera Infante's stories are usually situated somewhere near the intersection of autobiography, memoir, and fiction, without corresponding exactly to any of these categories."[5] Oviedo argues for the designation of "imaginary biography" as the literary genre to which many of Cabrera Infante's writings belong, and he points out that Cabrera Infante "does not tell us his life story but instead draws from his life to invent yet another and writes about it—or, to be more precise, he writes about the life he lives while he is writing it. Certainly the antecedents of this genre are well known: Laurence Sterne, Marcel Schwob, Gertrude Stein, and of course Borges."

Pursuing a similar line of reasoning but with a significant difference, Suzanne Jill Levine views *Infante's Inferno* as "a memoir, on the edge of autobiography, signaled already in the title by 'Infante.'"[6] It is significant that "Infante" appears in both the English and Spanish versions of the book and that Cabrera Infante insists that "Infante" be capitalized in the original Spanish title, *La Habana para un Infante difunto.* While imaginary biography can be applied to many of Cabrera Infante's writings in the sense that the self is presented as an other rather than as oneself, in the case of *Infante's Inferno* it is difficult to avoid completely labels that do not include some reference to autobiography, whether they are terms such as *autobiographical fiction* or *imaginary autobiography.* Although Cabrera Infante's attitudes toward the text in this regard are at best ambivalent, he is not above answering specific questions about his life with direct references to *Infante's Inferno,* and it is difficult to forget the photographs that grace his apartment.

For my own part, recognizing the need to acknowledge the self-referentiality of the text as well as the element of self-invention in the act of writing, I prefer the term *autobiographical fiction.* Cabrera Infante admitted in an interview with Julián Ríos that "although there are multiple games of illusions, there is a great autobiographical basis to the book. Perhaps the book could be considered a kind of *Bildungsroman.*"[7] The narrator of *Infante's Inferno* is not above teasing his reader about the ontological quandary he is creating. On one occasion he remarks that a particular memory will be used in another book "where I won't be me."[8] However, Oviedo's comments about writing are helpful because of the circumstances and motivations that surrounded the creation of this particular work.

Like most of Cabrera Infante's books, *Infante's Inferno* began as fragments that eventually evolved into an extensive work. After the death of Francisco Franco in 1975, Spain went through a period of liberalization and it was possible to distribute materials that would have been banned prior to the durable dictator's demise. Cabrera Infante published in *Flashmen* two narrations, "La plus que lente" and "Mi último fracaso," that were later incorporated into *Infante's Inferno.* The first-mentioned story concerns the narrator's meditations on the role that classical music has played in his love life and the source of a record collection that was used for that purpose. The second relates the narrator's first experience in a brothel, to which he has been taken by Carlos Franqui. After Cabrera Infante published these erotic stories, Miriam Gómez cleverly suggested that he expand them into a book. The creation of *Infante's Inferno* then became an extended exercise in the remembrance of things past.

After his electroconvulsive treatments, Cabrera Infante was faced with the task of overcoming gaps in his memory, and reconstructing the past through writing became a vehicle to this end. Each of the books he worked on immediately after 1972 became an additional step back into his personal history. Relying in part on texts that had been written many years earlier, he continued working in 1973 on the manuscript of *View of Dawn in the Tropics* and published the book the following year. That work chronicled a vision of Cuba's history and incorporated episodes in which Cabrera Infante had participated. In 1973 he also composed the first draft of the still unpublished "Ithaca Revisited," the narration of his difficulties in Havana in 1965. Even the three collections of essays he published during the 1970s contain many autobiographical elements. The first to appear, *O*, in 1975, is the most self-referential and includes a chronology of his life. That collection was followed the next year by *Exorcismos de esti(l)o*, which contains many personal anecdotes. The last collection launched during the decade, *Arcadia todas las noches* (1978), is a recompilation of lectures on movie directors originally given in Havana in 1962.

In *Infante's Inferno*, written between 1975 and 1978, Cabrera Infante exploited the body's tendency to have a memory of its own and transformed desire into a window to the past. The author has remarked that in this work nostalgia is used as "the whore of memory."[9] Eroticism, the movies, and writing became the means to penetrate the misty shrouds of remembrance. That is why so many variations of "to remember" appear in the pages of *Infante's Inferno*, especially in the first section, and why there are occasional gaps ("I look for him in my memory and don't find him" 10). In this regard, writing becomes a metaphor for the novel, because as he writes, the narrator simultaneously recaptures his past and turns it into a fiction. This is the origin of all the autobiographical ambiguity and ambivalence that characterize this text and the author's attitudes toward it.

Infante's Inferno and "Mi personaje inolvidable" ("My Unforgettable Character") were published in the same year and share a similar organizational strategy. The portrait of Pepe Castro begins with specific information about the writer's favorite relative and ends with a purely imaginary account of Pepe's death in the Yucatan. A similar device is employed in *Infante's Inferno;* the book opens with the family's arrival in Havana and ends with a fantastic voyage in which a woman's body becomes an entrance into another realm. A part of this section was originally published in Venezuela in 1969 as a short story based on an anecdote told to Cabrera Infante by Virgilio Piñera.[10] He later combined Piñera's anecdote with borrowings from Jules Verne's *A Voyage to the Center of the Earth* and transformed earth into the origin of existence. The narrator follows a flirtatious woman into a movie theater, seduction in mind. Strange things begin to happen when he succeeds in getting a hand under her dress. First he loses his wedding ring, then a watch, and finally some cufflinks. All these objects are linked to circle imagery or to elements that unite or bind. The watch is even identified as a present from his father. Significantly, they are all lost. When the narrator expresses concern over the disappearance of his possessions, the woman hands him a flashlight and continues to focus her attention on the screen. She becomes a figure of mythological proportions and the narrator disappears into her vagina, swallowed by his infernal obsession. He passes into another world, and after a succession of images of ascent and descent appear, he falls into a Hitchcockian vortex: "Then there was light, a streak lightning or street lighting, the freak bolt followed by something like a crash in a crack, a fall into the fault, a death rattle in the spelunca and when I was about to wake up screaming—I fell freely into a horizontal abbess, abyss!" (410).

Even in this fanciful fiction, there are self-referential subtleties. As the narrator enters the movie house in search of his prey, he passes "through the swing doors and under the sign that said 'NO SE ADMITEN INFANTES . . .'" (394). The sign causes the reader to recall the title of the novel. "Infantes" can be taken as a direct reference to the author, or, more obliquely, to those who have not yet lost their innocence. In the English rendering of this passage, the narrator comments that he did not see the placard at that particular time, an observation that points to the importance of memory. The origin of the sign belongs to another time and place and is described in a letter to Julio Cortázar dated 8 July 1969. While explaining his reluctance to travel outside of England because of visa problems, Cabrera

Infante commented: "I do not have any guarantee . . . that they will let me re-enter this country where in any moment, as in the movie houses in Belgium, they can place that little sign 'Enfants non Admis' which my daughter Carolita insisted in translating as 'Infantes no Admitidos,' believing it a regulation directed especially at her family: avatars of family paranoia."[11] The anecdote in the letter and its textual manifestation in the novel share a common characteristic, the denial of a desired realm.

The movement into imaginative fantasy in the last sections of *Infante's Inferno* and "My Unforgettable Character" is significant. Having revealed so many self-truths, the inner need to counteract the effect becomes intense, and the result is a flight into fantasy. When the narrator ends *Infante's Inferno* with the words: "Here's where I came in," he is not only echoing the words of another character (Eloy Santos) in an earlier episode in the work; he is also signaling his intent to get out of the novel. When he enters the movie theater, the light from the screen reflecting on the woman's white dress enables him to locate her. This movement from darkness to light is repeated in the narrator's voyage into the woman's body, and both can be regarded as recastings of birth or, more accurately, a rebirth or reconception. Having rediscovered the past, it is now time to cast off its odious burden, to start anew in a recaptured innocence and fresh beginning. In this regard, the novel can be regarded as an exorcism of parental legacies, particularly maternal authority, with its distaste for sexuality (an echo of the convent school), and paternal promiscuity. And in the shadows there lurks the most bitter inheritance, the irrationality of the paternal grandfather.

Rebellion against the father is a thread that runs through many aspects of Cabrera Infante's life and work. Sometimes it is humorously expressed as in the comment in the form of a verse that precedes his review of *The Bachelor Party* in *A Twentieth Century Job*:

> "cain
> always believed
> that his father's
> problems
> were not
> the serpent's
> fault, but
> eve's."[12]

The overcoming of the paternal represents a struggle against various forces including carnality, political fanaticism, and the imperative toward inadequacy (the disapproval of literary endeavors). At one point, early in his career, the young writer even signed his name Guillermo C. Infante to avoid confusion with his father's name.

His relationship to his mother is more complex and less rejecting, for she actively encouraged his choice of a career. Indeed, things that anchor his memory to the past, such as Zulueta 408 and the movies, are described in terms of maternal imagery: "Our phase at Zulueta 408, more than a season in hell, had been a whole lifetime and was to remain behind like night. But it was really an umbilical cord which, cut off forever, remains in the navel's memory" (75). "Some time later I returned to the movies with my mother (her temper tempered by my wit), this movie lover who took me to the town theater when I was twenty-nine days old, creating for me a second umbilical cord, a tether to the theater (movies mostly)" (98). Because of her nurturing nature, Zoila is a yearned-for entity rather than a rejected one.[13] Erich Neumann has explained that "the positive femininity of the womb appears as a mouth; that is why 'lips' are attributed to female genitals, and on the basis of their positive symbolic equation the mouth, as 'upper womb,' is the birthplace of the breath and the word, the Logos."[14] That is, in Cabrera Infante's writings Zoila is not only the source of life, but of creativity as well, the very essence of his lifelong career.

Infante's Inferno is a book of adolescence with all of the egocentricity and rebellion that term implies. The will to fragmentation, so prevalent in his previous works, is more subtly expressed in this work through the ontological challenges created by the dichotomy of fiction and autobiography. Another duality is that of the narrating self and the experiencing self. The first dwells mainly in the present and the second in the past, but at times the distinction becomes blurred and the two merge. The Spanish version of the text ends with the words "aquí llegamos"[15] ("here's where we came in,"), signaling the desire to integrate a fragmented being or to telescope fragmentation into unity. The English edition takes the longed-for synthesis a step further and closes with the words "here's where I came in" (410). Time and space collapse into a new beginning as the narrator leaves behind the novel and his past existence. His voyeuristic orgy has concluded in the visual realms of a movie house and in the mind's eye of recaptured and transformed memory. The only way to escape the burden of ontological plurality is to begin again. Although there has been an occasional "ontological orgasm" (246) along the way, the search for being through eroticism has concluded.

Infante's Inferno is a novel of sexual excess, or what might be termed the predatory relationships between the sexes. The narrator, who aspires to be a Don Juan Habanero, often is as victimized by some of the formidable women in his life as they are by him. As he remarks in one instance: "Mistress meant mystery. I didn't know then that it was only the feminine form of master" (27). Margarita, the Amazon, demonstrates her abilities as an actress when she convinces the narrator that she has poisoned him. His panicky reaction provokes her laughter and the boastful admission that all has been a ruse, leaving him feeling emotionally raped. Margarita is the most psychologically complex woman in the novel. Unlike Julieta, who represents unbridled passion, Margarita brings anxiety, guilt, and superstition to the world of adults at play. In the narrator's psyche, she is the superego that responds to Julieta's id.

The novel's rampant sexuality has proved problematical for many readers. It's a long way from Doris Day to the characters in *Infante's Inferno,* who relentlessly search for the Holy Grail of erotic experiences. Regina Janes, who regards the work favorably, has declared: "But in *Infante's Inferno* he has clearly gone too far. . . . It is a brilliantly funny, dirty book that simultaneously sends up, spoofs, our Don Juans, Casanovas, and machismo and explores with extraordinary psychological insight— not to mention physiological depth—the power relations between the sexes. It also creates some remarkable female characters. To my mind, the most stunning—in every sense—is Juliet, the most beautiful girl in the world, who introduces our hero to cunnilingus, and when he balks— some Romeo—she tells him, 'Dear, love is wet and doesn't smell good.'"[16] Three years after the appearance of the Spanish version of *Infante's Inferno,* Cabrera Infante remarked that "writing is like walking down the street naked."[17] It is understandable why one of the earlier titles considered for this book was "Las confesiones de Agosto" ("Confessions in August"), a play on Saint Augustine's autobiographical *Confessions,* a work that expressed regret for a reckless youth. The point is further emphasized in a reference to *Infante's Inferno* as a "confessional" (344), a remark not contained in the original Spanish edition.

Has Cabrera Infante gone too far in this work? For many contemporary readers he has, but I believe that future generations will not be so shocked. Flaubert's *Madame Bovary* and Joyce's *Ulysses* provoked stronger reactions and even legal proceedings in their day but are hardly considered scandalous now. *Infante's Inferno* is a good example of what Camille Paglia has termed the "symbiosis of art and pornography."[18] Following Faulkner's lead in his condemnation of *Sanctuary*, Cabrera Infante has not shied away from referring to his work as a dirty book, a tactic that has not discouraged the sale of the novel. In both cases negative commentary has a diversionary function; it diverts our attention away from a consideration of the personal and psychological problems the authors were working through in their writings.[19]

Despite *Infante's Inferno*'s emphasis on sexuality, the literary quality of the novel, especially the language, cannot be denied; it is one of Cabrera Infante's best-written creations. Rosemary Geisdorfer Feal, in *Novel Lives*, has commented: "With the ironic perspective afforded by the viewpoint of the autobiographer writing about a past self, the narrator's exploits in the movie theater, in Julieta's apartment, or in the *posadas* he frequents, while often a repetition of the same activity, are never presented in the one-dimensional prose of a 'dirty book.' It is precisely the language of literature that shifts the focus from the act to the artifice, or from the story to the discourse."[20]

In addition, *Infante's Inferno* offers some of the most compelling portrayals of male and female seekers of pleasure. The novel is unrelenting in its exposure of the male psyche, and women readers are often intrigued with the power of the feminine in masculine consciousness. The novel exposes the amorality of the instinctive life that lurks just below the veneer of civilization and points out, rather convincingly, that the integration of mind and body is a problem that has yet to be resolved. From the narrator's perspective, sexuality is not devoid of troublesome emotional baggage, the price he pays for reflective consciousness. Margarita becomes the most compelling woman in the life of the narrator and she is the one who brings neuroticism and guilt to the surface of their relationship. The narrator recognizes some of these characteristics in his own personality when he tells of a friend who calls him "a part-time puritan" (344).

Infante's Inferno also chronicles the narrator's lifelong interest in popular culture, the movies, and literature. Individual works operate as reference points, enabling him to associate a particular creation with a specific individual or a time and place in the past. As he traverses the corridors of memory, cultural artifacts (a song, a book, or a movie) operate as coordinates in the map of his personal history. Along the way, he reveals many of his aesthetic preferences, and one passage is so revealing that it is worth quoting at length:

> Nothing pleases me more than vulgar sentiments, vulgar expressions, vulgarity itself. Nothing vulgar can be divine, that's true, but all vulgarity is human. Concerning the expression of vulgarity in art and literature, I think that if I'm a movie addict it is because of the movies' moving, living, lively vulgarity. I've become less and less tolerant of those movies that demand to be called films—serious, significant, and selective in their expressive form and, what's worse, in their intentions. In theater, the movies' predecessor as entertainment, I prefer minor Shakespearean comedy to the steepest (is that usage suggested to me by the use of the cothurnus?) Greek tragedy. If there's something that makes *Don Quijote* immortal (besides its author's intelligence and the creation of two archetypes) it is its vulgarity. Sterne is for me *the* eighteenth-century English writer, not the moralizing Swift or, saddling the turn of the century, Jane Austen, so proper. I am charmed by Dickens's vulgarity and can't stand George Eliot's pretensions. Given a choice, I prefer *Bel Ami* to *Madame Bovary*—an example of that vulgar artifact that is the nineteenth-century novel, all art and facts. Fortunately Joyce is as vulgar as he is creative, better than *Bel Ami* married to *Madame Bovary*. In the second half of the twentieth century the raising of pop products to the category of art (and, what's more, of culture) is not only a vindication of vulgarity but in agreement with my tastes. After all, I'm not writing a history of culture but rather putting vulgarity in its place—which is close to my art. (262)

The above excerpt can be considered a declaration of the aesthetic creed of *Infante's Inferno*. Sexuality operates as the intersection of nature and civilization in human existence, the place where instinctive forces vie with repression and control.[21] The novel does not permit the reader to enjoy the luxury of evasion, a time-honored tactic in dealing with this dilemma. Rather, it vulgarizes the topic, in the sense that it popularizes it, by narrating explicitly the various stages of sensuality throughout the course of an individual life. The narrator frequently has to choose between frustration or guilt, and although he most often elects the latter, it is seldom entirely satisfactory. It can be argued that he spends a good deal of his time mired in adolescence, obsessed with his search for pleasure, a position with which Cabrera Infante would agree. The novel peers into the heart of darkness of human sexuality, into a realm of raw impulse and selfish egocentricity where restraint and denial are alien words. Sentimentality and the cruelty and violence inherent in lasciviousness form part of the web of vulgarity the novel explores.

The use of "dead Infante" in the Spanish title and a reference to a "death rattle" in the last lines of both the English and Spanish versions indicate that something has perished. Based, of course, on Maurice Ravel's *Pavane pour une infante défunte,* the title refers to the demise of childhood and the loss of innocence. On a more basic level, the narrator's journey at the conclusion of the novel relates his return to his favorite place, the site where existence began and where he would like to see it end. Death, of course, is the other side of carnality, and in *Infante's Inferno* this feared entity lurks just below the surface of the text—suicide is even considered on a few occasions. What is overcome is adolescence and mindless sensuality in a final exorcism of the father, a legacy that is both personal and cultural. The search for being through eroticism collapses into a return to origins and a symbolic reconception and rebirth by way of the purity of the cinematic image. It is as if the narrator were intent on leaving behind the materiality of the body. The fantastic voyage at the end of the work signals the narrator's intent to get out of the novel and out of the negative aspects of his existence. Having descended into the vertigo of memory, it is now time to overcome the past and the limits of the flesh, that is, to escape the forces that bind him to his human condition. And this imaginative liberation, this *reconceptualization,* is accomplished through the literary word and the cinematic image.

The Demonic Heart of Nature

CABRERA INFANTE'S DISTASTE FOR THE VIOLENCE OF NATURE FOUND
ample expression in "La voz de la tortuga" ("The Voice of the Turtle"),
which appeared in 1990 in an anthology of horror stories published in
Spain.[1] The title is from a passage from a biblical text, "The Song of
Solomon," that speaks of the awakenings of spring: "The flowers appear
on the earth; the time of the singing *of birds* is come, and the voice of the
turtle is heard in our land" (2:12). Also known as "Song of Songs" or
"Canticles," this book of the Old Testament consists of a collection of
love poems, a fitting reference for Cabrera Infante's work, which starts
out as a love story but evolves into a narration of lust and the violation of
a taboo. The subtitle of the story, "Una historia que mi suegra me
contó" ("A Story My Mother-in-Law Told Me"), refers to the source of
the story, Carmen Díaz, who recalled seeing the protagonist's fateful end

in Pinar del Río, on the southern coast of Cuba, when she was about seven years old. The subtitle also indicates that the text we read was already an oral story when it came into the hands of the narrator.

The subtitle is followed by two quotations, one from Rudyard Kipling's *The Phantom Rickshaw* and the other from the reference manual *Cuba en la Mano* (1936). The citation from Kipling refers to the nebulous distinction between fact and fiction, and the quotation from the manual describes the type of sea turtle in the story ("caguama"). This species is known for its enormous size, which can reach five hundred pounds and, as indicated in the story, for the fact that its "flesh is not very desirable" (9). The last-mentioned quotation is doubly ironic, because in the work desire overcomes prudence, on the one hand, and, on the other, the statement proves to be deadly true.

The quotations and the reference to the origin of the story serve two functions: they give an air of authenticity to an unusual event, persuading the reader to accept the veracity of what is being told, and they establish an ironic tone that is used effectively throughout the work. The latter is particularly important because it creates a distancing effect, which enhances the aesthetic form and style of the story and makes the contents emotionally palatable. To heighten the sense of distance, the narrator breaks into the story several times and directly addresses the reader. However, the pendulum also swings the other way, and a feeling of intimacy is created by shifts in the focalization—the reader often experiences events from the perspective of different characters. These fluctuations between intimacy and distance are important strategies in the narration of a horror story. They keep the reader suspended between fascination and repulsion and are designed to prevent a complete surrender to either emotion. The playful style, which often depends on reversals of thought or contradictions, also produces a similar effect. It should be mentioned that some of the narrator's intrusions are meant for a European audience. In one instance, a Native American means of transport, a travois, is described in detail.

"The Voice of the Turtle" begins in the first-person singular as the narrator speaks of Carmen Díaz:

> When I first met my mother-in-law she was called Carmela, but she hadn't been born with that name. At four years of age she was lost for several days and her mother made a promise to the Virgin of Carmen:

if they found her alive they would call her Carmen. On the third day they found the child on an island on the other side of the river, where there were still caimans at that time. In that same river, as a child, I had seen manatees and it was still wild. Carmela swears now that she crossed the river carried by a tall, thin man with long hair who walked over the water. Everyone in the family believed that no one less than Jesus had placed her safely on the island. Since then my mother-in-law is called Carmen, Carmela. (9)

The narrator's neutrality about the veracity of Carmen's first story induces the reader to surmise that the same attitude can be taken toward the second account, but the assumption is a trap, as devious as the one that awaits the protagonist of the fable. However, the intervention of an unknown figure in the first story prepares the way for the intrusion of another element in the second. In the latter, the unexpected force is savage nature. The mention of caimans and the wildness of the river in the above quotation are the first indications that the protagonists will confront a devouring reality.

"The Voice of the Turtle" narrates the fortunes of a young man in a coastal village who falls in love with "a local beauty" (10). She responds in equal fashion to his enchantment with her: "They wanted to get married, but he was very poor. She was also very poor. Everyone in the village was poor" (10). To resolve his dilemma, he and a friend decide to leave the village "in search of fame and fortune. Ironies of destiny, he found one but not the other, although for a moment he thought that he had encountered both" (10). Recalling that the carcass of a whale washed up on a beach had provided a profitable boon to the village, the young men head for a remote and deserted beach, Los Caletones, located to the west of Gibara. (Los Caletones was a forbidden area during Cabrera Infante's childhood.) They scour the shoreline looking for some bounty from the sea, but they become discouraged and weary after a long and fruitless search. Throughout this part of the story, the two young men are described and act as if they were almost a single entity; they even share similar thoughts.

After turning back, their luck changes and they spy a sea turtle between two sand dunes. At this point, there is a break in the story as the narrator addresses the reader. This interruption is followed by a long paragraph in italics that describes the appearance and nature of the turtle and indicates that *caguama* is an Indian word. The tone of the entry imitates that of an authoritative account, but the use of quotation marks, which record the opinions of a zoologist, and a reference to Achilles and Ulysses indicate that a literary sensibility is operating here. Cabrera Infante has actually transformed information from several sources, including *Cuba en la Mano* and the *Encyclopaedia Britannica,* into his own version. The entry ends with the following words: "When the caguama has just finished spawning, its sex acquires a curiously human aspect. It has always been believed that the caguama sees badly and hears nothing, although some species have a voice, particularly when in heat. Those who have been in close contact with a caguama claim that it possesses an intelligence only possible in a mammal" (11).

When the young men approach the turtle, it emits a sigh, but oblivious to the creature's panic, they succeed after great effort in turning it over on its back. Although upside down, the turtle continues moving its flippers helplessly in the air as if it were still mobile. The young men feel superior to their defenseless prey and consider it "an immobile fortune" (13). One of them leaves to borrow a travois that they plan to use to transport the turtle back to town. The other, the one who plans to marry, remains behind to watch over their catch. The suitor, who knows that he is intellectually superior to his friend, enjoys reveries of fortune, thinking of all the products that will be made from the turtle. In his thoughts, pride and cold commercial motivation mix as he conceptualizes the animal as a source of wealth.

While examining the turtle, the suitor makes a startling discovery:

> The sex of the caguama had suddenly become visible. After spawning, says a naturalist, due to the strain of laying dozens of eggs in very little time or perhaps due to a natural process, the vagina of the caguama is exposed to the air and, in this case, to indiscreet stares. Now the turtle was exhibiting its sex, which seemed virgin, and the youth felt that curiosity was giving way to what was no more than a pure urge. He decided (or sensed) that he had to penetrate the caguama, a ready female. Right there, right now. (14)

The young man indiscreetly gazes on an emblem of revealed femininity (in the sense that the internal or mysterious is brought to light), and this invasion by the eye will be followed by a physical intrusion. That is, he violates secret and moral thresholds and, by yielding to desire, exposes humanity's vulnerability to primitive and amoral urges. The sexual character of seeing is also highlighted in the above quotation. The apprehension of a desired object by the eye leads the suitor to mistakenly conclude that seeing can be equated with mastery.

As the suitor yields to his primitive impulse, the contrast between the darkness of his skin and the whiteness of the flesh of the turtle establishes a chromatic duality. Unlike Melville's *Moby Dick,* which links whiteness to masculinity, the color is associated with femininity and nature in Cabrera Infante's work.[2] The turtle is like a blank and passive page waiting to receive a carbon inscription. But demonic nature strikes back and bestiality is chastised by a sudden and harsh punishment. Unknown to the young man, the female caguama possesses a hidden hook or spur that is designed to grasp the male of the species during intercourse to insure that fertilization will occur. When nature springs its trap on the unsuspecting suitor, the curved spur pierces him "a little above the coccyx" and passes through his body, destroying the prostate and obliterating "the two testicles (or only one)." The spur terminates its passage "inside the penis which was doubly rigid" (17). This shocking development is as surprising to the reader as it is to the victim.

When the companion returns, he is terrified to find his friend attached to the turtle and bleeding profusely. In a desperate effort to save the unfortunate suitor, he hauls the turtle with its attached human appendage back to the village on the borrowed travois. When they reach the village, the strange phenomenon attracts a large and curious crowd, including the victim's fiancée. Although the suitor opens his eyes, "no one saw it because in that moment the caguama, which, like all turtles, was immortal, exhaled a kind of painful moan that did not seem to come out of the mouth of the beast, but from between the open lips of the fiancée in front of her suitor. The young man, still on top of the turtle, closed his eyes and, for a moment, he thought that he was dreaming about his wedding night" (18). At this point, the story combines positive and negative aspects of femininity. The references to the turtle as "immortal" and as a "beast" are indications of the transcendence of its signification.

The blending of the turtle's voice with the lips of the fiancée points to the association of the animal with femininity and nature. As the suitor perishes in the ecstasy of a reverie of his wedding night, he sinks into the womb-tomb of nature. In this story, nature is not a benevolent mother but rather a devouring vampire. The caguama's sex and spur suggest a primordial symbol, that of the toothed vagina, which is referred to in Lezama Lima's *Paradiso*.[3] Erich Neumann has explained that "the destructive side of the Feminine, the destructive and deadly womb, appears most frequently in the archetypal form of a mouth bristling with teeth. We find this symbolism in an African statuette, where the tooth-studded womb is replaced by a gnashing mask, and in an Aztec likeness of the death goddess, furnished with a variety of knives and sharp teeth. This motif of the *vagina dentata* is most distinct in the mythology of the North American Indians."[4] Following Neumann's observations, Paglia points out that "the North American Indian myth of the toothed vagina (*vagina dentata*) is a gruesomely direct transcription of female power and male fear. Metaphorically, every vagina has secret teeth, for the male exits as less than when he entered. . . . For the male, every act of intercourse is a return to the mother and a capitulation to her. For men, sex is a struggle for identity. In sex, the male is consumed and released again by the toothed power that bore him, the female dragon of nature" (13–14). However, in "The Voice of the Turtle," to the male's great surprise, he is not freed and the embrace becomes eternal.

When associated with *Infante's Inferno,* especially the ending, it can be argued that "The Voice of the Turtle" is an extension of some of the deeper concerns of that autobiographical fiction, but there is also a connection to the movie script "Wonderwall." In "Wonderwall," the main character associates the object of his erotic desire with a praying mantis, but the text veers away from a logical progression or conclusion in that the female never devours the male. In "The Voice of the Turtle," however, the male surrenders his life. *Infante's Inferno* ends with a metaphorical journey into origins and a flight into fantasy that allows the narrator to leave behind the materiality of the body and to escape the forces that bind him to his human condition—he returns to the source of the word and creativity. The suitor in "The Voice of the Turtle" attempts a similar strategy when he dreams momentarily about his wedding night, but this mental evasion never allows him to escape the materiality of his sorrowful circumstance as he sinks into primeval dissolution. He represents both naive eroticism (he is a virgin) and reckless and unrestrained masculine sexuality.

"The Voice of the Turtle" narrates an encounter with primitive forces that awaken in the reader feelings of primordial dread. It is a tale of a fall from innocence, and of a transgression and reprisal set in motion by carnality and sensuality. The grim ending recalls an observation by Eric Hoffer that the only punishment that nature knows is death. Cabrera Infante's shift of the story from Pinar del Río to the outskirts of Gibara and the reference to the fiancée as a "local beauty," a key phrase frequently associated with Zoila, are examples of autobiographical details that are woven into the story, but it should be pointed out that we are speaking here of the displacement of elements rather than of entire entities.

The story's vitality and persuasiveness owe much to the adept manipulation of language and form and the appeal to deep-rooted fears and anxieties. The story suggests that dangerous erotic legacies lurk in the dark recesses of human consciousness. The basic anecdote is transformed in Cabrera Infante's skillful hands into a tragic tale with mythic implications. "The Voice of the Turtle," a story in which the hunter becomes the prey, explores the fragility of human existence in the face of the awesome forces of nature. The protagonist of the story violates a taboo and is crucified by the mysterious and paradoxical dynamics of existence. "The Voice of the Turtle" is symptomatic of Cabrera Infante's own flight from the violence of nature and his embracement of civilization and culture. Throughout his fiction, eroticism is double-edged, both paradisiacal and infernal, an intersection where order and chaos meet. It is also the place where desire is transformed into ashes as well as delight. In "The Voice of the Turtle," sexuality becomes a trap where ecstasy is synonymous with death.

The Essayistic Narrator

CABRERA INFANTE'S CAREER AS AN ESSAYIST STARTED IN THE LAST years of the 1940s, when he began writing film reviews and an analysis of the movie *The Snake Pit* won him a scholarship for the 1949 summer term at the University of Havana. During his association with *Carteles* in the 1950s, his film reviews and commentaries established him as the leading cinematic critic in Havana, and he soon acquired a reputation as an incisive intellect whose humorous and mordant style was both admired and feared. His editorship of *Lunes de Revolución* in the early 1960s consolidated his presence in the intellectual life of the capital and extended his influence well beyond the borders of his own country. His editorial work on those journals also allowed him to facilitate the careers of many writers such as Heberto Padilla, Virgilio Piñera, and Severo Sarduy, and those activities led to the formation of friendships that have lasted a lifetime.

The publication of *A Twentieth Century Job* in 1963 marked the culmination of the first period of his essayistic career and it was not long before he was penning articles for *Mundo Nuevo* in Europe. Since then he has published six books of essays and hundreds of articles that are scattered in newspapers and journals throughout Europe and the Americas. The articles, like the film scripts, have provided him with a satisfactory income and have contributed considerably to his survival in exile. Both activities have allowed him to pursue his first love, writing, while providing the mundane necessities of everyday life.

Although he is apt to write about anything, most of his essays concern creativity, cultural trends, film, the literary world, music, painting, politics, and his own life and career. Occasionally, he will pen a necrological notice, particularly if it concerns someone he has known well or whose work he admires. After reading such an essay on Manuel Puig, Nestor Almendros was moved to comment that he would have to die soon to assure himself of such an accomplished testimonial. Almendros's macabre observation revealed his admiration for the quality of the piece as well as his awareness of his own impending demise. Whatever the topic, Cabrera Infante's essays are written with care and with an eye and ear to artistic elaboration. It is difficult for him to turn out a casual piece; only deadlines compel him to let go of an article before he feels it is ready for publication. His inclination to blur the distinctions between genres is as evident in the articles as in his fictional creations. Alliteration, puns, parody, and humor are used extensively in the essays and intellectual discourse often is blended with fictional and autobiographical elements. There is also a decided tendency to mix high and popular culture. His first criterion always has been artistic merit, wherever it is found. Zoila's disdain for elitist pretension lives on in his own iconoclastic bent.

´ Despite his considerable accomplishments as a commentator in books and journals, Cabrera Infante's reputation as a writer of fiction has overshadowed his essayistic achievements. This is not an uncommon occurrence in the careers of many creative writers. For example, the same can be said of Jorge Luis Borges, Carlos Fuentes, and Mario Vargas Llosa. In Cabrera Infante's case, international fame came with the publication of *Three Trapped Tigers* and was consolidated with *View of Dawn in the Tropics* and *Infante's Inferno*. However, his recent essays have been very successful. The first edition of *Mea Cuba,* in 1992, sold out in a month, and it appeared in an English translation in 1994. *Holy Smoke,* which was written and published in English in 1985, also did very well, and the publication of the English version of *A Twentieth Century Job* in 1991 attracted considerable attention and resulted in invitations to be guest director of the Telluride and Miami Film Festivals. He also served as a juror along with Clint Eastwood and Catherine Deneuve, among others, at the Cannes Film Festival of 1994. The jury's decision to give the best film award to *Pulp Fiction* raised a few eyebrows in the movie industry.

Mea Cuba brings together political essays written and published over a period of three decades and reflects the vicissitudes of his painful relationship with the Cuban revolution, an issue that still provokes considerable passion. Cabrera Infante has remarked that if one is Cuban, it is as impossible to escape Castro as it was for a Soviet to escape Stalin. The introduction of the Mexican edition of *Mea Cuba* during a public forum in Mexico City was marred by bomb threats.[1] There is undoubtedly considerable information in the book that is embarrassing to the Cuban government, such as a special request Haydée Santamaría made of Mario Vargas Llosa in 1967. Vargas Llosa was asked to donate the prize money from the Rómulo Gallegos literary award to Venezuelan rebels. Had he accepted the arrangement, he would have been reimbursed by the Cuban government through monthly payments.[2]

Several of Cabrera Infante's essayistic books are collections of diverse articles, a reflection of his interest in fragments. Many of the essays in *O* (1975), one of the more autobiographical volumes, were first published in *Mundo Nuevo. Exorcismos de esti(l)o* ("Exorcisms of Style") of 1976 is a potpourri of brief selections on the use and abuse of language and on the relations between linguistic expression and structure. One of the exercises even transforms a prose selection into different forms of poetry. There are also poetic selections in English, an indication of an intensification of his interest and proficiency in that language, inclinations that would find full expression in *Holy Smoke.* Although Haydée Santamaría, the former director of Casa de las Américas, is not mentioned by name, an unusual admission by her is narrated. For many years she had thought that "Marx y Engels were one person, like Ortega y Gasset," and this confusion becomes the basis for a series of humorous litanies.[3] The same incident is narrated with her name and more details in *Mea Cuba,* along with an account of her tragic suicide in July 1980.[4] The humorous tone of many of the segments in *Exorcismos* is a sign that Cabrera Infante was beginning to move out from under the long shadow cast by the events of 1972.

Although many of his articles have been gathered into books, literally hundreds remain scattered in newspapers and magazines, and some of his best can be found among them. A representative example is his droll "Borges y yo" ("Borges and I"), an obvious parody of the title of one of the Argentine's most anthologized pieces. Borges's playful discourse on identity comes as close to perfection as one can achieve in a selection of prose. Cabrera Infante has been an admirer of Borges since Carlos Franqui lent him the translation of Faulkner's *The Wild Palms* back in Havana in the 1940s. Two days after Borges's death in June 1986, Cabrera Infante published his article in the 16 June issue of *El País*.

In the opening of his playful and warm testimonial, Cabrera Infante mimics both the style and content of the original, synthesizing different times and identities through an adroit series of challenging verbal sequences: "It was to the other man, Borges, that things happened. I only relate them. At times I used to see his name in an English dictionary: 'Jorge Luis Borges. Argentinean poet and scholar.' We would then walk through London and we will stop at a square that Borges can no longer see and I tell him its name. Now Borges has come to offer a series of literary evenings in Central Hall at Westminster."[5] Cabrera Infante wages his own war against time by using verbs in several tenses. The introduction defies death with the immortality of the word, and it prepares the reader for what is to come, a portrait of an elusive and mischievous Borges.

In these pages two literary pranksters are on the loose. We see Borges downing a glass of brandy in one gulp to calm his nerves before a talk, imitating Mae West's famous "'come up and see me sometime'" and repeating, as if it were a new revelation, a bit of information that originated with him. For his own part, Cabrera Infante claims to have momentarily left the writer in the middle of a busy street at Berkeley Square to ascertain if he really could not see and to discover, once and for all, whether his blindness was merely a literary pretense designed to emulate Milton and Homer. Of course, Borges gets the last laugh. After all, how could Cabrera Infante expect to get the better of someone who always aspired to be an evil man? The article moves from anecdotal precision to speculative fancy, a strategy used in other works such as the portrait of Pepe Castro, "My Unforgettable Character," and the ending of *Infante's Inferno*. "Borges and I" closes with an imaginary conversation between Borges and his biographer Emir Rodríguez Monegal as they wander among some celestial clouds. It is a witty and affectionate portrait of an esteemed colleague.

As far as Cabrera Infante's books are concerned, his best essayistic endeavors, in my view, are found in *A Twentieth Century Job* and *Holy Smoke,* two of his most organically unified essays, although it is hard to top *Exorcismos* for sheer enjoyment or *Mea Cuba* for stark drama. His two most recent endeavors, *Holy Smoke* and *Mea Cuba,* contain a wealth of detailed information, an indication of the thorough research and prodigious memory that went into both creations. *Holy Smoke* deals with the history and cultural evolution of tobacco and its manifestations in everyday life and film. The volume marks a significant milestone in Cabrera Infante's career since it is his first book written in English, an impeccably crafted and pun-encrusted linguistic feat. In this regard, he has followed in the footsteps of writers such as Joseph Conrad, Arthur Koestler, and Vladimir Nabokov in their movement between different cultures and languages. In particular, he shares with Conrad and Koestler the acquisition of British citizenship.

Holy Smoke straddles the cultures of the English and Hispanic worlds and pays tribute to the Native American origins of tobacco. The essay begins with references to two scenes from *Bride of Frankenstein* and to the first encounter of two of Columbus's men, Rodrigo de Xeres and Luis de Torres, with tobacco in the vicinity of Cabrera Infante's native Gibara. He comments on the monster's being offered cigars in the film, first by a hermit and then by Dr. Pretorious. The good doctor remarks that smoking is his only vice as he attempts to induce the creature to become somebody by having a smoke. Cabrera Infante continues: "These two short sequences in a most felicitous film contain the entire history of the five-century-old relationship between the European gentleman and his smoke. It all started in the New World, where smoking was not for gentlemen but for sorcerers—and for the incumbent Indian chief: he who wore the feathers."[6]

The scenes in the film and the historic encounter in the New World become synecdoches of the continuing battle between smokers and nonsmokers, a conflict that began for Cabrera Infante in his own family, since Guillermo senior rejected the weed while Zoila embraced it. The book is dedicated to his father "who at age 84 doesn't smoke yet."

Cabrera Infante pursues this theme throughout the work and returns to the subject in the closing paragraph of his essay:

> Now I know why Dr Pretorius, a brazen brigand, sounded so apologetic when he confessed to the Monster that he smoked cigars—his only vice. It was simply because Dr Pretorius *was* apologetic. He had been reduced to smoke his cigar in an old, sunken decrepit crypt: *savoir vivre* is now possible among corpses only. Nevertheless, when everything is said ("Cigarettes can burn a hole in your pocket") and done ("Ban smoking now—and shoot the bastard when you see the grey of his smoke!"), I'll still be able to go back to our dawn again to try and regress and redress. There and then Chris Columbus, that Jewish-Italian stand-up comedian, a *primo cartello* in the New World, a top banana already, with his name above the title (*America, America!*), actually addressed the Shaman after the chamade, a showman finally accepting the fact that this cham was a sham and no kin to the Khan. He firmly but courteously rejected his offer of that second cigar in history—de Xeres was here, remember? Columbus changing colours like a chameleon with a gentle, sweet disposition, as a discoverer should, the first declared non-smoker on record, begging to be excused by genuflecting, said finally:
>   *Do you mind if I don't smoke?* (238)

The dichotomy of smokers and nonsmokers radiates throughout the text and provides a foil for much of the work's humor. In his 1985 interview with Nedda G. de Anhalt, Cabrera Infante pointed out that the quip attributed to Columbus in the above quotation really came from Groucho Marx.[7] In addition to Columbus, Bartolomé de las Casas and Gonzalo Fernández de Oviedo are among other historical notables cited who detested tobacco. Cabrera Infante also quotes a candidate for the most disgusting cigar smoker in history, Flaubert, who boasted that in his youth, he always bedded the ugliest prostitute in a bordello in front of a retinue of friends, with a cigar in his mouth. For his own part, like any good cigar smoker, Cabrera Infante gets into the act by expressing his hatred of cigarettes because he "cannot stand the smell of burning paper: it reminds me of *Fahrenheit 451,* a bad movie, and the book pyre, a bad dream" (69). Although the scenes from *Bride of Frankenstein* are quite appropriate as signature references, I personally would have preferred the episode from Mel Brooks's *Young Frankenstein* in which the blind hermit, played by Gene Hackman, no less, mistakenly lights up the monster's thumb rather than a cigar. This is, of course, the opinion of a nonsmoker who has been known to partake occasionally of a cigar. Cabrera Infante cites the scene from *Young Frankenstein,* but in support of his preference for the work of the cigar-smoking Brooks over that of the non-cigar-smoking Woody Allen: "God is always making us choose between two Jews: Cain or Abel, Jesus or Judas, Marx or Engels, Freud or Wilhelm Reich, Lou Andreas Salome or Alma Mahler, Gropius, Werfel, etc. etc. Now it's Mel Brooks or Woody Allen" (224).

The adversarial relationships fostered by tobacco are very much a part of the contemporary cultural scene, and Cabrera Infante even foresees the demise of his cherished hobby: "One day cigars too will be the smoke of yesteryear" (116). In fact, the book conveys the sense that he is writing the swan song of smoking—at least, of cigars. But, in his view, there has been conflict over the use of tobacco ever since the days of Columbus. This topic has been the theme of other works and none has been more delightfully executed than Sir James Matthew Barrie's *My Lady Nicotine* (1890), a work referred to in *Holy Smoke* as having "the most splendid title of all books on smoking" (64). The Scottish writer is best known for his play, *Peter Pan* (1904), about a boy who refused to grow up, but the narrator of *My Lady Nicotine* exhibits some of the same characteristics. Barrie's book is a droll account of a Victorian gentleman's infatuation with tobacco and of his momentary abandonment of his vice for the sake of matrimony: "The lady who was willing to fling herself away on me said that I must choose between it and her. This deferred our marriage for six months."[8]

Although the narrator professes to have joined the ranks of nonsmokers, all of his arguments against smoking are double-edged: "The very smell of tobacco is abominable, for one cannot get it out of the curtains, and there is little pleasure in existence unless the curtains are all right" (15). Barrie casts his narrative into an ironic struggle between the sexes in which bachelorhood is associated with smoking. Such a tactic would have carried little weight in Cuba or Spain at that time because of the wide use of tobacco among women in those countries. Barrie recounts with great relish his long relationship with tobacco and relates with mock solemnity the arguments offered by his smoking companions, who are scandalized by his decision. Among their pleas are assertions of the medicinal benefits of smoking, a claim that goes back to the magical attributes Native Americans associated with tobacco. The narrator even speaks of a doctor's description of an ailment known as "non-tobacco throat" (248). For his part, the narrator divides history into "the pre-smoking and the smoking" (106) and claims that the glorious achievements of the Elizabethan age are due to tobacco: "When Raleigh, in honour of whom England should have changed its name, introduced tobacco into this country, the glorious Elizabethan age began. . . . The whole country was stirred by the ambition to live up to tobacco" (106–107). In addition to its mordant wit, *My Lady Nicotine* contains a good deal of information about the smoking practices of Victorian England. Barrie's volume was a source of data as well as an inspirational model for *Holy Smoke*.

Sir Compton Mackenzie's *Sublime Tobacco* of 1957 combines his personal experience with smoking and an affectionate history of tobacco. It is the type of book that Cabrera Infante's maternal great-grandparents, Sebastián Castro and Caridad Espinoza, could have written—an unabashed and uncompromising affirmation of the vice. Caridad spent a good deal of her time chewing tobacco leaves and Sebastián smoked cigars all day: "He used to smoke a third of each cigar leaving the butts strewn all over the house. 'For later.' Then he would smoke the cold dead cigars but he always seemed to have a fresh cigar in his mouth. His wife, my great-grandmother, chewed tobacco leaves and went about the house carrying a glass cuspidor as if it were an opaline jewel."[9]

Mackenzie goes so far in his defense of smoking that he asserts that even if tobacco is the cause of some illnesses, its benefits far outweigh any negatives. Cabrera Infante is less sanguine and includes cancer as one of the New World's legacies to the Old. He also points out that a proper cigar smoker never inhales. Like Cabrera Infante's relatives, Mackenzie lived a long life despite his persistent use of tobacco; he seemed destined to smoke. Even his first experience did not produce the customary queasiness, perhaps, he speculates, because of a Native American ancestor in his past. "It was meet that I, with a long American ancestry on my mother's side back to the time of the first colonization of Maryland, should be allowed by an American cousin my first experience of the richest gift that the New World gave to the Old. I like to imagine that my immunity from any of the ill-effects which in moral tales always accompany childhood's first experiments with tobacco may have been an inheritance from some Red Indian ancestress of three centuries ago."[10] There was a time, of course, when smoking for the first time was a rite of passage for the young, and it has a long tradition in literature and lore. Unlike Mackenzie, Cabrera Infante opted for the traditional version of the event and relates how he vomited when he attempted to follow in the footsteps of Huckleberry Finn and made the mistake of inhaling the smoke of a cigar.

When Mackenzie's father discovered that he and his brother were smoking the stubs of discarded cigars in the father's Petersen pipe, he gave them each an entire cigar, believing that an induced illness would teach them a lesson. To his surprise, the cigars produced no ill effects. "I think my father may never have really got over his early attempt to cure us of premature smoking by parting with two of his best cigars to no good purpose. At any rate, he never offered me another until I was over twenty" (6). Cabrera Infante guards his cigars just as jealously. One of Miriam Gómez's most grievous faux pas during a long and successful marriage is immortalized in *Holy Smoke*. Carried away by the enthusiasm of a friend whose wife had just given birth, Miriam gave one of her husband's most cherished possessions to the jubilant father. It is a mistake that has not been repeated. During weeks spent in Cabrera Infante's apartment working with his papers, I was treated to many gracious amenities, but the offer of a cigar was never among them. Nor were any other acquaintances or family members tendered one of the jewels carefully stored in boxes in the most accessible section of the refrigerator. In his defense, it must be granted that nonsmokers have a notorious reputation for accepting cigars, and for such individuals a smoke is only a smoke, devoid of the passion a connoisseur experiences.

Why smokers, and specifically cigar smokers, guard their possessions so covetously is open to question, but there may be sexual connotations to their actions. Cabrera Infante speculates:

Since their invention cigarettes were lusted as a woman's thing. Freudians might contend that if the cigar is just a surrogate phallus, a cigarette is only a clitoris misplaced: it is now between the lips, not immediately above them. "*Le malade fume des cigarettes. Freud fume des cigars—voilà tout!*" said Alain Robbe-Grillet in conversation. (96)

Later in *Holy Smoke,* he declares directly that "a cigar is a sexual symbol in Cuba" and cites the title of a hit song in Cuba from 1958, sung by Beny Moré, "Se te cayó el tabaco" ("Your Cigar Went Limp"), "the Cuban way of saying that you have become impotent" (160). Such comments are reminiscent of *Infante's Inferno*, one of many indications that *Holy Smoke* is a joyous synthesis of elements found in many of Cabrera Infante's previous works. A number of old friends, literary and actual, appear in its pages, including Leopold Bloom, characters from Sterne's *Tristram Shandy*, members of his family, Carlos Franqui, and John Kobal. There are also references to the works of Raymond Chandler, Hemingway, and Faulkner. Even Chiquita Banana, who first turned up in the short story "A Ballad of Bullets and Bull's Eyes," the work that led to his imprisonment in Batista's Cuba, makes an appearance.

One of the most detailed sources of information for *Holy Smoke*, as well as of stylistic devices, is Fernando Ortiz's *Cuban Counterpoint, Tobacco and Sugar*, a key text in Cuban cultural interpretation. Specific information gleaned from Ortiz's work includes items such as the influence of Luis Marx on the cultivation of tobacco and all the aura surrounding *vitolas*, a word that can be loosely translated as cigar bands and/or the category and quality of brands. Cabrera Infante's own love for words and interest in history were stimulated by Ortiz's etymological curiosity and historical investigations. He makes good use, for example, of information provided by Ortiz about Rodrigo de Xeres and Luis de Torres, who are used in *Holy Smoke* as icons of discovery and misfortune. However, just as there are points of convergence between the two texts, there are also divergences and disagreements. For example, Cabrera Infante does not accept Ortiz's conclusion that Columbus's men first saw Native Americans smoking near what is now known as Manatí Bay, or that cigar rolling is a particular Cuban art, superior to that of all others. As he rewrites this and other texts, Cabrera Infante incorporates new information, interpretations, and mythologies into those that have preceded him.

Ortiz, in his classic study of the influence of the sugar and tobacco industries on Cuban history and culture, argues that "tobacco and sugar are the two most important figures in the history of Cuba," and that the relationship between the two is both complementary and antagonistic.[11] Ortiz's essay, which owes as much to literary imagination and tradition as to analytic discourse, associates a number of characteristics with the two products:

The one is white, the other dark. Sugar is sweet and odorless; tobacco bitter and aromatic. Always in contrast! Food and poison, waking and drowsing, energy and dream, delight of the flesh and delight of the spirit, sensuality and thought, the satisfaction of an appetite and the contemplation of a moment's illusion, calories of nourishment and puffs of fantasy . . . reality and deception, virtue and vice. Sugar is *she;* tobacco is *he.* Sugar cane was the gift of the gods, tobacco of the devils; she is the daughter of Apollo, he is the offspring of Persephone.[12]

Taking a cue from such passages, Cabrera Infante creates his own playful comparison of cigarettes and cigars:

Cigarettes are the perverse opposite of cigars: cigars are long, cigarettes are short, cigars are dark, cigarettes are white, cigars are thick, cigarettes are slim, cigars smell strongly, cigarettes are perfumed, cigarettes are for the lips while cigars are for both mouth and teeth, cigarettes never go out but burn up quickly, while cigars seem to last forever, cigars are big brutes, cigarettes are as feminine as jewels. Cigarettes are for chain-smoking, cigars must be smoked one at a time, peaceably, with all the leisure in the world. Cigarettes are of the instant, cigars are for eternity. (85)

In another selection in which he touts the virtues of the cigar over pipes and cigarettes, Cabrera Infante also uses the contrastive technique to good effect and associates one passion with another: "A cigarette is a dangling particule in your lips and the pipe is all clenched teeth and no fury. But a good cigar is like a passion: first it is set alight, then it burns red, then scarlet, scary, scarry—then it glows ember, grows amber and becomes ashes: a passion spent. Kipling was wrong. A cigar *is* a woman and a woman is a smoke" (30–31). Cabrera Infante directly refers to more than fifty books and articles in his exhaustive treatment of the relationships between tobacco and its human consumers, including, as a random sampling, Robert Burton's *Anatomy of Melancholy,* Count Corti's *A History of Smoking,* Raymond Jahn's *Tobacco Dictionary,* Sydney Clark's *All the Best in Cuba,* and the Comtesse de Merlin's *Voyage à la Havane.* The appendix includes quotations from many literary sources as well as brief commentaries from his own pen. He even quotes the infamous Bonnie Parker of *Bonnie and Clyde* fame.

The most brilliant and innovative aspect of *Holy Smoke* is the study of the role of smoking in the movies. Some of Cabrera Infante's observations are categorical declarations about individual actors and films, such as his claim that Edward G. Robinson was the "greatest cigar smoker ever" (193). Others point out how cigarettes and cigars could embody the personas of different actors: "A languid cigarette at the end of a limp wrist was to Marlene Dietrich what the tough stub between forefinger and thumb was to Humphrey Bogart: an extension of the persona, not a prop" (90). Then there are whole sections that analyze what an academic would call the semiotics of smoking in film. Particularly insightful are the comments on how Orson Welles introduced "the theme of smoking as character" in *Citizen Kane* (193). This commentary is carried out so skillfully and with such flair that the reader is left in a momentary quandary over the intentions of the passage. Is Cabrera Infante serious or is he simply mocking a cherished intellectual pretension? His last two sentences in this particular section add weight to the second conclusion: "The cigar could be a phallic symbol in *Citizen Kane*—and then again it could not. Auden, who should know, called our attention to a distinct possibility: 'Clearly even Freud said that a cigar could be simply a cigar' " (195).

The references to cinema in *Holy Smoke* are as extensive as the acknowledgments of written sources. Such a wealth of information is incorporated into the text by a procedure approaching free association. This technique is accentuated by the absence of division by chapters and the use of few headings. Because of these strategies, *Holy Smoke* is best read in segments. Like a good cigar, it is best appreciated in spurts similar to the puffs of a savoring smoke. The book began as a fragment, as an article originally intended for *The New Yorker,* but as Cabrera Infante became caught up in three of his consuming passions, Cuba, cigars, and cinema, it evolved into a more extensive text. In his search for the perfect smoke, he describes how "just before midnight the cigar becomes fragrance, then smoke, then myth, then ashes, then memory, then nothing" (126). This observation recalls an earlier comment in the text: "What Wilde said of music is also true of smoking: it always makes you remember a time that never was" (28). The same could be said of literature and of any of the images created by words in which memory precedes the void. It is easy to imagine Cabrera Infante smoking at midnight, peering at the world through diminutive, steel-rimmed glasses, his piercing eyes fixed on a momentary unease suspended in space. The graying hair and bearded chin frame the darker-colored moustache and the eyes. There is a hint of inquisitive menace in his gaze. The impassive face masks years of pain. He sits in his black leather chair, motionless in a cloud of smoke, a cigar coiled in his hand, like a crouching tiger waiting to strike a swift, staccato blow.

N O T E S

1. A Distant Place

1. Heberto Padilla, *Self-Portrait of the Other*, 34–35.
2. *Holy Smoke*, 25.
3. *Infante's Inferno*, 293.
4. Danubio Torres Fierro, "Guillermo Cabrera Infante," 65. This interview is also available in *Vuelta*, October 1977.
5. "Del gofio al golfo," 139.
6. *Infante's Inferno*, 231.
7. "Del gofio al golfo," 140.
8. "Del gofio al golfo," 140.
9. Interview, 19 June 1990.
10. *Infante's Inferno*, 22.
11. Interview, 19 June 1990.
12. Interview, 21 August 1991.
13. Torres Fierro, "Guillermo Cabrera Infante," 71–72.
14. Interview, 21 June 1990.
15. *Infante's Inferno*, 22.
16. Conversation with Miriam Gómez, 12 October 1993.

2. A Room Without a View

1. Interview, 19 June 1990.
2. *Infante's Inferno*, 3.
3. Interview, 19 June 1990.
4. Carlos Franqui, *Diario de la revolución cubana*, 51.
5. *Infante's Inferno*, 287.
6. "Holmes Sweet Holmes," 25.
7. Bob Dorian, *Bob Dorian's Classic Movies*, 189.
8. "Foreword, Portrait of a Tyrant as an Aging Tyro," in Carlos Franqui, *Family Portrait with Fidel*, x.
9. Heberto Padilla, *Self-Portrait of the Other*, 39.
10. Padilla, *Self-Portrait*, 41.
11. Mario Vargas Llosa, *El pez en el agua*, 283.
12. Frederick R. Karl, *William Faulkner: American Writer*, 603.
13. Walter J. Ong, *Orality and Literacy*, 29.
14. Anne Marie Mergier, "Entrevista con Guillermo Cabrera Infante," 62.
15. "Antonio Ortega vuelve a Asturias," 62.
16. *Infante's Inferno*, 100.
17. Julio Matas, "Guillermo Cabrera Infante: Caricaturas tempranas," 597.

18. "Antonio Ortega vuelve a Asturias," 62.

19. *Infante's Inferno,* 160.

20. *Así en la paz como en la guerra* (1974), 52.

21. The experience is narrated in "Obsceno" in the collection of autobiographical works *O* (1975) and in the translation "English Profanities." For the latter see *Writes of Passage* or Doris Meyer, ed., *Lives on the Line* (1988).

22. Acceptance speech of honorary doctorate, Florida International University, 3 May 1993.

23. Interview, 21 June 1990.

24. Interview, 21 June 1990.

25. *Carteles,* 15 August 1954 and 5 September 1954.

3. A Momentary Splendor

1. "A Portrait of Jesse," 35.

2. Georgie Anne Geyer, *Guerrilla Prince,* 184–85.

3. "Todd's Little Garden Party," *Life* (28 October, 1957): 149.

4. "A Portrait of Jesse," 35.

5. "Muerte en la barbería," 924.

6. A summary of the assault is contained in Hugh Thomas, *Cuba, the Pursuit of Freedom,* 923–931.

7. Heberto Padilla, *Self-Portrait of the Other,* 41.

8. "Foreword," in Carlos Franqui, *Family Portrait with Fidel,* xiii.

9. Franqui, *Family Portrait with Fidel,* 129. Other revealing accounts of the demise of the journal can be found in chapter 6 of Heberto Padilla's *Self-Portrait of the Other* as well as Cabrera Infante's "Bites from the Bearded Crocodile," "Cuba's Shadow," and *Mea Cuba* (1992), 641–86. See also K. S. Karol, *Guerrillas in Power,* 237–41; Seymour Menton, *Prose Fiction of the Cuban Revolution,* 126–29; and William Luis, "Autopsia de *Lunes de Revolución,* Entrevista a Pablo Armando Fernández."

10. "Bites from the Bearded Crocodile," 5.

11. Padilla, *Self-Portrait,* 57.

12. "Bites from the Bearded Crocodile," 5.

13. Ephriam Katz, *The Film Encyclopedia,* 452.

14. Letter dated 11 November 1966, Emir Rodríguez Monegal Papers, Manuscripts Division, Department of Rare Books and Special Collections, Princeton University Libraries.

15. Jorge Edwards Papers, Manuscripts Division, Department of Rare Books and Special Collections, Princeton University Libraries.

4. The Apprentice Storyteller

1. Since the English version of *Así en la paz como en la guerra* does not

contain the vignettes, I will use the Spanish title throughout the text. However, references to the stories will include English titles as they appear in *Writes of Passage*.

2. "Talent of 2wo Cities," 18.

3. *Writes of Passage*, ix.

4. "Talent of 2wo Cities," 18.

5. Marie-Lise Gazarian Gautier, "Guillermo Cabrera Infante," 51–52.

6. Seymour Menton, *Prose Fiction of the Cuban Revolution*, 171–72.

7. Jorge Luis Borges, *Labyrinths*, 43.

8. *Así en la paz como en la guerra* (1974), 10.

9. *Así en la paz como en la guerra*, 126.

10. *Writes of Passage*, 112.

11. Mike Benton, *The Illustrated Superhero, Comics of the Silver Age*, 197.

12. Jeff Rovin, *The Encyclopedia of Super Heroes*, 276.

13. Interview, 21 August 1991. In Gazarian Gautier's *Interviews with Latin American Writers*, 32–33, Cabrera Infante gave less precise information about the translation and explained: "Even the name of my surrogate in *Three Trapped Tigers*, Sylvester, comes from a fascinating comic strip of my youth called *The Spirit*. The Spirit used to live under a tomb in the Saint Sylvester Cemetery in a place called Metropolis."

14. Michael Barrier and Martin Williams, eds., *A Smithsonian Book of Comic-Book Comics*, 270.

5. Citizen Cain

1. Danubio Torres Fierro, "Guillermo Cabrera Infante," 79.

2. *A Twentieth Century Job*, 70.

3. Interview, 26 June 1990.

4. A commentary on the life of Varona, including his tragic suicide in 1970, can be found in Cabrera Infante's article "Entre la historia y la nada (Notas sobre una ideología del suicidio)" and under the same title in *Mea Cuba*.

5. Interview, 26 June 1990.

6. *A Twentieth Century Job*,

7. *Un oficio del siglo veinte* (1963), 246; *Tres tristes tigres* (1967), 215.

8. Kenneth E. Hall, *Guillermo Cabrera Infante and the Cinema*.

9. Interview, 26 June 1990.

6. The Elusive Tiger

1. Guillermo Cabrera Infante Papers, Manuscripts Division, Department of Rare Books and Special Collections, Princeton University Libraries.

2. *Mea Cuba*, 49.

3. Mario G. del Cueto, "El aporte del directorio revolucionario en la lucha

contra la tiranía," 59.

4. Heberto Padilla, *Self-Portrait of the Other,* 43.

5. Maria-Lise Gazarian Gautier, "Guillermo Cabrera Infante," 48. See also Cabrera Infante's "Entre la historia y la nada," 78.

6. *View of Dawn in the Tropics* (1988), 140.

7. "Meta-final," 18–22. For a translation and commentary on "Meta-End" see Roberto González Echevarría, *The Voice of the Masters,* 137–68.

8. Interview, 4 July 1990.

9. "Ella cantaba boleros," *Lunes de Revolución,* 8.

10. Interview, 19 June 1990.

11. Danubio Torres Fierro, "Guillermo Cabrera Infante," 90.

12. Interview, 19 June 1990.

13. José Lezama Lima, *Tratados en la Habana,* 372.

14. "Lives of a Hero," 24.

15. Cabrera Infante has chronicled the fate of Arcos in "Lives of a Hero." It is most readily available in the English and Spanish editions of *Mea Cuba.*

16. "Lives of a Hero," 28.

17. Interview, 20 August 1991.

18. Camille Paglia, *Sexual Personae,* 17.

19. Hugh Thomas, *Cuba, The Pursuit of Freedom,* 1376.

20. "Quien está cansado de Londres," 13.

7. A Nocturnal Rhapsody

1. I first learned of this origin from Cabrera Infante on 19 June 1990 in London. Suzanne Jill Levine reports a similar version in *The Subversive Scribe,* 98, which was confirmed by Miriam Gómez and Nestor Almendros.

2. Suzanne Jill Levine, *The Subversive Scribe,* 97.

3. The use of Marinello as a foil is mentioned in a letter Cabrera Infante sent to Emir Rodríguez Monegal dated 7 December 1966. Emir Rodríguez Monegal Papers, Manuscripts Division, Department of Rare Books and Special Collections, Princeton University Libraries.

4. Dwight Macdonald, *Parodies, An Anthology,* p. xiii.

5. Nedda G. de Anhalt, "Carlos Franqui," 237.

6. Ronald Segal, *The Tragedy of Leon Trotsky,* 392.

7. Rita Guibert, "Guillermo Cabrera Infante," 389.

8. *Mea Cuba* (1992), 378.

9. Robert Payne, *The Life and Death of Trotsky,* 441, 463–78.

10. Segal, *Tragedy,* 402.

11. Brian McHale, *Postmodernist Fiction,* 11.

12. *Three Trapped Tigers,* 213.

13. Roberto González Echevarría, *The Voice of the Masters,* 141.

14. Interview, 20 June 1990.

15. Gustavo Pérez Firmat, "Riddles of the Sphincter: Another Look at the Cuban *Choteo*," 73. See also William L. Siemens, "Deconstruction Reconstrued: Chaos Theory and the Works of Guillermo Cabrera Infante."

16. McHale, *Postmodernist Fiction*, 182–83.

17. Letter to William Siemens, 2 June 1978.

18. Levine, *The Subversive Scribe*, 21. Other noteworthy intertextual studies include Juan Goytisolo's "Lectura cervantina de *Tres tristes tigres*," Djelal Kadir's "Stalking the Oxen of the Sun," Alfred J. Mac Adam's *Modern Latin American Narratives*, Ardis Nelson's *Cabrera Infante in the Mennipean Tradition*, and William L. Siemens's "Mirrors and Metamorphosis: Lewis Carroll's Presence in *Tres tristes tigres*."

19. Walter J. Ong, *Orality and Literacy*, 159.

20. Alfred J. Mac Adam, "The Art of Fiction LXXV," 181.

21. *Three Trapped Tigers*, 287.

22. Gerald Astor, *The Baseball Hall of Fame*, 46.

23. Raymond Chandler, *The Long Goodbye*, 328.

24. These figures come from an unpublished inventory compiled for Cabrera Infante by John Kettlety.

25. These figures, like those in note 24, come from an unpublished inventory compiled for Cabrera Infante by John Kettlety.

26. M. M. Bakhtin, *The Dialogic Imagination*, 23.

8. Lowry's Ghost

1. Leslie Halliwell, *Halliwell's Film Guide*, 1066.

2. Letter, 8 July 1969. Cabrera Infante Papers, Manuscripts Division, Department of Rare Books and Special Collections, Princeton University Libraries.

3. Telephone conversation, 5 January 1991.

4. "Wonderwall," 2. Unpublished script, Cabrera Infante Papers, Manuscripts Division, Department of Rare Books and Special Collections, Princeton University Libraries.

5. "Wonderwall," 39.

6. Rita Guibert, "Guillermo Cabrera Infante," 403.

7. Ephraim Katz, *The Film Encyclopedia*, 1244.

8. "A Portrait of Jesse," 37.

9. "Pepito Grillo en el vientre de la ballena," 61.

10. "Vanishing Point," 41.

11. William Siemens has suggested to me that the blind DJ is another allusion to the *Odyssey*—Tiresias giving guidance to Odysseus.

12. Interview, 4 July 1990.

13. Katz, *The Film Encyclopedia*, 735.

14. David Caute, *Joseph Losey, A Revenge on Life,* 374.

15. "Joe Losey, americano," 124.

16. "Under the Volcano," 64. Unpublished script in possession of Cabrera Infante.

17. "Under the Volcano," 225.

18. "Un guión para la locura," 126.

19. "Scenario o de la novela al cine sin pasar por la pantalla," 10.

20. Interview, 21 June 1990.

21. Kay Redfield Jamison, *Touched with Fire, Manic-Depressive Illness and the Artistic Temperament,* 88.

22. Cabrera Infante Papers, Manuscripts Division, Department of Rare Books and Special Collections, Princeton University Libraries.

23. Caute, *Joseph Losey,* 346.

24. John H. Richardson, in "Dead Ends: The Films That Never Were," includes "Under the Volcano" in a list of remarkable scripts that were never filmed.

9.Images of History

1. Emir Rodríguez Monegal, Review of "Vista del amanecer en el trópico," 69.

2. Matías Montes Huidobro, "El montaje fílmico-histórico de *Vista del amanecer en el trópico,*" 380–84.

3. David William Foster, *Studies in the Contemporary Spanish-American Short Story,* 120.

4. *View of Dawn in the Tropics* (1978), 1.

5. *View* (1988), 1.

6. *View* (1978), 7.

7. *View* (1978), 13.

8. *View* (1978), 9.

9. Danubio Torres Fierro, "El eterno retorno de lo mismo," 47.

10. *View* (1978), 115.

11. Richard Whelan, *Robert Capa, A Biography,* 96.

12. Suzanne Jill Levine, *The Subversive Scribe,* 104.

13. Fernando Portuondo del Prado, *Historia de Cuba,* 70.

14. *Vista del amanecer en el trópico* (1974), 17.

15. *View* (1978), 6.

16. *View* (1988), 130.

17. *View* (1988), 131.

18. *View* (1988), 127.

19. See Hugh Thomas, *Cuba, The Pursuit of Freedom,* 1247–48.

20. *Holy Smoke,* 67–68.

10. The Vertigo of Memory

1. *Infante's Inferno*, 222.
2. Conversations, 2 July 1990 and 21 August 1991.
3. Brian McHale, *Postmodernist Fiction*, 203.
4. *Infante's Inferno*, 136.
5. José Miguel Oviedo, "Nabokov/Cabrera Infante: True Imaginary Lives," 560. See also Rosemary Geisdorfer Feal, *Novel Lives*.
6. Suzanne Jill Levine, *The Subversive Scribe*, 114.
7. Julián Ríos, "Una conversación entre G. Cabrera Infante y J. Ríos," 5.
8. *Infante's Inferno*, 82. Further quotations are noted in the text.
9. Mario Vargas Llosa, G. *Cabrera Infante with Mario Vargas Llosa*, ICA Video.
10. Vargas Llosa, "G. Cabrera Infante." Cabrera Infante indicated the title as "Facilis Descensus Averni" in Alfred Mac Adam, "The Art of Fiction LXXV," 172.
11. Cabrera Infante Papers, Manuscript Division, Department of Rare Books and Special Collections, Princeton University Libraries.
12. *A Twentieth Century Job*, 154.
13. The first critic to broach this matter was Emir Rodríguez Monegal in "Cabrera Infante: la novela como autobiografía total." René Prieto carries the concept to its Freudian limits in "A Womb with a View: Sex and the Movies."
14. Erich Neumann, *The Great Mother*, 168.
15. *La Habana para un Infante difunto*, 711.
16. Regina M. Janes, "Ta(l)king Liberties: On Guillermo Cabrera Infante," 236–37.
17. Conversation, 5 April 1982.
18. Camille Paglia, *Sexual Personae*, 498.
19. Frederick R. Karl, *William Faulkner: American Writer*, 351–57.
20. Geisdorfer Feal, *Novel Lives*, 71.
21. Paglia, *Sexual Personae*, 1.

11. The Demonic Heart of Nature

1. *La próxima luna*, 9–19.
2. See Camille Paglia, *Sexual Personae*, chapter 22.
3. "'Foción suffered from the complex of the toothed vagina, he saw a woman's vulva as an immense mouth that devoured the phallus,'" José Lezama Lima, *Paradiso*, Rabassa translation, 319.
4. Erich Neumann, *The Great Mother*, 168.

12. The Essayistic Narrator

1. See Jorge Luis Espinosa, "Bajo la amenaza de una bomba que nunca explotó."
2. *Mea Cuba* (1992), 381–82.

3. *Exorcismos de esti(l)o*, 221–25.

4. *Mea Cuba* (1992), 34, 181.

5. "Borges y yo," 34.

6. *Holy Smoke*, 2. Further quotations are noted in the text.

7. Nedda G. de Anhalt, "Guillermo Cabrera Infante," 22.

8. James Matthew Barrie, *My Lady Nicotine*, 12. Further quotations are noted in the text.

9. *Holy Smoke*, 25.

10. Compton Mackenzie, *Sublime Tobacco*, 2. Further quotations are noted in the text.

11. Fernando Ortiz, *Cuban Counterpoint*, 4.

12. Ortiz, *Cuban Counterpoint*, 6. For studies of the literary sensibility in the works of Ortiz, see Gustavo Pérez Firmat's "The Philological Fictions of Fernando Ortiz"; and Edward J. Mullen's "'Los negros brujos.'"

The most important collections of Cabrera Infante papers are at the Firestone Library (Manuscripts Division, Department of Rare Books and Special Collections) of Princeton University and his London apartment. Manuscripts of published and unpublished works as well as letters can be found at both locations. The Princeton collection includes correspondence with John Barry, Calvert Casey, Julio Cortázar, Joseph Losey, Alberto Mora, and Virgilio Piñera, among others. Letters can also be found at Princeton in the papers of Reinaldo Arenas, José Donoso, Jorge Edwards, and Emir Rodríguez Monegal. Not all of the correspondence in the Princeton collection is open to the public at the time of this writing. As files are made available and additional papers are acquired and cataloged, other materials will undoubtedly appear.

The following bibliography is divided into two basic sections, the works of Cabrera Infante and all other studies, and is organized as follows:

> I. Works by Cabrera Infante
>> A. Books
>> B. English Translations of Books
>> C. Articles and Stories by Cabrera Infante
>> D. Unpublished Film Scripts
>> E. Interviews with Cabrera Infante
> II. Criticism, History, and Other Interviews and Literary Works

Recent bibliographies of Cabrera Infante's publications and criticism of his works are listed in Section II below under Patricia Rubio and William L. Siemens. Also useful is the bibliography in Kenneth E. Hall's *Guillermo Cabrera Infante and the Cinema*.

I. Works by Cabrera Infante

A. BOOKS (LISTED CHRONOLOGICALLY)

Así en la paz como en la guerra. 1960. Barcelona: Seix Barral, 1974.

Un oficio del siglo veinte. Havana: Ediciones R, 1963. Spanish edition, Barcelona: Seix Barral, 1973.

Tres tristes tigres. Barcelona, Seix Barral, 1967.

Vista del amanecer en el trópico. Barcelona: Seix Barral, 1974.

O. Barcelona: Seix Barral, 1975.

Exorcismos de esti(l)o. Barcelona: Seix Barral, 1976.
Arcadia todas las noches. Barcelona: Seix Barral, 1978.
La Habana para un Infante difunto. Barcelona: Seix Barral, 1979.
Holy Smoke. London: Faber and Faber, 1985.
Mea Cuba. Barcelona: Plaza y Janés, 1992.

B. ENGLISH TRANSLATIONS OF BOOKS (LISTED CHRONOLOGICALLY)

Three Trapped Tigers. Translated by Donald Gardner and Suzanne Jill Levine with the author. New York: HarperCollins, 1971.

View of Dawn in the Tropics. Translated by Suzanne Jill Levine with the author. New York: HarperCollins, 1978.

Infante's Inferno. Translated by Suzanne Jill Levine with the author. New York: HarperCollins, 1984.

View of Dawn in the Tropics. 1988. Translated by Suzanne Jill Levine, revised by the author. London: Faber and Faber, 1990.

A Twentieth Century Job. Translated by Kenneth Hall and the author. London: Faber and Faber, 1991.

Writes of Passage. Translated by John Brookesmith, Peggy Boyars, and the author. London: Faber and Faber, 1993.

Mea Cuba. Translated by Kenneth Hall and the author. London: Faber and Faber, 1994. U.S. edition, New York: Farrar, Straus & Giroux, 1994.

C. ARTICLES AND STORIES BY CABRERA INFANTE

"Antonio Ortega vuelve a Asturias." *Los Cuadernos de Asturias* (March–April 1985): 62–65. Also in *Mea Cuba.*

"At the Great 'Ecbo.'" Translated by J. G. Brotherston. *Latin American Writing Today.* Edited by J. M. Cohen. Baltimore: Penguin Books, 1967, 203–15. Included as "The Great Ekbo," in *Writes of Passage.*

"Bajo el volcán o la vida vista desde el fondo de una botella de mescal." *Los Cuadernos del Norte* (March–April 1981): 60–65.

"Balada de plomo y yerro." *Bohemia* (19 October 1952): 23-24, 127–29.

"La belleza de la bomba." *Carteles* (5 August 1956): 58–60.

"El bikini tiene más de 2,000 años." *Carteles* (5 September 1954): 51.

"Bites from the Bearded Crocodile." *London Review of Books* (4–17 June 1981): 3–8. Also in *Quimera* (July–August 1984): 66-82; and *Mea Cuba.*

"Borges y yo." *El País* (16 June 1986): 34.

"Brubú." *El País* (22 September 1988): 15.

"El censor como obsexo." *Espiral* 48 (1979): 167–84.

"Cuando Emir estaba vivo." *Vuelta* (September 1986): 53–56. Also in *Diario 16* (19 October 1986): 4–5; and *Homenaje a Emir Rodríguez Monegal.* Edited by Roberto Andreon. Montevideo, Uruguay: Ministerio de Educación y Cultura, 1987, 39–43.

"Cuba's Shadow." *Film Comment* (May–June 1985): 43–45.

"Del gofio al golfo." *Jornadas de Estudios Canarias-América* 1, no. 4 (1984): 131–43.

"Delito por bailar el chachachá." *Mundo Nuevo* (July 1968): 59–71. Also in *Guillermo Cabrera Infante*, edited by Julián Ríos. Madrid: Fundamentos, 1974, 217–53.

"Desde el Swinging London." *Mundo Nuevo* (August 1967): 45–53.

"Ella cantaba boleros." *Lunes de Revolución* (23 October 1961): 8–10.

"Ellos vivieron en Kensington." *El País Semanal* (21 August 1977): 9, 26.

"En el gran ecbó." *Carteles* (6 September 1959): 58–60, 71–72.

"English Profanities." Translated by Peggy Boyers. *Lives on the Line, The Testimony of Contemporary Latin American Authors.* Edited by Doris Meyer. Berkeley: University of California Press, 1988, 59–71. Also in *Writes of Passage.*

"Entre la historia y la nada (Notas sobre una ideología del suicidio)." *Escandalar* (January–June 1982): 69–83. Also in *Vuelta* (January 1983): 11–22; and *Mea Cuba.*

"Los espectadores las prefieren rubias." *Carteles* (15 August 1954): 4–6, 8.

"Foreword: Portrait of a Tyrant as an Aging Tyro." In Carlos Franqui, *Family Portrait with Fidel, A Memoir.* Translated by Alfred Mac Adam. New York: Random House, 1984, vii–xix.

"La guerra civil de todos." *Vuelta* (November 1986): 74–75.

"Un guión para la locura." *Cambio 16* (15 October 1984): 126–28.

"Hemingway y Cuba y la Revolución." *Lunes de Revolución* (14 August 1961): 16–19.

"Holmes, Sweet Holmes." *El País* (11 January 1987): 25.

"La isla partida en dos." *Carteles* (18 January 1959): 100–103.

"Joe Losey, americano." *Cambio 16* (2 July 1984): 124–26.

"Josefina, atiende a los señores." *Ciclón* 2.3 (May 1955): 31–33.

"Lives of a Hero." Translated by Peggy Boyers. *Salmagundi* 67 (1985): 13–33.

"Mar, mar, enemigo." *Carteles* (27 June 1954): 30–32, 82.

"Meta-End." Translated, with an introduction, commentary, and notes by Roberto González Echevarría. In Roberto González Echevarría, *The Voice of the Masters, Writing and Authority in Modern Latin American Literature.* Austin: University of Texas Press, 1985, 137–68.

"Meta-Final." *Alacrán Azul* 1.1 (1970): 18–22.

"Mi personaje inolvidable." *Escandalar* (July–September 1979): 8–25.

"Mi querido censor." *La Nación* (Buenos Aires) (25 September 1988) sec. Letras 4a: 1–2. Also in *Tres tristes tigres.* Caracas: Biblioteca Ayacucho, 1990, x–xiii.

"Miriam Gómez va de compras." *El Nuevo Día* (6 November 1988): 6–11.

"Mis mejores lecturas." *Diario 16* (20 April 1989): i–ii.

"Mi último fracaso." *Flashmen* no. 40 (n.d.): 33–35, 79–80, 82.

"Muerte en la barbería." *Carteles* (10 November 1957): 22–24.

"Nest, Door, Neighbors." *Review* (Winter, 1973): 18–26. Also in *Contemporary Latin American Stories.* Edited by Pat McNees Mancini. New York: Fawcett, 1974, 385–402; and *Writes of Passage.*

"A Nest of Sparrows on the Awning." Translated by Suzanne Jill Levine. *The Eye of the Heart.* Edited by Barbara Howes. Indianapolis: Bobbs-Merrill, 1973, 357–63.

"Un nido de gorriones en un toldo." *Carteles* (25 September 1955): 74–75, 125.

"Pepito Grillo en el vientre de la ballena." *Los Cuadernos del Norte* (September–October 1983): 52–61.

"The Phantom of the Essoldo." *London Tales.* Edited by Julian Evans. London:

Hamish Hamilton, 1983, 108–43. Also in *A Hammock Beneath the Mangoes, Stories From Latin America*. Edited by Thomas Colchie. New York: Dutton, 1991, 382–415; and *The Penguin Book of Latin American Stories*. London:Viking, 1992, 382–415.

"La plus que lente." *Flashmen,* no. 38 (n.d.), 51–54, 80. Also in *Plural* (February 1976): 6–9.

"Por el camino de West, mi memoria de Mae." *El País* (29 November 1980): 8.

"Portentos, magias y maravillas de la tecnología." *Vuelta* (July 1988): 63–65.

"A Portrait of Jesse." Translated by Alfred J. Mac Adam. *Review* 39 (1988): 35–37.

"Quien está cansado de Londres." *El País* (1 June 1987): 13–14.

"¿Quién mató a Calvert Casey?" *Quimera* (December 1982): 42–53. Also in *Mea Cuba.*

"Un rato de tenmeallá." *Lunes de Revolución* (28 March 1960): 29–30.

"Remington Visits with Edison." *American Film* (January–February 1986): 52–53.

"Resaca." *Bohemia* (5 October 1952): 23–24, 114. Also in *Antología del cuento en Cuba, 1902–1952.* Edited by Salvador Bueno. Havana: Ministerio de Educación, 1953, 385–92. Published in English as "How Revolution Begins." *Viñetas del Caribe.* Edited by Alan Soons. London: George G. Harrap, 1970, 156–65.

"Scenario o de la novela al cine sin pasar por la pantalla." *Revista de Occidente* (September 1984): 7–19.

"Seseribó." *Casa de las Américas* (September–October 1965): 43–59.

"Talent of 2wo Cities." *Review* 35 (1985): 17–19.

" 'Time,' 'Life' & Co. Mentiras la por mayor importadores y exportadores." *Lunes de Revolución* (2 November 1959): 6–7.

"Tres tristes tigres." *Mundo Nuevo* (May 1967): 28–37.

"La última traición de Manuel Puig." *El País* (24 July 1990): 22.

"Vidas de un héroe." *Vuelta* (December 1984): 5–11. Also as *Vidas de un héroe.* Washington, D.C.: Cuban American Foundation (n.d.); and in *Mea Cuba.*

"El viejo y la marca." *Ciclón* 2.5 (September 1956): 51–54.

"La voz de la tortuga. Una historia que mi suegra me contó." *La próxima luna.* Barcelona: Tanagra, 1990, 9–19.

D. UNPUBLISHED FILM SCRIPTS (LISTED CHRONOLOGICALLY)

"El Máximo" (1966), ts.

"The Mercenary" (1966), ts., Princeton University Libraries. Later titled: "Universal Soldier."

"On the Speedway" (1966), ts. Princeton University Libraries. Later titled: "The Jam."

"Wonderwall" (1967), ms. & ts., Princeton University Libraries.

"The Gambados" (1967), ms.

"The Jam" (1968), ms. & ts., Princeton University Libraries.

"Birthdays" (1968), ms. & ts., Princeton University Libraries.

"Vanishing Point," (1970), ts., Princeton University Libraries.

"The Salzburg Connection" (1970), ts.

"The Hero" (1970?), ts.

"Under the Volcano" (1972), 214-page ms., Princeton University Libraries.
"A Taste for Larceny" (1973?), ms.
"The Lost City" (1991), third draft, ms.

E. INTERVIEWS WITH CABRERA INFANTE

Alvarez-Borland, Isabel. "Viaje verbal a La Habana, ¡Ah Vana! Entrevista de Isabel Alvarez-Borland con G. Cabrera Infante, arquitecto de una ciudad de palabras erigida en el tiempo." *Hispamérica* 11, no. 31 (1982): 51–68.

Anhalt, Nedda G. de. "Guillermo Cabrera Infante: *Holy Smoke:* Pun y Humo." *Rojo y naranja sobre rojo.* Mexico:Vuelta, 1991, 17–34. Also in *Sábado* (1 March 1986): 1–4.

Esteva, Jordi. "Guillermo Cabrera Infante." Photos by Germán Puig. *Ajoblanco* (Barcelona) 52 (May 1993): 38–47.

García M., Eligio. "Guillermo Cabrera Infante: el más triste (y alegre) de los tigres." *Son así, reportaje a nueve escritores latinoamericanos.* Bogotá, Colombia: Oveja Negra, 1982, 181–231.

Gazarian Gautier, Marie-Lise. "Guillermo Cabrera Infante." *Interviews with Latin American Writers.* Elmwood Park, Ill.: Dalkey Archive Press, 1989, 27–54.

Guibert, Rita. "Guillermo Cabrera Infante." *Seven Voices.* Translated by Frances Partridge. Introduction by Emir Rodríguez Monegal. NewYork:Vintage Books, 1973, 341–436.

Hoyos, Bernardo. "Guillermo Cabrera Infante." *Revista Diners* (Colombia) (October 1988): 88–93.

Janes, Regina M. "From 5 to 7: An Interview with Guillermo Cabrera Infante." *Salmagundi* 52–53 (1981): 30–55.

Mac Adam, Alfred. "The Art of Fiction LXXV: Guillermo Cabrera Infante." *Paris Review* 25.87 (1983): 154–95.

Mergier, Anne Marie. "Entrevista con Guillermo Cabrera Infante." *Huellas, Revista de la Universidad del Norte* (Barranquilla, Colombia) 32 (August 1991): 58–64. Also in *Proceso* (Mexico) 3 (June 1991): 48–51.

Pereda, Rosa M. "Habla Cabrera Infante: Una larga entrevista que es una poética." *Guillermo Cabrera Infante.* Madrid: EDAF, 1978, 99–141.

Ríos, Julián. "Una conversación entre G. Cabrera Infante y J. Ríos, La Habana para un Infante difunto," 59–61. Unattributed Xerox copy.

Rodríguez Monegal, Emir. "Las fuentes de la narración." *Mundo Nuevo* (July 1968): 41–58.

Torres Fierro, Danubio. "Guillermo Cabrera Infante." *Memoria Plural, Entrevistas a escritores latinoamericanos.* Buenos Aires: Editorial Sudamericana, 1986, 60–103. Also available in *Vuelta* (October 1977): 18–27.

Vargas Llosa, Mario. *G. Cabrera Infante with Mario Vargas Llosa.* ICA Video, The Roland Collection, Institute of Contemporary Arts, London, 44 min.

Wilson, Jason. "Guillermo Cabrera Infante: An Interview in a Summer Manner." *On Modern Latin American Fiction.* Edited by John King. New York: Farrar, Straus & Giroux, 1987, 305–21.

II. Criticism, History, and Other Interviews and Literary Works

Anhalt, Nedda G. de. "Carlos Franqui: El Reposo del Guerrero." *Rojo y naranja sobre rojo*. Mexico: Vuelta, 1991, 230–61.

"Announcing the Jam." *Variety* (10 April 1968): 25.

Astor, Gerald. *The Baseball Hall of Fame*. Englewood Cliffs, N.J.: Prentice-Hall, 1988.

Atlas de Cuba. Havana: Instituto Cubano de Geodesia y Cartografía, 1978.

Bakhtin, M. M. *The Dialogic Imagination*. Edited by Michael Holquist, and translated by Caryl Emerson and Michael Holquist. Austin: University of Texas Press, 1981.

Barrie, Sir James Matthew. *My Lady Nicotine*. London: Hodder and Stoughton, 1890.

Barrier, Michael, and Martin Williams, eds. *A Smithsonian Book of Comic-Book Comics*. New York: Smithsonian Institution Press and Harry N. Abrams, 1981.

Benton, Mike. *The Illustrated Superhero, Comics of the Silver Age*. Dallas: Taylor, 1991.

Borges, Jorge Luis. *Labyrinths, Selected Stories and Other Writings*. Edited by Donald A. Yates and James E. Irby. New York: New Directions, 1962.

Caute, David. *Joseph Losey, A Revenge on Life*. New York: Oxford University Press, 1994.

Chandler, Raymond. *The Long Goodbye*. 1953. Reprint, New York: Vintage Books, 1988.

Cueto, Mario G. del. "El aporte del directorio revolucionario en la lucha contra la tiranía." *Bohemia* (11 January 1959): 56–59.

Dally, Peter. *Chemotherapy of Psychiatric Disorders*. New York: Plenum Press, 1967.

———. *Elizabeth Barrett Browning, A Psychological Portrait*. London: Macmillan, 1981.

Dorian, Bob. *Bob Dorian's Classic Movies*. Holbrook, Mass.: Bob Adams, 1990.

Espinosa, Jorge Luis. "Bajo la amenaza de una bomba que nunca explotó, fue presentado *Mea Cuba*." *Uno Más Uno* (28 May 1993): 31.

Feal, Rosemary Geisdorfer. *Novel Lives: The Fictional Autobiographies of Guillermo Cabrera Infante and Mario Vargas Llosa*. Chapel Hill: North Carolina Studies in Romance Literature, 1986.

Foster, David William. *Studies in the Contemporary Spanish-American Short Story*. Columbia: University of Missouri Press, 1979.

Franqui, Carlos. *Diario de la revolución cubana*. Chatillon-sous-Bagneux, France: Ruedo Ibérico, 1976.

———. *Family Portrait with Fidel, A Memoir*. Translated by Alfred Mac Adam. New York: Random House, 1984.

Gardner, Martin. *The Annotated Alice*. 1940. Reprint, New York: Bramhall House, 1960.

Geyer, Georgie Anne. *Guerrilla Prince, The Untold Story of Fidel Castro*. Boston: Little, Brown, 1991.

González Echevarría, Roberto. *The Voice of the Masters, Writing and Authority in Modern Latin American Literature*. Austin: University of Texas Press, 1985.

Goytisolo, Juan. "Lectura cervantina de *Tres tristes tigres*." *Disidencias*. Barcelona: Seix Barral, 1978, 193–219.

Hall, Kenneth E. *Guillermo Cabrera Infante and the Cinema*. Newark, Del.: Juan de la Cuesta, 1989.

Halliwell, Leslie. *Halliwell's Film Guide,* 7th ed. Great Britain: Grafton Books, 1989.

Jamison, Kay Redfield. *Touched with Fire, Manic-Depressive Illness and the Artistic Temperament*. New York: Free Press, 1993.

Janes, Regina M. "Ta(l)king Liberties: On Guillermo Cabrera Infante." *Salmagundi* 82–83 (1989): 222–37.

Kadir, Djelal. "Stalking the Oxen of the Sun and Felling the Sacred Cows: Joyce's *Ulysses* and Cabrera Infante's *Three Trapped Tigers*." *Latin American Literary Review* 4.8 (1976): 15–22.

Karl, Frederick R. *William Faulkner: American Writer*. New York: Weidenfeld & Nicholson, 1989.

Karol, K. S. *Guerrillas in Power: The Course of the Cuban Revolution*. Translated by Arnold Pomerans. New York: Hill and Wang, 1970.

Katz, Ephraim. *The Film Encyclopedia*. New York: HarperCollins (Perennial Library), 1990.

Levine, Suzanne Jill. *The Subversive Scribe, Translating Latin American Fiction*. Saint Paul, Minn.: Graywolf Press, 1991.

Lezama Lima, José. *Paradiso*. 1966. Mexico: Era, 1968.

———. *Paradiso*. Translated by Gregory Rabassa. New York: Farrar, Straus & Giroux, 1974.

———. *Tratados en La Habana*. 1958. Buenos Aires: Ediciones de la Flor, 1969.

Luis, William. "Autopsia de *Lunes de Revolución*. Entrevista a Pablo Armando Fernández." *Plural* (March 1982): 52–62.

Mac Adam, Alfred J. *Modern Latin American Narratives: The Dreams of Reason*. Chicago: University of Chicago Press, 1977.

Macdonald, Dwight, ed. *Parodies, An Anthology from Chaucer to Beerbohm and After*. 1960. New York: Da Capo, 1990.

McHale, Brian. *Postmodernist Fiction*. New York: Methuen, 1987.

Mackenzie, Sir Compton. *Sublime Tobacco*. London: Chatto & Windus, 1957.

Matas, Julio. "Guillermo Cabrera Infante: Caricaturas tempranas." *World Literature Today* 61 (Autumn 1987): 593–97.

Menton, Seymour. *Prose Fiction of the Cuban Revolution*. Austin: University of Texas Press, 1975.

Montes Huidobro, Matías. "El montaje fílmico-histórico de *Vista del amanecer en el trópico*." *Encuentro de la literatura con la ciencia y el arte*. Edited by Juana Alcira Arancibia. Instituto Literatura y Cultura Hispánico, 1990, 379–91.

Mullen, Edward J. "'Los negros brujos': A Reexamination of the Text." *Cuban Studies* 17 (1987): 111–29.

Nelson, Ardis. *Cabrera Infante in the Menippean Tradition*. Newark, Del.: Juan de la Cuesta, 1983.

Neumann, Erich. *The Great Mother*. Translated by Ralph Manheim. Princeton, N.J.: Princeton University Press, 1963.

Ong, Walter J. *Orality and Literacy, The Technologizing of the Word*. London and New York: Methuen, 1983.

Ortega, Antonio. *Ready.* Havana: Editorial Lex, 1946.

———. *Yemas de coco y otros cuentos.* Santa Clara, Cuba: Universidad Central de las Villas, 1959.

Ortiz, Fernando. *Contrapunteo cubano del tabaco y el azúcar.* 1940. Barcelona: Editorial Ariel, 1973.

———. *Cuban Counterpoint, Tobacco and Sugar.* Translated by Harriet de Onís. New York: Vintage Books, 1970.

Oviedo, José Miguel. "Nabokov/Cabrera Infante: True Imaginary Lives." *World Literature Today* 61 (Autumn 1987): 559–67.

Padilla, Heberto. *Self-Portrait of the Other.* Translated by Alexander Coleman. New York: Farrar, Straus, & Giroux, 1990.

Paglia, Camille. *Sexual Personae, Art and Decadence from Nefertiti to Emily Dickinson.* New York: Vintage Books, 1991.

Payne, Robert. *The Life and Death of Trotsky.* New York: McGraw-Hill, 1977.

Pérez Firmat, Gustavo. "The Philological Fictions of Fernando Ortiz." *Notebooks in Cultural Analysis* 2 (1985): 190–207.

———. "Riddles of the Sphincter: Another Look at the Cuban *Choteo.*" *Diacritics* (Winter 1984): 67–77.

Portuondo del Prado, Fernando. *Historia de Cuba.* 6th ed. Havana: Minerva, 1957.

Prieto, René. "A Womb with a View: Sex and the Movies." *World Literature Today* 61 (Autumn 1987): 584–89.

Richardson, John H. "Dead Ends: The Films That Never Were." *Daily News* (Los Angeles) (19 April 1987): 20–21.

Rodríguez Monegal. Emir. "Cabrera Infante: la novela como autobiografía total." *Revista Iberoamericana* 47.116–117 (1981): 265–71.

———. "Review of 'Vista del amanecer en el trópico.' " *Plural* (May 1975): 66–70.

Rovin, Jeff. *The Encyclopedia of Super Heroes.* New York: Facts on File Publications, 1985.

Rubio, Patricia. "Bibliografía." In Guillermo Cabrera Infante, *Tres tristes tigres.* Caracas: Ayacucho, 1990, 365–73.

Segal, Ronald. *The Tragedy of Leon Trotsky.* London: Hutchinson, 1979.

Siemens, William L. "Deconstruction Reconstrued: Chaos Theory and the Works of Guillermo Cabrera Infante." *Ometeca* 1:2–2:1 (1989–90): 53–59.

———. "Mirrors and Metamorphosis: Lewis Carroll's Presence in *Tres tristes tigres.* *Hispania* 62 (1979): 297–303.

———. "Selected Bibliography (1960–1987)." *World Literature Today* 61 (Autumn 1987): 535–38.

Thomas, Hugh. *Cuba, The Pursuit of Freedom.* New York: HarperCollins, 1971.

"Todd's Little Garden Party." *Life* (28 October 1957): 149.

Torres Fierro, Danubio. "El eterno retorno de lo mismo." *Los territorios del exilio.* Barcelona: La Gaya Ciencia, 1979, 47–64.

Vargas Llosa, Mario. *El pez en el agua, memorias.* Bogotá: Seix Barral, 1993.

Whelan, Richard. *Robert Capa, A Biography.* Lincoln: University of Nebraska Press, 1994.

INDEX

Permission to quote from the following sources is gratefully acknowledged:

Guillermo Cabrera Infante for quotations from published and unpublished materials, interviews, and for photographs from his collection.

Department of Rare Books and Special Collections, Princeton University Libraries for quotations from Guillermo Cabrera Infante, Emir Rodríguez Monegal, and Jorge Edwards.

Guillermo Cabrera Infante and the Agencia Literaria Carmen Balcells, S.A., for selections from *Vista del amanecer en el trópico*, copyright © 1974; *La Habana para un Infante difunto*, copyright © 1979; and *Holy Smoke*, copyright © 1985.

Faber and Faber Limited Publishers for *A Twentieth Century Job*.

Farrar, Straus and Giroux, Inc., for Heberto Padilla, *Self-Portrait of the Other*.

Graywolf Press for Susan Jill Levine, *The Subversive Scribe: Translating Latin American Fiction*.

Metheun for Brian McHale, *Postmodernist Fiction*.

Graduate School of International Studies of the University of Miami for permission to reproduce Raymond D. Souza, "Citizen Cain," *Ideas* 92:10 (Spring 1991): 11–16.